# Straight Talk About Criminals

# Straight Talk About Criminals

## Understanding and Treating Antisocial Individuals

*Stanton E. Samenow, Ph.D.*

JASON ARONSON INC.
*Northvale, New Jersey*
*London*

Production Editor: Elaine Lindenblatt

This book was set in 11 pt. Times Roman by Alabama Book Composition of Deatsville, AL, and printed and bound by Book-mart Press, Inc. of North Bergen, NJ.

**Library of Congress Cataloging-in-Publication Data**

Samenow, Stanton E., 1941–
    Straight talk about criminals : understanding and treating
antisocial individuals / Stanton E. Samenow.
        p.  cm.
    Includes bibliographical references.
    ISBN 1-56821-875-3 (alk. paper)
    1. Criminal psychology.  2. Deviant behavior.  3. Antisocial
personality disorders.  I. Title.
HV6085.S215    1998
364.3—dc21                                    97-40385


Printed in the United States of America on acid-free paper. For information and catalog write to Jason Aronson Inc., 230 Livingston Street, Northvale, NJ 07647-1731. Or visit our website: http://www.aronson.com

To my wife

*Dorothy K. Samenow*

With appreciation for her devotion and forbearance
during my travels over the last two decades
while I accumulated all the questions
upon which this book is based

# Contents

# Preface

I am a clinical psychologist with the kind of practice that few others have or want to have. During the past twenty-seven years, I have interviewed, evaluated, and counseled hundreds of men, women, and children who have committed crimes—everything from a housewife apprehended for shoplifting to a man sentenced to death for lethally assaulting a total stranger with a baseball bat to rob him of a few dollars. I have met with these people in juvenile detention centers, in psychiatric hospitals, in county jails, in penitentiaries, and in my office in Alexandria, Virginia. In most instances, they have not sought me out voluntarily. Judges ordered them to see me. Defense attorneys told their clients that it was in their best interest to undergo evaluation. Probation and parole officers required them to receive counseling. Child Protective Services mandated that child abusers meet with me for evaluation or counseling. Beleaguered teachers and school administrators referred children whom they found incorrigible. Mental health professionals who customarily do not work with this difficult offender population urged recalcitrant clients to consult me. At their wits' end, husbands and wives warned their antisocial spouses that unless they saw me and changed, the marriage was over. And frustrated, sometimes desperate, bewildered parents dragged their delinquent sons and daughters to me, hoping that I could turn them around.

I began full-time clinical practice in 1978. For eight years, before I opened my office, I was a research psychologist working for Dr. Samuel Yochelson, a psychiatrist who headed the Program for the Investigation of Criminal Behavior based at St. Elizabeths Hospital in Washington, D.C. To my knowledge, that program remains the longest in-depth research–treatment study of offenders ever conducted in North America. Throughout the project's seventeen years, we studied more than 200 criminals, spending as many as 8,000 hours with some and, in many cases, interviewing others who knew them well. Coming from extremely varied backgrounds, these men had committed nearly every type of crime. We discovered that factors we were certain cause crime were, to our surprise, not causal at all. They merely served as excuses for the criminal. We therefore shifted from our earlier emphasis on causation to identifying specific thought patterns of the criminal as he functions from day to day. Once we understood how criminals view themselves and other people, we were successful at developing a method to help some of them correct errors of thinking and thereby become responsible citizens.

Since 1977, I have spoken about the crime problem in forty-eight states and the District of Columbia. My travels have taken me to the big cities (e.g., Los Angeles, Houston, Denver, Cleveland, Seattle), to smaller cities (e.g., Butte, Montana; Jackson, Mississippi; Wichita, Kansas; South Bend, Indiana), to towns (e.g., Ligonier, Indiana; Eau Claire, Wisconsin; Coos Bay, Oregon; Statesboro, Georgia), and to suburban areas. My presentations have ranged from delivering a one-hour keynote address at a conference to speaking eight hours a day for three consecutive days while presenting workshops to professionals who work with juvenile or adult offenders. Among those in my audiences have been judges, attorneys, police officers, school counselors, teachers, social workers, psychologists and psychiatrists, probation and parole officers, men and women who work in jails and penitentiaries and juvenile detention centers, drug and alcohol counselors, and politicians. I have often addressed groups of parents and other concerned citizens. Occasionally, I have spoken at prisons to assemblies of inmates.

Groups attending my talks, lectures, and workshops usually

number in the hundreds—too large for responding to questions from the floor. Consequently, I ask those in attendance to write down their questions, objections, and need for clarification, and to submit these during breaks. This procedure is not to make it easy for me to skip the tough questions or the ones I simply prefer not to answer. Rather, it is to organize questions and to avoid repetition and the frustration when the questioner cannot be heard by others in a large meeting hall. Since 1976, I have saved these written questions. Numbering in the thousands, they spill out of two large cardboard cartons. I had no particular reason for saving them. I just did. Having accumulated two decades of questions, I decided that it is time to answer them for a larger audience. Thus my decision to write this book.

The people who asked the questions come from all over America. Most of their questions arise from their professional work in the criminal justice field. However, there is a deep personal interest as these individuals are also concerned citizens of their communities, worried parents, and frustrated taxpayers. In selecting questions to answer, I chose those that were asked most frequently. However, I also included some of the more offbeat queries, and a number resonated with regard to my own interests and reactions to criminals. I did not discover differences by region, state, or size of the town or city. There are no discernible differences in substance or attitude between questions asked in Peoria or those asked in Pittsburgh.

The format will be to present questions organized by topic. In answering them, I shall convey a perspective, provide information, and recommend urgently needed approaches for combating crime in America. I hope that this book will interest the vast number of Americans who are fed up with failed approaches. As a psychologist, I have no axe to grind on the subject. My work is free of ideological slant. It is based on twenty-eight years in this field during an era that has spanned both so-called liberal and conservative approaches. While answering each question, I shall provide straight talk and a workable approach to a problem that touches everyone.*

---

*In referring to the criminal in my answers, I use only the masculine *he/him*, solely for the sake of consistency.

# Acknowledgments

I wish to thank Dr. David B. Cohen, Professor of Psychology at the University of Texas, and friend since graduate school days. David read the manuscript and made valuable conceptual and editorial suggestions.

I also deeply appreciate the time and thought given to reading the manuscript by the following people who offered their ideas as well: Mary Jane Adcock, Marcia Kerchner, and Kathy Robbins.

# The Criminal Personality:
# An Introduction

Does a member of your family constantly get into trouble? This person may be an adult who, despite repeated arrests, seems to learn little from his experiences. Predictably, he blames other people or circumstances for any predicament. Rarely does he accept responsibility for what he has done.

Maybe your child behaves as though rules do not apply to him. He skips school, sneaks out of the house, steals from you, and uses drugs. Unresponsive to discipline, he keeps the family in turmoil, playing one person against the other while he persists in doing exactly as he pleases.

Perhaps you know people who don't break the law, yet continually victimize others. The nonarrestable person with a criminal personality is unprincipled in taking advantage of others. Gregarious and engaging, he charms people and insinuates himself into their lives so that they trust him totally. Then, like a snake, he strikes, exploiting them financially, sexually, or for other personal gratification.

I've written this book to help you understand more about antisocial adults, juveniles with severe conduct disorders, and people who are criminal in the broadest sense of the term even if they have not been arrested. All these individuals have an antisocial or criminal personality, and I shall refer to them in these writings simply as "the criminal." (*Antisocial*, as I am using the term, has nothing to do with how gregarious or sociable a person is. Rather it has to do with a propensity to victimize other people.)

Before I answer the many questions addressed to me over the years, I shall briefly describe a man or woman who has a criminal personality. Bear in mind that the features I mention exist in most people to varying degrees. For instance, nearly everyone has told a small lie if for no other purpose than to spare someone else's feelings. If your best friend asks how you like her new dress, and you think it is hideous, you are nevertheless likely to be complimentary. A person who occasionally tells a white lie is very different from an individual who lies as a way of life to avoid being caught for a crime or to bail himself out of a jam. By lying even about inconsequential matters, this person feels superior thinking he has successfully pulled the wool over the eyes of others.

The person I refer to as a criminal is a creature of extremes. Any of us may inadvertently hurt someone's feelings or, once in a while, even do so deliberately out of spite. The criminal has no concept of injury to others. He does what he pleases, eliminating from his thinking potential consequences. To him, the world is a chessboard, and people and objects are pawns to be moved about at will.

The criminal is uncompromising. He seeks to control others for the sake of control. Human relationships are opportunities for him to make conquests and get what he wants. Whether operating by deception, intimidation, or brute force, he is determined to prevail. He demands respect, but not necessarily on the merits of hard work or by treating others well. The criminal's pretensions outstrip his achievements. He does whatever seems easy or expedient at the time and is prone to balk at doing what others require. If you put nine of these people on a baseball team, each would think he was the captain and attempt to give orders. When a task becomes difficult or disagreeable, the criminal slacks off or quits altogether, then blames others for the results. Thinking something makes it so. Success at any enterprise is guaranteed just because the criminal thinks it is, not because he is willing to do the necessary work.

Criminals come from all walks of life—rich and poor, educated and illiterate—and from all ethnic, racial, and religious groups. They are not immediately recognizable; they do not announce their presence. Rather, they scheme and connive to gain an advantage. When they encounter opposition, they become more deceptive or respond violently.

The criminal cases out others to identify vulnerabilities, then preys upon them. When apprehended, he evaluates his interrogators in order to feed them what he thinks they want to hear. The criminal perennially renders himself as the victim. Whatever happens invariably is someone else's fault. After the fact, he always offers an explanation that he hopes his listeners will find plausible. Usually, it has little or nothing to do with his true motives.

The criminal is changeable. A violent individual can appear to have a winsome personality and seem very sincere about his good intentions. He may worship in a church at nine, yet two hours later terrorize a store clerk during an armed robbery. With roses and champagne, he may profess love to his wife but later beat her unmercifully because she insisted on knowing why he came home at two in the morning.

The criminal is very fearful but he conceals this aspect of his personality. He is afraid of getting caught, convicted and confined, or injured or killed in a highly risky crime. The criminal also has internal reservations about some of what he does. However, he has a remarkable capacity to shut off both fears of external consequences as well as qualms of conscience long enough to do as he pleases, with just enough fear emerging so that he looks over his shoulder for the police or any other potential witness. This individual can and does learn from experience. He just doesn't learn what family, teachers, and others want him to learn. From a past event, he can learn how to be more careful and take fewer risks. Only if he suffers severe consequences is there a possibility that he will conclude that "crime doesn't pay." Otherwise, in his experience, crime does pay, because he gets away with far more than is ever known.

In this book you will learn a lot more about these people as I answer questions posed by men and women who, every day, encounter the criminal personality in their work and perhaps in their personal lives as well.

# 1

# Criminal Behavior Is a Result Not of Environment but of an Individual's Choices

## Role of Environment

> *Do you entirely dismiss the influence of environment?*
> [LINCOLN, NEBRASKA]

> *I have always believed in the bucket theory dealing with the environment. Our environment decides what gets into the bucket. How can you say that the environment does not have anything to do with whether a person becomes a criminal?* [INDIANAPOLIS, INDIANA]

> *How do you justify negating the impact of social ills toward the contribution of developing the so-called criminal?* [BEDFORD, TEXAS]

Virtually every conceivable aspect of the individual's environment has been implicated as causing criminal behavior. Perhaps the best example of the thinking that has been with us for most of this century is the idea that poverty causes crime. Ingrained in theory and at the foundation of social policy and numerous programs is the belief that poverty propels citizens into a life of crime. Ostensibly, people who live in dire poverty lose hope early in life. Although they see success and all its trappings depicted in the movies and on television, they cannot envision it for themselves. Consequently, out of frustration and despair, they conclude that the only way to get what they want is to take it. Some sociologists even have asserted that committing crimes is a normal and adaptive way for deprived and frustrated individuals to gain both the respect and material items that they crave. They find it understandable that an inner-city youngster sells drugs to obtain designer clothes, jewelry, and other items that he is convinced he will never have otherwise. Of course, if this thinking were correct, then virtually all residents of poor neighborhoods would be selling drugs.

Most poor people are not criminals, and many people from affluent circumstances are. But those who see the environment as causing crime have an explanation for this as well. They contend that individuals who have been indulged by growing up in affluent circumstances develop a sense that they are entitled to the good life. These individuals eventually realize that what has been handed to them when they are young must be earned. Rather than work hard, they resort to easier ways to attain what they want. So the theory goes. If this were true, most members of the upper middle class would be criminals, which clearly is not the case.

In understanding criminal behavior, a person's environment is not the critical factor. It is, rather, *how* the person chooses to deal with that environment. For many people, growing up and having little provides a strong incentive to work hard and overcome adversity. During their darkest moments, when discouragement is intense, the thought of committing a crime to get what they want is repugnant or may not occur at all. Their solution is to work harder.

I could interview any readers of this book and find that they had to overcome some adversity from their environment while growing up. If they had followed a criminal path, after the fact, I could explain why, because that is what many people do. After the fact, they can explain anything. And, in doing so, they are more clever than they are correct.

When he is held accountable, the criminal focuses upon any adversity in his environment to explain why he acted as he did. He may claim that he had little choice in growing up, that he turned to crime because he came from a bleak situation where all his buddies stole, fought, and used drugs. What he won't reveal so readily is that his own brother and many other kids in his housing project rejected the temptations of the street, attended school, came home, and stayed out of trouble. However, these were not the kids he chose to be with because he looked down on them as "lame," "sissy," and "weak."

I do not totally discount the role of environment. Opportunities to commit and get away with crimes may be greater in one area of town than in another. In one part of a city, the drug trade flourishes. Still, most residents of that area choose not to use drugs. It has been claimed that conditions in many low-income housing projects virtually spawn criminal behavior. But there is no evidence that most residents of these projects are criminals. Living in fear for themselves and their children, law-abiding residents have been known to implore the police to enter the projects to make them safe.

Over the years, I have heard people say that I am letting society off the hook and, worse, that I am providing ammunition to those policy makers and politicians who are turning their backs on our country's neediest citizens. This is not the case. Certainly, we should assist people who lack opportunity. What I am saying is that we must be realistic as to who will be helped by such efforts. A person who already is responsible will utilize the assistance he is given to improve himself. If you teach him computer skills, he will be equipped to support himself and will likely do so. If you give an antisocial person such an opportunity, what you will have is a criminal with computer skills rather than a criminal without such skills. Providing this individual with more opportunities does not by itself change fundamental thinking patterns. In fact, offenders have bragged to me that, because they acquired new skills, they were better equipped to commit new crimes.

Basing our attempts to fight crime on a theory that the root causes lie in social conditions has gotten us nowhere. Many years of perpetuating the myth that people turn to crime because they are victims of circumstances has been extremely costly. The toll runs into billions of dollars as well as into human costs that cannot be measured in dollars.

> *Is there more of a chance that a child growing up in a bad environment is more likely to think in erroneous ways and become delinquent?* [GRAYSLAKE, ILLINOIS]

> *John lives in the inner city. Before his father left, he beat John and his three brothers and one sister. The mother was unable to give warmth and nurturing to her children. Does the combination of circumstances—child abuse, poor role model, inner city environment, lack of supervision—make it more likely that John will become involved in crime?* [POUGHKEEPSIE, NEW YORK]

What constitutes a bad environment is largely a matter of opinion. Let us assume that the individual lives in a chaotic household where basic needs often go unmet. He resides in a squalid tenement, is malnourished, and lives with a single mother who is so preoccupied with her own problems that she gives him little attention, supervision, or support. Sometimes she is loving, but often she considers him a burden and treats him harshly.

This child requires material assistance, emotional support, and numerous other services. He has a lot to overcome. However, there is no compelling reason automatically to assume that he will attempt to escape his circumstances by committing crimes. A teenage girl in a Los Angeles juvenile correctional facility told me that in her neighborhood gangs roamed streets where drugs were as easy to obtain as candy. She had seven siblings, and they all lived in poverty. When I asked her whether her brothers and sisters were involved in crime as she had been, she looked at me incredulously and replied, "I have a little brother who's starting to act up but the rest, they don't want no part of no trouble." She had chosen to gravitate to the youngsters whom she found exciting. The world of gangs, sex, and drugs was far more appealing to her than spending time at home, attending school, and generally living by the rules. Had she actually been a gang member, a social scientist or counselor would likely have ascribed it to her environment.

> *Have you ever known a serial killer to have a good loving family and environment?* [SALT LAKE CITY, UTAH]

Like other offenders, serial killers come from a variety of environments. Most seem to be from troubled families. However, millions of people grow up under deplorable social and familial circumstances. They do not become serial killers or criminals of any sort.

## Environmental Stress and Crime

> *Can stress, in your opinion, play a role in causing a person to become a criminal?* [PORTLAND, OREGON]

> *Isn't it possible (probable) that many persons who are predisposed with a "criminal mind" will not exhibit these antisocial behaviors (i.e., commit a crime) unless there is a precipitating event outside the person?*
> [AUSTIN, TEXAS]

Just living is stressful. People can create problems by the way that they respond to situations, then turn around and complain about the stress. This question is about individuals who, through no fault of their own, find themselves in extremely stressful circumstances.

This notion that stress may cause a responsible person suddenly to do something totally out of character does not stand up to clinical scrutiny. People develop ways of responding to stress that are in line with their personalities. For example, one individual's characteristic reaction may be to avoid stress, whereas another person immediately tries to grapple with the problem. Still another pattern may be for a person to try to wipe out the source of stress through intimidation or physical attack.

Imagine a highly stressful situation at work. One employee might react by taking leave. Another might approach his supervisor to address the problem directly. And still another, in an attempt to annihilate the source of the stress, might punch his supervisor. A videotape of these three individuals' lives would most likely reveal that each had dealt with previous sources of stress in a similar manner.

To assume that a particularly stressful situation will push a person over the brink so that he commits a crime ignores the fact that, before he encountered the current dilemma, he had developed a characteristic way of dealing with stress. Perhaps any person, no matter how responsible, under extreme stress may fantasize a violent response. However, what the person actually does will conform to his past patterns. Only those who know him well may be aware of what those patterns are. I interviewed a man who, after brutally beating his wife, was court-ordered into counseling. He had been married for many years, had two grown children, and had held the same job for more than a decade. It appeared that he was a highly responsible individual who snapped under stress, but I learned otherwise after interviewing his wife and one of his sons. This fellow had been a domineering, belligerent, threatening husband and an abusive father. On previous occasions, when he grew intensely frustrated at things not going his way, he had exploded in rage, screamed, thrown things, and hit family members. Nobody knew this except those who lived with him and had never dared confide in anyone outside the family.

## The Military and Criminality

> *Does military training, intense combat and stress, and approval for murder and savagery have potential for creating a psychopath out of a normal adolescent?*
>
> [SEATTLE, WASHINGTON]

The answer to this is simply "No." If a person enlisting in the military is already a criminal, he may find dangerous situations highly exciting and have few qualms about killing. Such a person could be an asset in combat. However, during peacetime service, he may prove hard to get along with. Bored and disgruntled, such an individual may fail to comply with rules and regulations and may commit crimes on or off base. If he drank and used drugs previously, he may do more of the same. The point is that, if he was not a criminal before he went into the military, serving in the military would not make him into one.

## Permissiveness in Society and Crime

> *Address the relationship of crime to a permissive society.*
>
> [VAIL, COLORADO]

I stated earlier that the environment can provide greater or fewer opportunities for crime to occur, although the environment does not cause a person to become a criminal. One price of an increasingly free society seems to be more crime. As totalitarian regimes have fallen and given rise to more democratic forms of government, crime has risen. No doubt we could decrease crime by stationing a policeman on every corner and by making penalties for crimes more severe. However, it is debatable whether most people would desire to live in a society that would be so oppressive.

I like to use school truancy as an example. Once there were serious consequences for skipping school. I recall that one time during my senior year of high school, I thought of skipping a particular class I found boring. But that was as far as it went—a thought. I believed that if I actually skipped the class, I would be caught. They did take attendance then. I also believed I would be in big trouble because my parents would be notified and would be terribly disappointed in me. I also thought that my school would notify Yale University, which had just accepted me, and that Yale would rescind its acceptance. Whether I was right about all this or not, the deterrents were so strong that I thought the world would fall in just for skipping one class.

I remember interviewing a mother whose son had skipped two full weeks of school. She would drop him off in the morning and watch him enter the building. After she left, unknown to her, he would leave. When she arrived home after work, her son would be there with his book bag and would even talk about school. She learned of his truancy only because she happened to call the school to leave a message and discovered that not only was he absent on that day, but he also had failed to attend for two weeks. The school did not cause her son to be truant. The school's lax policy (i.e., failing to notify parents) made it easier for him to skip because he knew he could get away with it. Some children will go to school, no matter what the truancy policy; others will skip school, no matter what. In the middle of these two extremes are students who react to a lax policy by succumbing to temptation and skipping. Rather than causing them to skip school, the lack of deterrents makes it easier for them to choose to do so. Clearly, some children will be responsible, no matter how permissive the environment. The child who is becoming increasingly antisocial will exploit a permissive attitude or policy. In the end, it is the child who makes the choice. The environment only makes that choice easier or more difficult.

## Egocentrism in Society and Crime

> *Some of the attitudes described as typical of criminal*
> *thinking seem to be widespread in today's cultural climate*
> *(e.g., violence can be a solution, egocentrism, manners*
> *viewed as irrelevant and inhibiting). Do these social*
> *attitudes contribute to an individual's becoming a criminal?*
> [LOUISVILLE, KENTUCKY]

> *How have the "me" generation and "do your own*
> *thing" philosophy influenced antisocial behavior?*
> [WICHITA, KANSAS]

We must not confuse a cause of criminality with an excuse for criminality. We live in times where there appears to be less civility, a dwindling sense of community, and more of a tendency to resort to violence rather than to amicably mediate. While living amidst conditions that are far from ideal, we develop different methods of coping, but most of us do not turn to crime. Bear in mind that persons who commit a crime decide to do so because they wanted to, not for abstract reasons that they may conjure up later.

## Cultural Relativity and Crime

> *Are some or all of the "errors in thinking" of the antisocial*
> *person fostered by characteristics of a particular culture?*
> [SEATTLE, WASHINGTON]

It has been argued that the definition of what is "criminal" depends on the laws or the customs and mores of a particular culture. To an extent, this is true. Marijuana possession may be a crime in one place, but not in another. My focus is not on laws or cultures but on minds. There are people who would be criminals, regardless of when or where they exist on this planet. They seek to dominate others, appropriate what is not rightfully theirs, and abuse people in pursuit of their own objectives. As one man said, "If rape were legalized today, I wouldn't rape, but I'd do something else." His statement reflected that the excitement of doing whatever is forbidden mattered above all else.

# 2

# Environmental Factors Do Not Cause Crime

## Media Violence and Crime

> *Do you really believe violence as televised or portrayed*
> *in other media forms has as much impact on criminal*
> *behavior as the public is led to believe?*
> [BRADFORD, PENNSYLVANIA]

Television and the movies, in my experience, have never made a criminal out of anyone. Critical is not what is shown on the screen, but what is in the mind of the viewer. Millions of people have watched countless films and programs laden with violence, whether they are cartoons, prize fights, science fiction, or the nightly news. They do not imitate the criminality that they see. However, there is such a thing as a "copycat crime." If a criminally inclined person watches a crime being enacted, his already fertile mind absorbs what he is seeing. The individual may dwell on the scene, fantasize about it and, given the opportunity, may commit the crime. Other viewers will regard the program merely as a diversion or entertainment and will give it no more thought. The program or movie is not what "causes" the viewer to behave in a criminal manner. The seeds were there long before he sat down to watch television or the film.

> *Are you concerned about the explosion of movies and*
> *TV shows about serial killers? These shows seem to*
> *glorify serial murder and demonstrate violence far more*
> *severe, cunning, and thought-out than most serial killers*
> *carry out in reality.* [FT. MYERS, FLORIDA]

The issue of my personal concern about violence in the media is separate from the question of whether the media cause people to become violent. Personally, I think there is too much gratuitous violence in entertainment. Nonetheless, I must emphasize that millions of people of all ages and backgrounds flock to see programs and films about serial killers and other perpetrators of violence. It is entertainment for them; few seek to emulate the violence they watch.

> *Does [society's] glamorization of criminal activity (e.g.,*
> *movies, books) send a mixed message to criminals?*
> *Does it matter?* [AUSTIN, TEXAS]

No question about it: violence sells! The public has a hearty appetite for crime in what it reads and watches. Some criminals thrive on this attention that the media give them. Their excitement is heightened by news reports about how they manage to elude apprehension. Putting criminals in the spotlight with a magazine interview or television appearance adds to their sense of being important. However, glamorizing crime does not send a mixed message to criminals in terms of the acceptability of their behavior. They are fully aware of what is illegal and know that if they are apprehended, punishment is likely to follow.

## Pornography and Crime

> *What part does pornography play in sex crimes?*
> [BILLINGS, MONTANA]

Some sex offenders are avid consumers of pornography. Again, a distinction must be made between cause and effect. Millions of Americans have watched X-rated films or read sexually explicit publications, but they do not become perpetrators of sex crimes.

My response to the question is similar to the one I gave about television. The critical factor is the mind that consumes the pornography. Two individuals may view the same materials yet, depending upon their personalities, respond very differently. Whereas one person may fasten onto pornography to increase his arousal during sex with a consenting partner, another may seize upon a particular scene and rehearse it over and over in his mind, fueling fantasies he already has had of victimizing another person. The pornography does not cause the individual to commit a sex offense. Antisocial features of the personality must already be present for the crime to occur.

## Free Time and Crime

> *Is free time a problem? In other words, does a young offender commit crime because he or she has too much free time?* [KANSAS CITY, MISSOURI]

Youths do not commit crimes because they have too much free time. They commit crimes because they want to. I have heard more than one juvenile offender claim that he acted as he did because he had nothing to do. A responsible youngster may feel bored and also assert that there is nothing to do. However, the individual either remains bored for a while or is resourceful enough to occupy himself. Committing a crime does not enter his mind as a way to relieve boredom.

A youth with a criminal personality may claim he has nothing to do when in fact many activities are available. He may have homework assignments or chores. He could watch television, go to the playground, kick a ball around, or ride a bike with a neighbor. Still, he maintains he has nothing to do because he has no interest in such activities. They do not offer the high voltage of hanging out with his buddies and engaging in illicit activities.

## Nutrition

> *Does a high sugar diet have a significant impact on*
> *perpetuating delinquency?* [ABILENE, TEXAS]

> *Have you any useful hunches regarding causation [with*
> *respect to] nutritional deficits?* [SALT LAKE CITY, UTAH]

There is no conclusive evidence that a particular nutritional deficiency or a diet high in sugar is contributory to juvenile delinquency. In fact, some studies suggest that sugar can have a calming effect rather than inciting kids to commit crimes. Millions of children do not eat nutritiously, but there is no evidence that they commit crimes because of their diet.

## Full Moon and Crime

> *Have you heard the theory that when the moon is full,*
> *crime and violence increase? Is there any connection?*
> [BILLINGS, MONTANA]

This notion has been around for a long time, but I know of no scientific evidence that supports it.

## Gangs: A Sense of Belonging?

> *Do adolescents get involved in gangs because of their*
> *need for a sense of belonging and identity, or is gang*
> *involvement related more to the need for the excitement?*
> [DALLAS, TEXAS]

Adolescents have told others that, by joining a gang, they found a family. With membership came a sense of acceptance and belonging that they had not found elsewhere, even at home. This is a self-serving explanation by youths who are in trouble and being held accountable.  It is also a theory of some social scientists.

Many youngsters in gang-ridden neighborhoods do not belong to gangs and want no part of them. Gangs have spread into suburbs where children have families and a variety of groups to belong to. Their members do not care about acceptance by church groups, scout troops, athletic teams, or other school and neighborhood organizations. No matter where they live, gang members willingly defy the social order and take risks so that they can participate in the exciting street life and criminal activity of a gang. They are not joining a gang because they like to play chess, go skating, or engage in some other highly "prosocial" activity.

## Birth Order and Crime

*What are your views on the birth order theory as a component of the development of or contribution to antisocial behavior?* [BOISE, IDAHO]

I know of no correlation between birth order and the development of a criminal personality.

# 3

# Bad Parenting Does Not Cause Crime

ized to the point that the child will do horrible things and turn into a criminal. To varying degrees, children are vulnerable to what their parents say and do. I have met adults who told me that, as children, they were determined to prove their parents wrong. These youngsters who were told they'd amount to nothing were anything but failures. I know people whose parents showered them with love and encouragement, but they still ended up in prison.

A criminal may tell a counselor that his parents were always down on him. He will relate how his mother and father yelled at him, how punitive they were, and how they never praised him. Hearing this tale of woe, the counselor will believe that this client had harsh, unsupportive parents. If the counselor were to ask the parents what this client had done that prompted parental condemnation, he might gain a different perspective. The counselor would learn that the criminal's parents had berated him for skipping school, grounded him for taking the family car without permission, and repeatedly warned him that he would be a failure in life when he refused to do homework and hung out with friends late at night.

## Antisocial Child as Family Scapegoat?

*One theory that I have heard frequently is that a maladjusted youth can be the "symptom bearer" for the family—that he or she is acting out the difficulties of the family system. Please comment.* [RALEIGH, NORTH CAROLINA]

*What do you think of the family–systems theory that says that one child, often the second-born, is picked as a family scapegoat and therefore acts out to help the family maintain a "stably unstable" system?* [BOISE, IDAHO]

It depends on what you mean by maladjusted. If this term is being used synonymously with criminal, I have not found this to be true. The criminal is more likely to make the family a scapegoat. If you have a criminal in your family, I can guarantee that all members will be maladjusted because people with a criminal personality keep families in turmoil. Such a person will cite family problems (even the ones he has created) and attempt to blame his antisocial behavior on them. Well-intentioned but uninformed counselors may find the criminal convincing and sympathize with him. Rather than confront him for victimizing the family, they chastise family members for being unfair, uncompromising, or insensitive.

I have read numerous case files filled with accounts of how such individuals had severe difficulties because they were misunderstood and mistreated by parents. One might conclude that these youngsters had never done anything wrong, but whatever befell them was a result of the awful things their mothers or fathers did. A counselor may be highly sympathetic because he does not regard the criminal as a criminal at all but, instead, perceives him as a victim of a "dysfunctional family." The reality is that rather than being mistreated as a scapegoat, the criminal is a person who continually mistreats others.

## Latchkey Children and Crime

> *If a parent stays home from work (giving up a career),*
> *will it make a difference?* [WICHITA, KANSAS]

Millions of children, so-called latch-key children, spend hours unsupervised every day. Most play in the neighborhood, do homework, watch television, and responsibly take care of themselves, but others exploit the freedom they have and get into trouble. In one family, the mother worked at two jobs and could not get home until eight o'clock at night. She arranged for her two sons to go next door where a parent would be home to watch them and give them dinner. Each afternoon, the boys' mother called to talk to them. If they wanted to do anything out of the ordinary, they had her telephone number at work and were expected to call for permission. One son did precisely what his mother expected, while his brother started to hang around older youths, disappearing sometimes for hours. One day, a call came requesting that he be picked up at the police station where he had been detained for stealing.

The circumstances were identical for both boys: the same family, the same neighborhood, the same rules applied to each. The critical factor was not the mother's absence, but the fact that the two boys made different choices as to how to use their freedom.

## Permissive versus Authoritarian Parenting and Crime

> *How much of an influence on criminal behavior in children is a parent who accommodates the child when he or she sees the child does not try and expects things to come easily?* [EL PASO, TEXAS]

> *Do you feel parents are at fault when they continue to cover for their children's mistakes?* [NORFOLK, VIRGINIA]

> *Couldn't it be possible that a well-behaved child can be encouraged toward criminality by permissive "rescue parenting"?* [SALT LAKE CITY, UTAH]

Fearing that their children will fail, parents sometimes step in too quickly and do for their offspring what they could eventually accomplish for themselves. Or they may rush to bail a child out of a jam that he created by his own irresponsible behavior. Such attempts by parents to accommodate their children are ill-advised, because they can deprive a child of an opportunity to learn something worthwhile. A child might procrastinate or ignore a task if he thinks he can count on a parent to step in and resolve the problem for him. Or if he is rescued and spared some unpalatable consequence, he may expect that someone will always be available to bail him out. I do not see this as having any bearing on crime. The outcome of what I have described may be a spoiled child or a child who fails to believe in himself and then fails to utilize his potential. It is an unwarranted leap to assume that such behavior by a parent will create a criminal.

> *Is it possible that the "concentration camps" that overly strict parents set up for their teens actually cause more acting-out behavior?* [SALT LAKE CITY, UTAH]

When parents are rigid and highly authoritarian, there are any number of possible responses by their offspring. Some children simply buckle under an authoritarian regime and meekly submit. They may identify with their parents and even defend them. Others, while resenting their parents, still substantially conform to their expectations. Another response is for a youngster to secretly circumvent parental restrictions. Then there is the youngster who overtly pits his will against that of his parents and defies their restrictions.

The question of cause and effect is complicated. With more moderate and reasonable parents, there would be less conflict. There is no evidence that most criminals are raised by highly punitive parents. Juvenile offenders come from all sorts of homes. If their parents were unreasonably strict, they are faulted for fostering conditions that foment rebellion and antisocial behavior. If they were permissive, they are criticized for failing to set limits with appropriate consequences. And if they were fairly democratic in their approach to child rearing, they are seen as wishy-washy or as not having taken a strong enough hand. The focus in psychological analysis usually seems to be on what the parents did or failed to do, not on the child and how he chose to deal with whatever the circumstances were.

## Parental Attention and Crime

> *Isn't it possible that the children in a family were not given the same type of attention or amount of attention? Since each child has a distinct personality, is it realistic to expect that the same treatment is necessarily appropriate for each child?* [PITTSBURGH, PENNSYLVANIA]

Because no two children are exactly alike, it is reasonable to expect that parents treat each of their offspring differently. I have found no pattern of child-rearing practices in one family that accounts for a youngster's becoming a criminal while his siblings become responsible citizens.

## Parental Untruthfulness and Crime: An Example

> *A 6-year-old child is being told that his or her father who is in prison is there because the police and the judge have made a mistake and that the father is innocent. Is this breeding an antisocial child?* [GRAYSLAKE, ILLINOIS]

Without knowing more about the particular youngster, it would be hard to predict the outcome, but one thing is clear. It takes a lot more than this to breed an antisocial child. A parent might say this to protect the child at an age when it is difficult for him to comprehend the situation. Believing his father is innocent, the child may feel less self-conscious or embarrassed, especially when his friends ask. I think what the question is getting at is whether the youngster might grow up experiencing resentment toward authorities (police, courts). That is a possibility, at least until he discovers that his father was actually guilty. He might also harbor resentment against a mother who lied to him. In my experience, one event or set of circumstances does not create lasting antisocial patterns.

## Is the Child to Blame for Crime?

> *In saying that certain children, by their behavior, cause*
> *their parents to react negatively, isn't it true that we seem*
> *to be removing parents' fair share of responsibility?*
> [DENVER, COLORADO]

> *Are you shifting all the responsibility onto the child with*
> *no consideration of parenting skills?* [BEDFORD, TEXAS]

> *How can a 3-, 4-, or 5-year-old child really be*
> *considered to be making choices? How might the way in*
> *which he or she interacts with the parents contribute to*
> *the choices he or she is making?* [RALEIGH, NORTH CAROLINA]

For decades, counselors and other advisors have blamed parents for whatever problems their children develop. Mothers and fathers have heard that it is their fault if they have a child who is maladjusted, emotionally disturbed, or badly behaved.

A distortion of my findings has been to say that by "blaming" the child, I absolve parents of all responsibility. What I have been pointing out is that the child does not enter the world like a formless lump of clay to be haplessly shaped and molded by his parents. Rather, children have distinct temperaments. Any parent who has more than one youngster knows that, from infancy, each differs from the others in alertness, activity level, fearfulness, sociability, and in other ways. Parents react in accord with their children's temperaments. A mother or father responds differently to a cranky, colicky baby than to a cooing, contented baby.

To discuss the problem of criminality in terms of ascribing blame neither illuminates child development nor facilitates solutions to problems. We must recognize that children influence the behavior of parents as well as the other way around. From the time they are toddlers, children make choices in the way they respond to their environment. A mother warns her son, "Don't touch the stove. Hot!" Obediently, the child draws back, much to the mother's relief. Another child may respond to the same admonition by jabbing a finger at the stove and feeling the heat, but then never touching it again. A lesson was learned. Then there is the venturesome, daring child who continually defies his mother, fiddling with the dials and switches. The mother is a nervous wreck and has to keep watching her child whenever he draws near the stove. In this rather simple example, each child shapes a parent's behavior.

What parents do *does* matter. We need to do our best! Fortunately, most children do internalize the responsible norms, standards, and values their parents try to teach them. However, being a responsible parent does not guarantee that a child will make responsible choices. Nor does failure to be a good parent ensure that a child will turn out to be a juvenile delinquent.

## Crime as a Choice

> *So now that you have debunked various theories about what makes a criminal, are you saying people become criminals through conscious choice?* [ST. LOUIS, MISSOURI]

Yes! From a very early age, human beings embark on a lifetime of making choices. We choose how to deal with outer circumstances. We also choose how to react to our own emotions and thoughts. The criminal knows right from wrong, yet chooses to do exactly what he wants, even if it involves pushing aside considerations of conscience or external consequences. The excuses as to what made him act a certain way come later, when he is taken to task by others.

# 4

# People Do Not Become Abusers and Criminals Because They Were Abused

## Victim or Victimizer?

> *If socialization has nothing to do with crime, how do*
> *you account for the fact that the huge majority of sexual*
> *offenders were victims?* [STEAMBOAT SPRINGS, COLORADO]

> *Don't statistics show that a high percentage of individuals*
> *who sexually abuse others were themselves abused?*
> [LANSING, MICHIGAN]

Let us examine the claim that the huge majority of sex offenders are victims. What is the source? It is the sex offenders themselves who, when they have to account for their conduct, are often untruthful. They may assert they suffered abuse when it never happened. People who truly are victims of sexual abuse react in different ways. Most do not become criminals. Some bear lasting psychological scars that impair their functioning. Others are amazingly resilient and move on with minimal disruption to their lives. What happened to them would be the last thing they would consider inflicting upon another person.

The antisocial child is open to temptations and opportunities that most of his peers would shun. This includes sexual activity that the child is receptive to or even chooses to initiate. In one case, a boy had sex with his scoutmaster on numerous occasions. The latter was convicted and incarcerated for having sex with minors. Later, the boy and his family sued the scouting organization, claiming psychological damages. They asserted that, because of the sexual abuse, the youngster's personality had changed so that he had become a delinquent. There is no question that, as the adult, the scoutmaster was legally and morally responsible, no matter what the boy wanted. Yet, the youth was not exactly an unwilling victim. So eager was he to pursue the sexual encounters that he skipped school. Not only had he found sex exciting with this man, but he also had been involved in other illicit activities having nothing to do with the scoutmaster.

Studies indicate that, rather than having been abused, some sex offenders began seeking out sexual contacts and abusing others at a very early age. Only when held accountable did they claim that they had been the ones who had been approached and victimized.

> *As a therapist we use background to understand. It seems you are discounting all mental health theory.*
> [SEATTLE, WASHINGTON]

> *Don't you agree that "choosing" is subject to the same principles of behavior as other behaviors, and it is simply our not understanding the learning history that puzzles us?*
> [MINNEAPOLIS, MINNESOTA]

I am not discounting all mental health theory. I am questioning how background is used in understanding and evaluating criminals. I recall an offender who, in a moment of rare candor, declared to my colleague and mentor, Dr. Samuel Yochelson, "If I didn't have enough excuses for crime before psychiatry, I certainly have enough now."

When the criminal is accounting for what he does, he feeds others what he thinks they want to hear and what he hopes will exonerate him. His approach may be to make up things that never happened, magnify the significance of an event, or simply use what actually did happen to justify past, present, and even future behavior. In citing an adversity, the criminal may minimize any contribution he made in creating it or omit how he compounded it by his reaction.

I am not maintaining that psychiatrists, psychologists, social workers, and other professionals all are gullible. I recall my own naiveté. As I discovered, the antisocial person does not wear a sign announcing his personality. He presents himself in the best possible light, contending that he is little different from anyone else except that he "made a mistake" or suffered "bad breaks." His presentation of himself as a victim is often subtle. Early in my career, as a well-intentioned and empathic psychologist, I gathered information in order to "understand" and to treat. The outcome was that I had, at the end of treatment, offenders who were psychologically sophisticated. They still were criminals, and they used the entire psychotherapeutic process in a self-serving manner. They did not change one iota.

I became aware that in fact I did not have an understanding of this population. By focusing on background, as they presented it, I thought I was dealing with people who truly were victims. Recognizing that these people were far more victimizers than they were victims resulted in my taking a very different and more effective approach.

> *Would you comment on an adolescent, in a psychiatric hospital by court order, who killed his father in cold blood while he was asleep after enduring years of physical and emotional abuse. This occurred after years of petty crime by the adolescent.* [DALLAS, TEXAS]

Whereas I cannot comment on this specific case (because I do not know the particulars), it raises the question as to whether I believe that everyone who kills his abuser has a criminal personality.

I would respond in the negative if the abused person has no escape other than to eradicate his tormenter. Homicide in such a case would be tantamount to self-defense.

Consider a different sort of situation. I consulted in a case where a woman shot her husband to death. The lady claimed that her marriage had been a living hell because her spouse tried to control her every move. One afternoon, a petty disagreement escalated, and her husband started taunting, then threatening her. Because he had struck her before, she became terrified as he advanced toward her. When she grabbed a gun, he dashed into a room and slammed the door. She was actually safe at the time she fired the weapon. The bullet passed through the door, striking and mortally wounding him.

An analysis of the marital relationship revealed that the wife was not a helpless victim. She was able to leave her residence and, against her husband's wishes, she frequented bars where she drank and played pool. She was independent enough to hire a sitter and go to work. She had numerous opportunities to leave and plenty of places to seek refuge, but instead she chose to remain in this volatile relationship.

In evaluating situations where an abused person takes the life of the abuser, one must carefully investigate the circumstances and evaluate the personality of the killer. How did this individual previously deal with difficult situations? What options other than homicide were available, and why did the person not avail himself of them?

In the case mentioned in the question, why didn't the teenager leave the home and seek help while his father was asleep? Clearly, he did not kill his father because he was being terrorized at that very moment. How long had he harbored the wish to kill his father, even rehearsed it in his mind until the opportunity presented itself? Information in the question asked above indicates that the boy already was engaging in petty crimes. How much more was there that had not come to anyone's attention?

Many questions in such cases need to be answered by a careful psychological investigation before one concludes that the homicide was justifiably perpetrated by a helpless victim. The individual with a criminal personality has expertise in rationalizing whatever he does. He can build a case to convince others that he was in such jeopardy that, to save his own life, he had to kill. The truth is that other alternatives existed.

> *[You spoke of] antisocial juveniles calling 911 as a weapon to victimize their parents, teachers, or relatives. How do we know if the juvenile making the call is truly an abused child or a juvenile abusing his parents? Do we do psychological evaluations on all youths reporting cases of abuse?* [AUSTIN, TEXAS]

Antisocial youngsters constantly defy and threaten their parents. In some cases, they commit crimes in the home. When an exasperated parent does anything physical—a slap, a push, a shove, or anything else—the child goes on the offensive. He may threaten, "I'm going to call 911," or "I'm going to report you for child abuse." I have known more than one case in which the parents were investigated by a state agency while the child's conduct, which precipitated the incident, was completely ignored.

I recall one family in which the daughter had been incorrigible. She turned every request into a battleground. Rarely did she consider the needs or wishes of anyone else in the family. Only what she wanted at the time mattered. She became embroiled with her parents over her failure to study, her involvement with a boy much older than she, and her staying out late. Toward the end of a particularly exasperating weekend, an argument erupted over putting away dishes. The girl started spewing curse words at her father. Having had his fill of her nastiness, he slapped her across the face. Within a few days, he was under investigation by social services because his daughter had complained to a school counselor about being abused by her father. This normally patient, loving father had done everything he could to try to help his daughter, including hire a private psychotherapist. Now his job, with its security clearance, was imperiled unless he could clear himself of his daughter's charges. I helped him do just that, explaining to authorities the entire picture. I did not condone the father's slapping his daughter, but I did explain what had preceded it. The case for abuse was dropped by the investigators.

I am not advising that those who man hot lines or who work in protective services assume that a report of child abuse is fabricated, but workers who investigate these cases must allow for the possibility that, in certain instances, the person claiming abuse has actually been the one to wrong another.

## Corporal Punishment and Violence

> *Do you feel that corporal punishment with children leads to violent behavior?* [AUSTIN, TEXAS]

This is highly unlikely. What qualifies as corporal punishment can be discipline ranging from a light slap to a severe spanking. Beating, not corporal punishment, is abuse.

It is another one of these glib cause–effect formulations to assert that children become violent because they were physically punished. It is reasonable to wager that most children who have been spanked become loving parents and law-abiding citizens. They do not turn into violent criminals.

I do know of cases where a child was violent and, in response, the parents became physical. Consider the child who throws temper tantrums, attacks his siblings, and destroys property. To restrain him when he endangers himself or others may require physical measures. Such a child may elicit a spanking by a parent who has found that less severe disciplinary measures proved ineffective. When he finds a sympathetic ear, the child relates that his parents "beat" him for no reason. Hearing one side of the story and a highly exaggerated one at that, the listener confuses cause and effect and thinks that the child was a victim of abuse. He may go a step further and conclude that the child's violence was a direct outcome of the way that his parents disciplined him—a real inversion of cause and effect. It was the violent behavior that elicited the corporal punishment, not the other way around.

*I am often called upon to be a spokesperson for abused
children. At the end of every interview, I am asked,
"What will become of these children without
intervention?" Since most grow up to be responsible,
mature citizens, how do I answer this without risking
discouraging interest in funding treatment programs?*
[DALLAS, TEXAS]

I am responding to this question mainly because I do not want to
be seen as indifferent to the plight of abused children. Abused children
have problems, but most do not become criminals. Some become
withdrawn, some feel guilty and blame themselves, and some become
depressed to the point of trying to take their own lives. They need help!
To assume that a child in need of services will eventually be fine and
will "grow out of it" is unwarranted and irresponsible.

# 5

Biological/Genetic
Contributions to
Criminality Need Not
Preordain Incarceration

> *If environment has little impact on decisions to commit criminal acts, do you believe that there is a "criminal gene" that makes crime innate in the individual?* [AUSTIN, TEXAS]

> *When you talk to parents whose child has committed a crime, how often do they tell you, "This child has been different since his or her birth"?* [ST. CLOUD, MINNESOTA]

Whereas there is no evidence that a single "criminal gene" exists, we must be receptive to evidence that genetic or biological factors can contribute to criminality. In speaking with parents of criminals, I have been struck by their observation that a particular child was different from others in the family long before peer, school, and other outside influences had a chance to play a significant role. One mother said that, no matter how loving she was, her toddler seemed to reject closeness, a pattern that became more pronounced as he got older. Another described the destructiveness of her 3-year-old, behavior that turned out not to be a stage as she had hoped, but an intensifying aspect of his personality. A mother recalled that, among her children, her daughter always seemed to be the malcontent, perpetually complaining, dissatisfied, bored, and uncooperative. Many a family event was ruined by the child's sulking and negativity. Whatever she did that got her into trouble, she blamed on someone else.

Many children are strong-willed, but that is not the problem. What the strong will is directed toward is the problem. The parents of an antisocial child have to cope with their youngster's unrelenting nagging, bullying, threatening, and even physical attacks on others to achieve his objective.

As parents have described being locked into power contests with their child, they recalled their own reactions as initially ranging from amusement to toleration at what seemed to be childlike strides for independence. When the child did not respond to the setting of limits and imposing of consequences, the parents' frustration and apprehension mounted. What would the child do next? Could they take him anywhere without some crisis? What could they do to help turn his behavior around?

All children can be difficult at times. Their aggressive or deceptive behavior is episodic and tends to diminish as they become socialized and develop a concept of injury to others. Not so with the antisocial child whose patterns expand and intensify the older he gets.

How does one explain a child being so unmanageable and destructive at an early age? At this point, we simply do not have definitive answers. Factors in the child's environment do not seem to account for this. Surely, the possibility of there being a significant genetic or biological basis for criminal behavior is worthy of further investigation.

> *If there is a genetic predisposition to criminal behavior,*
> *are criminals then responsible for their acts or should they*
> *be no more blamed for their condition than the diabetic?*
> [INDIANAPOLIS, INDIANA]

If a person has a genetic predisposition toward a particular condition, it does not mean that he inevitably will develop that condition or that, even if he does, it will run its full course. There are indications that people may be genetically predisposed to a number of illnesses: breast cancer, prostate cancer, alcoholism, or manic-depressive (or bipolar) illness. Preventive measures can be taken and, if the condition is discovered early, interventions can occur before the condition fully develops. A person does not choose to have prostate cancer run in his family. The genetically vulnerable individual can be careful with diet, undergo medical tests to detect early evidence of the disease and, if it is discovered, treatment can be initiated to prevent the disease from spreading.

Even with a genetic predisposition toward criminality, a person's inevitable destination need not be the penitentiary. With early detection, children can learn to make responsible choices. This will be discussed later in this book.

# 6

# The Alleged Increase in Crime: It Is Not Human Nature but Laws, Law Enforcement, and Deterrents that Change

## Inner-City Crime Rate

> *How do you make sense of the supposedly high crime
> rate reported in inner-city areas if environment is
> relatively unimportant?* [PETERSBURG, VIRGINIA]

Most people who live in inner-city areas are not criminals. Criminals congregate in areas of instability and low deterrence—characteristics of many inner-city locations. Suburbanites enter these environments to purchase "hard drugs" such as crack cocaine and heroin. They obtain firearms as well. All too often, the people in inner-city neighborhoods who are confined are not the criminals. They are the law-abiding people who are barely able to protect what little they have. Just walking on the streets of their own neighborhoods can be lethal. The majority of these law-abiding inner-city residents are at the mercy of the law-breaking minority.

## Multiple Antisocial Offspring

> *Would you comment on multiple antisocial youngsters in one family?* [OMAHA, NEBRASKA]

There are families in which more than one youngster is antisocial. Nevertheless, most of these families have other members who are law-abiding. The family in which everyone is antisocial is rare in my experience. Whether there is a significant genetic contribution to this, we do not know.

## An Increase in Antisocial Personalities?

> *Why does it seem that these antisocial personalities are on the increase in our society?* [COLORADO SPRINGS, COLORADO]

Human nature does not change, but social conditions do, making it easier or more difficult for people to commit crimes. There has been a rise in crime in nations where totalitarian regimes have given way to democracy. The citizens of those countries are freer, including those with criminal personalities. Consequently, we hear of crime increasing in countries whose populace was controlled by a dictator. The antisocial people were always there but, in a police state, they had fewer opportunities to commit crimes.

In addition, our awareness of crime is much greater because of rapid communication. No sooner does a shocking crime occur than we hear about it instantly, often with an on-the-scene radio or television report.

## Female Crime

> *Would you comment on the reported increase in violent*
> *offenses by teenage females?* [TULSA, OKLAHOMA]

There have been and still are many more correctional institutions for males than for females, chiefly because women commit less crime than do men. Both juvenile and adult female offenders have been treated differently from males by the juvenile justice system. The policy has been to divert them to programs offering social and psychological services.

A surge in female crime has occurred in the 1990s in the United States. Certainly, in their temperament and psychological makeup, teenage girls are no different now than ever before. However, they have gained greater freedom and have more opportunity in society. Like teenage boys, more are left to their own devices by working parents, and fewer restrictions are placed on where they go and what they do. As is the case with males, they have more access to drugs and guns.

## More Law Enforcement as a Cause of Crime?

> *During my childhood, many of the pranks I did escaped*
> *the gaze of the police. My son has gotten into trouble*
> *for doing the same things I got away with. Is an*
> *increased level of law enforcement creating crime?*
> [ST. GEORGE, UTAH]

There are two questions: first, does law enforcement create crime; second, does law enforcement create criminals?

A conscientious law-abiding person might get arrested for inadvertently committing some minor infraction that is on the books but rarely enforced. In such a situation, one could say that an increased level of law enforcement led to identification of a crime (another officer might have ignored the offense or given a warning). A criminal was created in the sense that a person had to pay a penalty. Such an incident, however, does not create a criminal in the deeper sense that I have been using the term: a person who lives his life doing whatever he wants with little regard to consequences.

The individual posing this question seems to acknowledge that he and his son both did things that were wrong, although I do not know specifically what he means by "pranks." In this particular context, the misconduct was there. The police did not create it. Apparently, his son was apprehended and prosecuted whereas when he did the same thing as a child, either he was not caught or the police let him off with a warning.

In many places, social policy has taken the direction of decriminalizing certain offenses. The misconduct occurs, but it is not prosecuted. Youngsters are no longer criminally prosecuted for what are called status offenses, such as truancy and running away. In some states, possession of small amounts of marijuana is penalized no more seriously than a motor vehicle violation. Rather than creating crime, police often are criticized for not enforcing laws that already exist.

> *How does the way the police treat someone who engaged in criminal behavior affect the possibility of future bad conduct (i.e., police may consider behavior by one child as a prank and the same behavior by another child as a crime)?* [RICHMOND, VIRGINIA]

Granted that there is a certain amount of discretion left to the arresting officer, the offender's reaction depends upon his personality prior to the crime. If a child is warned, but not prosecuted, for shoplifting, he may become emboldened to steal again. Another youngster may be so terrified that he never repeats the offense.

## A One-Time Criminal?

> *Is there such a thing as a one-time criminal, someone*
> *who made a bad choice, who truly regrets his or her*
> *crime, and who wants to change? Can there be a person*
> *like this, or do we label all criminals (convicted felons)*
> *and treat them with a blanket approach to behavior?*
> [LARAMIE, WYOMING]

Every person who steals a candy bar does not become a professional shoplifter. I have met people who told me about a very distasteful aftermath when they were caught stealing during their childhood. The embarrassment and the punishment were sufficient to deter them from ever repeating the offense.

When it comes to committing a major crime, the offense for which the person is caught usually represents the tip of an iceberg. I remember a judge who commented, "When I have a person who is convicted for a felony for the first time, it usually is the first time he has been caught, but not his first offense." Hypothetically, a person might commit a single felony, stand trial, and never commit a crime in the future. Such an individual is unlikely to come to the attention of a psychologist.

Only a careful evaluation can determine whether a person truly is a one-time offender or an individual who successfully has concealed numerous crimes but has finally slipped up and been apprehended.

# 7

# Individuals with a Criminal Mind View Life Differently Than Do Responsible People

## Pursuit of Excitement

> *Are there people who really want to lead this lifestyle?*
> [DALLAS, TEXAS]

> *Is there an element of the "adrenaline junkie" in an antisocial person—one who has not channeled the need for speed into being a cop, firefighter, paramedic, circus performer, or whatever?* [BOISE, IDAHO]

A career criminal commented, "If you take my crime away, you take my world away." He declared he would rather be dead than live an ordinary life where you adhere to the rules.

From a criminal's perspective, to be a worthwhile person involves overcoming others, gaining an advantage deviously or ruthlessly. This involves activity a lot more insidious than the adventure sought by the adrenaline junkie who finds excitement in a legitimate risk-taking occupation or in legal recreational activity, such as skydiving, surfing, or rock climbing.

The criminal seeks excitement at the expense of other people, building himself up by tearing them down and exploiting trusting individuals for his own selfish purposes. Contemptuous of people who conform to laws and social customs, he pursues excitement by engaging in what is illicit or forbidden.

"Why buy something if you can steal it!" exclaimed a 15-year-old. His point was that anyone can purchase an item, but it takes someone special to pilfer it.

One young man told me he despaired of living in a "McDonald's world," his term for a conventional life. A bright student with advanced computer skills, he could have successfully completed college and been highly sought after by potential employers. Instead, he had chosen to apply his intelligence and ingenuity to discovering ways to buck the system. By tinkering with pay phones, he found a way to make free calls. He prided himself on defrauding the phone company and on being more clever than the suckers who paid.

## Intelligence, Achievement, and Crime

> *Does low intelligence play a role?* [ANOKA, MINNESOTA]

As is the case with most groups, there is a wide range of intelligence among criminals. Many are more intelligent than test scores reveal. Subtests of one of the most widely used intelligence tests (the Wechsler Intelligence Scales for Children and Adults) are divided into two categories: verbal and performance. If a criminal has not applied himself in school, which frequently is the case, he may score poorly on vocabulary, arithmetic, and information subtests. Scores on performance subtests depend in part on whether a person is motivated to focus on the tasks and persist as they become increasingly difficult. Asked to assemble a complicated design, a criminal may make only a token effort because he simply does not care.

I have interviewed offenders whose scores on intelligence tests were so low as to indicate that they were mentally retarded. Despite performing poorly on comprehension, vocabulary, and other items, they were extremely resourceful and effective in pursuing their day-to-day objectives. They were street-smart, savvy men and women who could assess other people for their own purposes and carry out elaborate schemes. I was a consultant in a case where an inmate was closely following the legal proceedings at his own trial. He was overheard bragging to a correctional officer that he might escape the death penalty because he was mentally retarded.

> *One of my clients once told me, "I was never good at school or work. The only thing I was ever successful at was selling drugs." Is this a common thought process?*
>
> [CHICAGO, ILLINOIS]

Many criminals accomplish little academically or professionally. Usually this has nothing to do with a lack of ability or talent. As the criminal grows up, he is likely to hear people telling him over and over that he is not utilizing his potential and assuring him that he could be successful if only he would pay attention, stick with tasks, and do what others asked. He disregards such encouragement and advice because, from his perspective, there is no reason to attend to and persist with what is boring. Consequently, he rejects school and jobs before they ever reject him. A reflection that he excelled only in an unlawful enterprise such as selling drugs may be accurate. If he makes such a self-assessment, it often includes blaming others for what he chose to do. He explains that he had a learning disability, that teachers would not help him, that he was treated unfairly by his boss, that he wasn't given a fair chance.

A man who had sold drugs for nearly a decade spoke to me of his enormous success in that "business." He had bales of marijuana stored away and had connections for sales throughout the western hemisphere. He prided himself on his contacts, on his ability as a salesman, and on his availability to provide prompt service to his customers at any time of the day or night. When I inquired about the danger to which he subjected himself, his wife, and his child, he replied that the risks were well worth taking. Always flush with cash, he was able to afford things he never would have had were he to have worked at a regular job. Once apprehended, he hoped to improve his own legal situation by helping law-enforcement authorities. He bragged that he had "helped bring down" kingpins of the drug trade. Other than in drug sales, during his forty years of life, he never had known such success. This was not because he was deprived of opportunity. Ever since he was a little boy, he had despised school and regarded regular work as for suckers. Acknowledging that he could have used his business skills in a legitimate occupation, he said that he would never have had such an exciting life. With not a trace of regret, this man asserted, "I've lived the lives of ten men."

## A Time Bomb of Anger

> *Would you comment on the role of anger as an underlying cause for criminal behavior?*
> [LEXINGTON, KENTUCKY]

The criminal is always angry because the world rarely meets his expectations. Think of it this way. If every day of your life you expected everything to go exactly as you wanted and you counted on people treating you as you believed they should, you would experience countless disappointments. The criminal expects things to go his way, and thinking something makes it so. The slightest disparity between his expectations and reality constitutes a severe blow to his self-esteem. His thinking runs in extremes so that no middle ground exists between being number one and being a zero.

In an auditorium, a youngster is saving a chair for his buddy. In his mind, he owns that chair. When another boy takes it, this act offends him, for it runs counter to his estimation of who he is and how the world should treat him. The criminal's entire self-concept is on the line in what appears to be a very minor slight. It is as though one pierced a balloon with a pin, and the whole thing deflated.

A normal day has more than one incident when things do not go as we expect. A driver cuts in front of us on the freeway. The cleaning isn't ready. The car isn't repaired correctly the first time. A store is out of merchandise it advertised. A tape gets stuck in the VCR. Constantly, we have our encounters with Murphy's Law, which ordains that if anything can go wrong, it will. The responsible person copes with Murphy, sometimes calmly, other times less effectively. The criminal makes no allowance for Murphy. A setback that a responsible person takes in stride threatens to make the criminal less of a person. His entire self-image is on the line every time an expectation is not met. Since this happens constantly, he is perpetually angry. Consequently, he is a walking time bomb that can be detonated at any moment by some tiny slight or by the one disappointment that he considers too awful to endure. Because he thinks someone is staring at him, he's ready to fight. A motorist cuts him off. With an obscene gesture, he speeds in pursuit intending to do the same to him. The most extreme expression of rage at a world that does not suit him occurs when he takes out a gun and fires. From being a nothing, he has again become a force to be reckoned with.

## A Tattered, Threadbare Conscience

> *Are these people who do horrible things without a conscience?* [HOUSTON, TEXAS]

> *Do you believe people with criminal personalities experience guilt?* [PORTLAND, OREGON]

> *Is remorse present and, if so, how is it expressed?* [PHOENIX, ARIZONA]

How, you might wonder, could a person have a conscience when he has entered a woman's home, abducted, raped, and strangled her, and felt not a trace of remorse?

Surprisingly, the perpetrator of such a crime has a conscience, but he is able to ignore it long enough to do whatever he intends. Every offender has told me, usually with pride, that he has a conscience that prevents him from engaging in particular offenses that he considers abhorrent. Most criminals find child molestation repugnant. A teenager declared that his conscience never would allow him to attack an elderly person on the street and snatch her purse. He said that anyone who was so low as to do that should be shot. Nonetheless, he had no compunction about entering an elderly lady's home while she was asleep and ransacking it.

Remorse may follow a particular crime. A man broke into a widow's home and carried off priceless heirloom jewelry. Upon finding out that the victim was suffering from cancer, he became so conscience-stricken that he arranged for the return of the items. His remorse in this situation did not deter him from additional burglaries. The criminal has enough of a conscience to make him dangerous. It governs only his attitude toward specific acts and fortifies his view that he is a good person.

## Fear of External Deterrents

> *Do these people ever consider that they might get caught and incarcerated?* [FAIRBANKS, ALASKA]

The criminal is totally aware of the occupational hazards of crime; he might be apprehended, convicted, confined, or even injured or killed. Not only do criminals know of potential consequences, but most have had direct experience with them. They have been arrested, spent time in jail, and sustained injuries. You could ask the toughest inmate in a penitentiary, "Didn't you think you could get caught?" Most likely, his response would be, "Sure, but not this time." When the criminal commits a crime, he is certain he has everything under control. What comes into play is his striking ability to shut off deterrent considerations from his thinking long enough to do whatever he has in mind.

The criminal could advise someone else of the potential consequences of the very crime he plans to commit. However, as he is on his way to the crime scene, he is thinking of none of this, so absolutely positive is he that he will achieve his objective.

## Shutting Off Feelings

> *Can they shut their feelings off and on at will?*
> [THOUSAND OAKS, CALIFORNIA]

It is amazing how sentimental even the most violent criminal can be. A man who murdered a store clerk would not step on a bug because he refused to kill anything that was alive. Then there was the man who, after raping a woman, engaged her in an emotional discussion about religion. I interviewed a teenage drug dealer who described his mother as though he worshipped her. When she removed his phone from his room, he screamed and cursed as though she were his worst enemy. More than one felon has helped a disabled or homeless person and, within minutes, committed a violent crime.

The criminal is a study in stark contrasts in that savage brutality and maudlin sentimentality often go hand in hand. "I can change from tears to ice," reflected one individual. I remember that my colleague, Dr. Yochelson, would ask criminals in his program, "Who are you today?" This was not a reference to a multiple personality or a crisis in personal identify; rather, he addressed this query to men who were extremely changeable in their moods, thoughts, and deeds, not just from day to day but sometimes from hour to hour. These individuals are not mentally ill. Rather, they are quite purposeful in their behavior but changeable in their objectives. A heroin user adored his little boy and doted on him whenever he happened to be home. This very father went out with his buddies and missed his son's birthday party. If you asked him, he would say that being a good father was extremely important, but the competing desire to hang out and use drugs prevailed. He was able to shut off all feelings for his son in order to do what offered excitement at the time.

## Vulnerability and Dreams

> *Do you know if vulnerability shows up in the dreams of*
> *criminals?* [CHICAGO, ILLINOIS]

If, by vulnerability, you mean finding themselves in situations that make them break into a nervous sweat, the answer is yes. Criminals have told me of dreams in which they were in the midst of committing crimes but were about to be thwarted either by the police or by the potential victim.

## Lack of Intimacy

> *What causes the lack of love relationships—lack of*
> *ability to express intimacy? Do criminals feel love but*
> *cannot express it?* [SPRINGFIELD, ILLINOIS]

The criminal rarely uses the word *love.* When he does, it usually has one of two meanings. He may mean it in a sentimental vein toward someone who cares for him and helps him out. The other use of the word is to refer to sex. He loves someone whom he can sexually subjugate or someone who will consent to having sex with him.

The criminal does not share with others but, instead, maneuvers to gain an advantage. He is a taker, not a giver. Unless it is an expression of momentary sentimentality, his giving is predicated on an expectation of how he will benefit in return. The criminal rarely maintains an intimate relationship because he seldom considers anyone's point of view but his own. What he wants is paramount, no matter at whose expense. He professes to love a person so long as the individual does what he wants. That person is not regarded as a separate individual with his or her own needs.

A 19-year-old in a county jail had been charged with several counts of sexual assault. He told me of the wonderful relationship he had with his girlfriend. As it turned out, the girl was an emotionally unstable, insecure person who had no idea that her boyfriend had committed sex offenses. After conflicts with her own parents, she had moved out and had become emotionally dependent on this youth. What he characterized as an intimate relationship was based on his lying and controlling her. She thought that she knew him, but she knew only the image he had created. Asked if he thought his girlfriend deserved to hear the truth about him, the young man responded that if she knew, she would break off the relationship. Intimacy requires a mutuality and  honesty that are antithetical to the criminal's way of doing things.

## Group versus Individual Criminality

> *Is there a difference in the thinking of an individual who commits a crime alone and the thinking of a person who commits a crime only in a group? Or would the person who commits a crime in a group eventually do this alone? Or has he or she probably already done such things alone?* [LARAMIE, WYOMING]

Granted that people sometimes behave differently in groups than they might otherwise, they do not lose the power to think for themselves and make choices. Regardless of what the group does, the individual still can behave responsibly. Individuals who commit crimes with other people usually have not been paragons of virtue in their own personal lives. The group provides support for and creates new  opportunities for the individual to seek excitement.

An otherwise responsible youth conceivably might go along with a group of adolescents who commit a crime. If this were so, certain questions would arise about his personality and character. Why did the young person associate with this particular group? Once it became clear what was intended, why didn't he leave rather than participate in criminal activity? What does it say about him that he dismissed considerations of right and wrong and ignored his own knowledge of potential consequences both to himself and to his victims? It is the individual who chooses to affiliate with the group and then makes further decisions about whether to join in its particular activities.

## Low Self-Esteem

> *I have heard both that criminals have low self-esteem, and that is why they are the way they are, and that they have an elevated self-esteem— "grandiose"—and that is part of their problem. Which is the case?* [NEW ORLEANS, LOUISIANA]

 The criminal regards himself as powerful and unique. His self-esteem fluctuates in line with how successful he is at controlling other people and attaining his other objectives. Those who do not understand how the criminal thinks believe that he suffers from low self-esteem. From their point of view, criminals are failures because they are so destructive to themselves and to innocent people. Many have alienated their families, dropped out of school, or lost jobs, and some have even failed in crime as evidenced by the fact that they got caught.

When criminals appear depressed, their desperation is usually not about themselves but about their situations. Picture an offender talking to a police investigator, a social worker, or a correctional officer while at a police station, hospital, or detention center. He glumly looks at his adversary, responds monosyllabically, and appears genuinely depressed.

Just because a criminal is in prison does not mean that his self-esteem has nosedived. Although he is unhappy about being incarcerated, he remains the person he always was and is inclined to behave in confinement as he did on the streets. He seeks out other inmates and boasts of past crimes and plans others in the future. Although confined, he still maneuvers to build himself up and pursue excitement. Correctional facility staff members routinely cope with inmates gambling, fighting, stealing, trafficking in contraband, and using illegal substances. Confinement may have no impact on the criminal's self-esteem. Ending up there was always a risk and, once in the "big house," the criminal will make the best of it consistent with his past patterns.

## The Criminal and God

> *Since the criminal sees himself as all-powerful, how does he view God? You talk about the criminal praying. Does he or she ask for things?* [PORTLAND, OREGON]

Some criminals profess to be deeply religious. They attend religious services, read the Bible, and celebrate special holidays. Some even construct shrines in their own homes. The fact that they are religiously observant reinforces their opinion of themselves as decent human beings.

Some offenders claim to be inspired by Biblical passages that they glibly quote to others. Nonetheless, they fail to incorporate the principles and teachings of their faith into daily living. The way they treat others is the antithesis of the foundation of virtually any religion. While praying to a supreme being for something they want (perhaps a clean getaway from a crime scene), they remain a law unto themselves in their daily activities, recognizing no authority, earthly or divine, to which they need be beholden.

## Suicide

> *You say that criminals perceive themselves as good. If that is so, why do so many say they are "bad" or "outlaws" or "rotten to the core"?* [AUSTIN, TEXAS]

> *Does the antisocial youngster ever view himself or herself as a loser?* [ST. CLOUD, MINNESOTA]

> *How common is suicide or suicidal ideation in the*
> *antisocial person?* [CHICAGO, ILLINOIS]

There are occasions when, temporarily, the criminal's view of himself as a good person collapses and he sees himself as a loser or, worse yet, as a total zero. Usually this occurs when he is forced to confront the harm he has done, especially to people about whom he cares. At such a time, he may admit that he needs to change, acknowledge that he is unfit to be in society, or conclude that he has no redeeming features and does not deserve to live.

In a "zero state," the criminal perceives himself as without merit, is convinced that others share his view, and believes that his life has no hope of improvement. The despair can reach such intensity that the criminal contemplates ending his life. Although suicides do occur under such circumstances, the zero state is short-lived. Relief is available by renewing the search for excitement. It may only take a phone call to an old friend, a female, or a drug connection. Just the anticipation of excitement makes life again worth living.

**Paranoia**

> *Could you please explain the paranoia characteristic of*
> *the antisocial criminal mind?* [SAN FRANCISCO, CALIFORNIA]

Paranoia is a mental disorder in which a person is suspicious of others and regards them as intending to harm him. The thinking is delusional because the suspicions are not based on reality. One example of such delusional thinking would be a law-abiding person being overwhelmed by fear because he is convinced that at any moment the local police or FBI might detain him.

If a criminal harbors such a belief, his fears are based on reality. Having done any number of things that could result in his arrest, it would be foolhardy for him *not* to be guarded. There is quite a difference between a person being apprehensive for good reason and one living in fear that arises from irrational beliefs.

## Career Choice of Criminals

> *What occupations or careers are attractive to the type of persons we are talking about?* [PETERSBURG, VIRGINIA]

In the long-term study at Saint Elizabeths Hospital, we asked adult criminals how they would have answered this question when they were youngsters. Their responses fell mainly into two categories: law enforcement or an occupation in which they would personally influence or instruct others, such as a clergyman or counselor. The appeal of these occupations lies in the criminal's perception of being a big shot—a person in charge of or directing others. Some of the men recalled they were attracted to becoming police officers by the uniform and weapons, the fast cruiser, and the thrill of pursuing the "bad guys."

Some actually took steps to become clergymen, enrolling in a seminary. Their motivation was less a desire to serve God than to be god-like in the pulpit and to have people respect and admire them. Ordained as a minister, one fellow used his position to attract women and have sex with them. Another, without any training or credentials, founded his own church and solicited money, clothing, and furniture from residents of his community who were eager to help the needy. The "minister" appropriated the contributions for his personal use.

In my clinical practice, I have found that many juvenile and adult offenders want to become counselors. Because of their own experiences, they assert that they are uniquely qualified to advise young people and save them from following in their footsteps. Some of these men are charismatic and may have a positive impact on their counselees. While thriving on the authority and influence that they wield as counselors, many remain irresponsible in their own lives. Some have gotten into difficulty right at the job site because they took sexual liberties with clients, misappropriated funds, or used drugs.

## Is the Criminal Immature?

> *Is it possible that moral and personality development*
> *stopped at age 2 in the criminal personality?*
> [EL DORADO, KANSAS]

Because the criminal fails to develop empathy and demands that his desires be catered to, he appears to be fixated at an early stage of development. I have heard individuals with a criminal personality compared to a 2-year-old who expects the world to revolve around him and who has not yet developed a conscience. However, there is a major distinction between the morality of the 2-year-old and that of the criminal. The toddler is only starting to encounter the socializing forces from which he will learn how to get along and empathize. The juvenile and adult offender have been presented with these influences time and again, but they have chosen to reject them. They are able and often eager to identify what constitutes moral behavior in a situation in which they are not directly involved. They frequently offer advice concerning the right thing to do. However, they often fail to apply to themselves the moral standards that they tout to others.

## Male–Female Differences among Criminals

> *What differences have you observed between male and*
> *female offenders?* [WILLIAMSBURG, VIRGINIA]

> *How does [your concept of] the criminal personality*
> *relate to the female criminal?* [PULLMAN, WASHINGTON]

> *Please address women offenders (nonviolent). They do not*
> *appear to have an ownership view, sense of uniqueness,*
> *lack of concept of injury, and so forth. They generally do*
> *not appear to be excitement seekers. Are they different*
> *from the males you have described?* [ST. CLOUD, MINNESOTA]

The thought patterns are the same for both sexes. There are occasional differences in the interpersonal tactics that male and female offenders deploy. Correctional officers have told me that, in dealing with men, female offenders frequently resort to flattery and seductive behavior. To gain sympathy with either sex, some female offenders appear to turn tears off and on virtually at will.

I can understand why female offenders appear to have a different set of mental processes. It is because they can present themselves so differently. For example, one woman in jail told me of the predicament from which she and her baby had to escape. Her boyfriend had deserted her, leaving her so destitute that she had no money for infant formula and diapers. She knew that she could obtain money quickly by selling drugs, which she did, and then she was arrested. With tears streaming down her cheeks, she claimed that she was a good mother. Although she committed a crime, she asserted she was not a criminal. As she related her story, there appeared to be no element of excitement seeking and certainly no intent to harm anyone. She represented herself as a conscientious woman who just wanted to care for her baby. So how can I ascribe her thought patterns to those of a criminal?

We must question why this young mother found herself in the dilemma that she so poignantly described. Then we might discover the following. At the age of 15, she had skipped classes at school, hung out with an older crowd, and become sexually active. She dropped out of high school and refused to tolerate the restrictions of her deeply concerned mother and father. To her parents' dismay, she left home and moved in with a drug-using boyfriend. She became pregnant, and they agreed that she should have the baby. Because of his drug use, the father often failed to show up for work and was fired from one low-paying job after another. He finally decided that he no longer could stand being nagged by her and being burdened by a child even though it was his. So he vanished, leaving her to fend for herself and their offspring.

Since early adolescence, this young woman had made a series of choices to reject her family and had lived a completely irresponsible life. Even when she and her baby became destitute, instead of seeking help from social services or from some other legal source, she chose what was expedient and illegal. By possessing and selling drugs, she put at risk that which she valued most, her child. The thinking processes and resulting behavior were little different from those of male offenders. In her decision to sell drugs, she shut off all deterrent considerations, confident that everything would turn out as she intended.

> *Do you believe that some women may gravitate toward these men because of their own criminal personality? After all, the criminal offers a much more exciting lifestyle—drugs, parties, crime—than does the straight Joe checking groceries or working at some other mundane, stable job.* [BOISE, IDAHO]

> *What is your opinion about the females who assist in criminal activities of their male partners in terms of their personality structure?* [COLORADO SPRINGS, COLORADO]

"Us kinds find each other," noted one man. He was reflecting the fact that male offenders often are attracted to women like themselves. Some female criminals seek out their male counterparts because they have money, are readily available for sex, and seem to be free spirits, not bound by rules or other constraints. These women may aid and abet their male counterparts in criminal activity. They disdain the "straight Joe" who is a dutiful provider, lives within his means, and abides by the law. When two antisocial people become involved with each other, the relationship invariably is stormy, as each person tries to control the other, arguing over the most trivial matters, with conflicts occasionally escalating into physical violence. Most of these relationships are short-lived. Some couples go through periods of breaking up and reconciling, but the emotional volatility increases each time. Neither partner changes, and each blames the other for the dissension.

## Responsible Girlfriends of Criminals

> *What kind of personality do the girlfriends of antisocial people have?* [DENVER, COLORADO]

Some criminals seek a partner who is virtually the diametric opposite of them. They prefer a quiet, submissive, and highly moral woman to settle down with. Frequently, they are attracted to a person who is naive and lacking in self-confidence.

I interviewed the daughter of a minister who thought she had found the man of her dreams. She described him as handsome, charming, adventurous, and full of surprises. She remembered his showing up one day, directing her to close her eyes as he blindfolded her and then led her to his car. After a short drive, he removed the blindfold, and she found herself in a secluded park whereupon her boyfriend spread a blanket and set on it a basket with wine and a picnic lunch. The two became increasingly intimate, and he initiated her into her first sexual relationship.

The young woman came from a small town where she had worked as a grocery checker and had little experience with men. The only reservation she had was that she noticed that her lover had very expensive tastes. One weekend when he took her camping, she asked how he could afford all the elaborate gear, for she knew that he had just started a new job with a very modest salary. His cryptic response to her was, "Don't ask any questions that you might not want to hear the answers to." She thought this odd, but he said it in such an offhand, good humored manner that she brushed aside any qualms. Although she had known him only a few months, she allowed him to convince her that the two of them were meant for each other and should marry.

One night, not long after the wedding, she was home and the phone rang. She was shocked when her husband informed her that he had been arrested for stealing. Dutifully, she drove to the police station and helped get him released.

In her attempt to make sense of the incident, she thought that had she been a better wife, this never would have happened. Subsequently, to avoid conflict and to minimize the stress that he had complained of, she vowed to do everything her husband wanted. As time passed, he started staying out late, often failing to call, and offering no explanation of his whereabouts. She continued to think that somehow she was the problem. When she questioned where he had been and what he had been doing, he became enraged. This was a side to his personality that she had not seen.

No matter how she accommodated him, his behavior did not change. Increasingly, she felt hurt and resentful but dared not risk upsetting him. Finally, another call came. This time the charge was rape, and her husband received a long prison sentence. With counseling, she finally realized that she was not to blame, that she had not ever really known the man to whom she was married. She divorced him, learned from the experience, and found a more responsible, although less exciting, partner.

 The criminal is an abuser of women. As long a female does precisely what he wants, the relationship is smooth. If she ceases to be a doormat and asserts herself, she is likely to be mistreated. Enduring whatever her partner dishes out, she may think that she deserves it. Lacking self-confidence, some of these women prefer to live in a situation that is familiar, no matter how unpleasant or dangerous, rather than cope with loneliness, uncertainty, and financial insecurity.

## Fear and a Shootout

> *Would the fear of being put down ever drive the criminal into a knowing fatal confrontation with police, to wit, an escapee who attempts to shoot it out with large numbers of police?* [PORTLAND, OREGON]

> *What benefit is it to the criminal to do himself in after murdering somebody else (e.g., as in the case of disgruntled workers)?* [ST. CLOUD, MINNESOTA]

If a criminal is convinced he is cornered, he might choose to go down in what he would perceive to be a blaze of glory rather than face the ignominy of surrendering and being imprisoned, perhaps for life. Seeing no way to escape, this individual might assert himself in the final moments by trying to take someone down with him. An alternative is to kill himself. Either way, true to form, he strives one last time to remain in control of what happens to him. He will end his own life rather than allow someone else to do it.

## Do Criminals Reform on Their Own?

> *Does aging or maturing change the antisocial personality?* [LONG BEACH, CALIFORNIA]

> *When I was young, 16 years old, I nearly killed a friend with a knife. Now I'm a judge. Where does growing up fit into your theory of criminality?* [BILLINGS, MONTANA]

> *Why would a career criminal with a long and serious history improve after his second or third incarceration in the state penitentiary? Did he simply get tired of serving time?* [PIERRE, SOUTH DAKOTA]

Aging cannot be counted on to eradicate criminality. As a person grows older, the criminal personality remains intact. The individual may no longer engage in extremely risky activities that require great agility and a quick getaway. Just because an offender has slowed physically does not mean that there has been a transformation in his thought processes. I interviewed a 55-year-old man who, by the time he turned 40, was no longer "rippin' and runnin'" in the streets brandishing guns and selling drugs. On his own, he ceased using heroin. Nonetheless, at 55, he was victimizing more people than he did earlier, but the type of crime changed. He stole from every job he had and, in his community, he solicited from door to door falsely representing himself as an agent for a charitable cause. He was so charismatic and persuasive that people readily opened their wallets and contributed. Although he was no longer using hard drugs, he increased his consumption of alcohol and smoked marijuana.

I have heard accounts of criminals deciding on their own to reform and being successful. These are not the individuals whom I see in my practice. An interesting and worthwhile study would be to examine in depth these men and women. Such an investigation would explore why they decided to change, the process by which they did it and, most important, how extensive and enduring the changes were. I have interviewed people who no longer are breaking the law, but they continue to behave criminally in that they are dishonest, ignore obligations, and persist in attempting to control other people.

*As a youth (6–14), I did most everything that was risky to an adolescent: shoplift, steal money from parents, smoke cigarettes, smoke pot, try other drugs, try to get laid, and so forth. At 16, I found religion and made a 180-degree turn. At about 21, I began turning back little by little. Now married, with children, I sometimes lie to my wife in order to avoid conflict, and I cheated on her once. I've even shoplifted (a music tape, a tool, maybe a couple of other things). I struggle with such things. I'm at a point where I see progress, especially with shoplifting—a very stupid thing to do, but I wonder if I am just a classic criminal, a recovering criminal, hopelessly lost, or what? And how many people in the room would share my same problem?*

[SALT LAKE CITY, UTAH]

This report of self-observations underscores the point that growing older does not automatically temper or eradicate criminality. I have seen male and female offenders make a "180-degree turn" practically from one extreme to another. Having engaged daily in criminal activity, they resolve that they are going to be pure. They become imbued with religion or a cause and intensely focus on it. When the excitement and novelty wear off, they become disenchanted and lose interest. The resumption of old patterns may commence as they behave in ways that are not arrestable—lying, cheating, increased drinking. From the question, this man sounds like he is, in fact, "a classic criminal." However, he has struggled, at times with some success, against his own criminality. There is no reason to conclude that he is "hopelessly lost," especially if he continues to scrutinize his own thinking, deters criminal behavior, and seeks help. As to how many people in the room of close to 200 people share his dilemma, there may be any number who are struggling with similar problems. As to how many individuals at a workshop on criminality are themselves criminals, I have no idea.

# 8

## The Criminal Mind Exists Independent of Particular Laws, Culture, or Customs

## Universal Criminality

> *Does this type of individual cross national and ethnic boundaries (i.e., universal among all nationalities and races)?*
> [ROCKFORD, ILLINOIS]

In using the term *criminal*, I have not restricted the definition to a person's breaking particular laws. Rather, I have been describing a mentality that exists no matter what the laws are. The individual with this mentality is a victimizer who injures others in pursuit of his own objectives. Unprincipled, predatory human beings have existed throughout the ages in a variety of cultures and societies.

## Defining Criminality

> *Do you believe that in every human being there is a certain amount of criminal activity in the mind?*
> [PETERSBURG, VIRGINIA]

> *How do you define criminal behavior? Don't most of us cheat—like use the telephone at work for non-business purposes, appropriate office materials for our own use, or try to get away with certain things?* [CHICAGO, ILLINOIS]

> *On TV, a preacher cited a study that said America is a culture of lying. This study said at least 99% of Americans intentionally lie. Is this connected to the crime level in the United States?* [SALT LAKE CITY, UTAH]

Any human being is capable of committing a crime. This is indisputable, but of what significance is it? To assert that a moral, responsible individual *could* murder someone means virtually nothing, because unless he must do so in self-defense, he will never do it. His characteristic way of dealing with an adversary is not to annihilate him, but to negotiate with him, ignore him, or address the problem in some less drastic way. A responsible teenager is capable of rape, but his character is such that there is virtually no likelihood that he will ever rape anyone. Although he may be intent on having sex, his thoughts about finding a partner do not include the use of force.

Justifying his own behavior, the criminal claims that he is no different from anyone else, because everyone has done something wrong. He equates a white lie by a responsible person with his lying as a way of life. I recall one accomplished thief who asserted that his mother was as guilty of larceny as he because she kept extra change that the cashier mistakenly gave her. He asserted that he was no worse a person than his mother because both had broken the law. A teenager equated his daily use of illegal drugs with his dad drinking one beer each night after work.

Everyone has done something wrong, whether it was stealing a candy bar as a child or going to the beach while taking sick leave from work. Every person who has stolen an item does not become an habitual thief. And a person who lies one time about being sick does not lie as a way of life in order to conceal numerous illegal activities.

People who are responsible may fantasize about committing a crime, but they differ greatly from the criminal in terms of the extent that they encourage such thoughts, dwell on them, or act on them.

> *Is not wearing your seat belt breaking the law or a criminal act?* [HOUSTON, TEXAS]

Failure to wear a seat belt in the front seat is against the law in most states. If you look at the thinking processes underlying the violation of this law, you will see that errors in thinking play a role. The person who does not fasten his seat belt knows better, but he discounts the possibility that harm will come to him on this particular automobile trip. He ignores the fact that he is violating the law. He also fails to consider the multiple consequences that could befall him and his passenger in an accident. And he further ignores the potentially devastating aftermath of an accident on people not directly involved, such as the family and friends of the injured. The mental processes here differ only in degree from the criminal who, while knowing what the law is, believes he will get away with a violation and does not think about possible adverse consequences.

> *What is your opinion of people who daily run red lights, speed through school zones, or park in handicap parking, yet see themselves as better than a mugger, bank robber, or any other criminal?* [ANCHORAGE, ALASKA]

> *Is the behavior of a chronic traffic offender, who otherwise appears to be law-abiding, due to a criminal personality?* [LEXINGTON, KENTUCKY]

The key word is "daily," because a person who violates laws repeatedly shares something in common with the person who commits felonies. Both behave as though laws do not apply to them. Determined to do solely what they please, both eliminate considerations of possible consequences to themselves and to others.

One could go overboard in making comparisons. It would be absurd to equate a mugger's calculating violent victimization of an individual with the violation of a shopper who parks one time in a handicapped space to dash into a store and purchase a few groceries. The person who repeatedly parks in handicapped spots clearly has the attitude that he is above the law and is impervious to consequences of violating it. I believe that if you looked at how that individual lived from day to day, you would find a similar attitude expressed in other circumstances.

> *What about incidents like the Los Angeles riots, Dallas riots after the Super Bowl, and Chicago riots after the Bulls won the championship? Not all these people are criminal. How can it be explained?* [BOULDER, COLORADO]

There are many forms of protest and many ways to celebrate. People who victimize other human beings while doing either are criminal. They are exploiting the particular occasion for their own personal excitement and gratification. Protests and celebrations provide ripe opportunities for criminal activity. It is easier to remain anonymous and get away with crimes when crowds congregate in the streets, and the attention of the police is diverted by security and public safety concerns. Responsible people who are protestors or celebrants do not take to the streets and burn buildings, assault innocent people, and loot unprotected businesses.

> *If we take guns away from criminals, would they then turn to baseball bats—the weapon may change, but the person will not?* [BILLINGS, MONTANA]

A person can always grab any available object and use force to overcome his adversary. When juveniles and adults have easy access to firearms, a conflict that might otherwise have erupted into a fistfight or been "settled" by the individual's grabbing a baseball bat now gets quickly and lethally resolved by a bullet.

Guns do not cause crime any more than do bows and arrows or knives. Individuals choose whether to use them and for what purpose. The key factor is the personality of the human being who has these instruments at his disposal.

> *Do you see wife batterers as antisocial personalities?*
> [COLORADO SPRINGS, COLORADO]

> *Does the profile of thinking for the criminal mind seem to fit partner/spousal domestic violence?* [MESA, ARIZONA]

Wife batterers are criminals. They are uncompromising individuals who try to control others both away from home and even more so at home. In the privacy of his family, the wife batterer is likely to be far more ruthless than he is elsewhere. He emotionally abuses his spouse by criticizing her constantly, isolating her from relatives and friends, and undermining her self-confidence. If she asserts herself, he feels threatened and reacts, perhaps resorting to physical violence.

The same is true for females with a criminal personality. The psychological battering occurs as the woman orders her spouse around and then, when he does not do as she demands, humiliates and ridicules him. If successful in provoking him to retaliate, she may react by taunting him further, then assaulting him. I know of cases in which men, attacked and injured by their wives, nevertheless did not file criminal charges either because they did not want to have their wives arrested or because they thought that no one would believe what they reported.

The victims of spouse abusers live in a private hell in which they walk on eggshells, never knowing when their partners will become infuriated and lash out at them verbally or physically. Intimidated into silence, they struggle to put up a good front. I recall the wife of a physician whose friends envied her for what appeared to be an idyllic home life. She hid her bruises well, both the psychological scars and the black and blue marks. Her husband was certain that she would never leave for several reasons. She was opposed to divorce. She dreaded the humiliation of having to explain to others that her marriage had failed. She had become completely dependent financially upon her spouse. If she left with the children, she would have to assume the entire burden of child care. Finally, her husband had ample resources to engage in a protracted legal battle for custody of the children. He proceeded to do this, asserting that his wife was emotionally unstable and therefore unfit to care for the children. Suffering from depression, she sought psychiatric treatment over the years. Her husband subpoenaed her mental health and pharmacy records. To build his case, he had kept detailed records of incidents during which, he claimed, she had assaulted him. What he omitted were the atrocities he had perpetrated to instigate her fighting back. In evaluating this case, I concluded that this abused spouse was an excellent mother. Her husband's assassination of her character and emotional health failed, and the court awarded her sole custody of her children.

> *Consider an unjust law. If responsible people choose to break it, how do we differentiate them from criminals?*
> [INDIANAPOLIS, INDIANA]

People who conscientiously strive to rectify injustice differ from individuals who prey upon others for their own self-aggrandizement. The reader should remember that, in using the word "criminal" throughout this book, I am referring to a particular mentality. It would be absurd to equate an individual who broke a law in the 1960s while trying to racially integrate a restaurant with a person who held up that very establishment at gunpoint and made off with the day's proceeds.

In 1967, while I was working on my doctoral dissertation on college dropouts, I interviewed a young man who had participated in a civil rights march in the South. Listening to his account of events, I was struck not by his commitment to the civil rights movement, for he hardly spoke of that, but by the excitement he experienced at defying the police, which he described in vivid detail. A drug user and thief before he ever thought of heading south, he had become bored with college, dropped out, and attached himself to a cause for the sheer adventure.

## Nonarrestable Criminals

> *Is it possible for some people to have a criminal mind/predisposition but never get into any trouble or be arrested?* [KANSAS CITY, MISSOURI]

Certain people whom I term *nonarrestable criminals* behave criminally toward others, but they are sufficiently fearful so that they do not commit major crimes. We all know them: individuals who shamelessly use others to gain advantage for themselves. Having little empathy, they single-mindedly pursue their objectives and have little remorse for the injuries they inflict. If others take them to task, they become indignant and self-righteous and blame circumstances. Such people share much in common with the person who makes crime a way of life. Although they may not have broken the law, they nonetheless victimize others.

> *Please differentiate the narcissistic personality disorder from the criminal mind.* [ST. CLOUD, MINNESOTA]

This topic is covered under the previous question. The person with a narcissistic personality is identical to what I am calling the nonarrestable criminal.

> *Are there juveniles who are disruptive and ungovernable*
> *in the home to an extreme, but who do not become*
> *involved in crime?* [SALT LAKE CITY, UTAH]

The key words are "to an extreme." Boys and girls who pursue what they want at an extreme cost to other family members have characteristics of the criminal personality. By their lies, temper tantrums, threats, and outbursts of physical violence, such youths create a climate in which the family feels virtually under siege. Hypothetically, such a person could be the proverbial "street angel, house devil." However, it is far more likely that this personality expresses itself similarly outside the family, even if in a more subdued form. At home, the youngster operates at full throttle as family members try in vain to contend with him. Many demoralized parents have told me how they had tried everything—grounding, forbidding use of the telephone, removing favorite possessions from the child's room, refusing to sign for him to obtain a driver's license, restricting him from participating in certain activities—and nothing worked. Some of these parents seek family counseling, but the youth either refuses to attend or else sulks at sessions, volunteering little information. Asserting that others need to change, he is impervious to suggestions that he be more accommodating and cooperative.

This youngster deprives his parents and siblings of any semblance of a normal family life. His responsible brothers and sisters spend their childhood growing up amidst wrangling and yelling. Their privacy is constantly invaded as he "borrows" their clothes and money and appropriates their possessions. The younger or smaller children constantly face intimidation or attack. Beleaguered mothers and fathers are so distraught and weary that they have little energy, time, or enthusiasm to attend conscientiously to their other children. In the situations that I have studied, a child who is causing so much trouble at home likely is behaving irresponsibly in other places. He may not yet have been taken to task because his misbehavior is not concentrated in any one setting.

> *What about the individual who steals money to help*
> *other members of the family financially? Is he or she*
> *still a criminal?* [AUSTIN, TEXAS]

There are individuals who struggle but still are unable to take care of basic needs of their family. The critical issue is not poverty, but character: how they choose to deal with their circumstances.

> *With patterns such as lying, insensitivity to the suffering of*
> *others, and perhaps an obsessive drive for power, what*
> *leads one to the status of criminal and leads another to the*
> *status of Pentagon executive? Neither is monetary.*
> [PITTSBURGH, PENNSYLVANIA]

I have heard the question put in terms of, "In order to be successful, isn't it essential to be a devious and ruthless seeker of power like the criminal?"

Power and control are neither good nor bad. It is how one pursues and uses them that is critical. The criminal values power and control as ends in themselves. Some people succeed because they resort to deception, breach the trust of others, and do not care whom they hurt while pursuing their objectives. This does not mean that deviousness and ruthlessness are requirements for success. People do obtain positions of power and authority through working hard, showing concern for others, and conducting themselves ethically in their business or profession.

### Does Psychological Testing Detect Criminality?

> *Is psychological testing helpful to recognize these people?*
> [COLORADO SPRINGS, COLORADO]

Skillful interviewing of the individual and of others who know him well is far more efficient and yields more useful information than implementing psychological tests, especially projective tests, which are extremely time-consuming (and therefore expensive) to administer, score, and interpret. To conduct interviews and obtain valid information, one must be well-trained in identifying and understanding the thought processes and tactics of the criminal.

Many psychological tests rely on the criminal's self-reporting. Because he customarily cases out any situation to figure how to make the best impression, he does the same with psychological tests. If he is intent upon convincing others that he should not be held responsible for his conduct, he can respond in a manner suggestive of mental illness. As a young psychologist, I mistook a hardcore juvenile delinquent's haphazard guessing at items on an IQ test for a thinking disorder; his responses seemed arbitrary, if not bizarre. Months later, after I knew this individual better, I realized that the responses were outlandish because they were consistent with his pattern of never admitting that he did not know something. At the time, I was just starting in my career, but over the years I have seen criminals fool even well-trained, experienced clinicians who relied on psychological tests to make their assessments.

## Incidence of Criminal Personality
## in Criminal Justice System

*What is your estimate of the percentage of all offenders in the criminal justice system who would resemble your concept of the criminal personality?* [HOUSTON, TEXAS]

I suspect that most offenders in the entire criminal justice system satisfy at least some of the criteria for having a criminal personality. Convicted felons who have made crime a way of life would satisfy all of them.

# 9

## The Criminal's After-the-Fact Excuses Rarely Reflect His True Motives

## An Unconscious Desire to Get Caught, or a Cry for Help?

> *You say none of the criminals wanted to get caught. I have known of some who commit a crime in a way that ensures that they get caught. What do you think?*
> [BURLINGTON, VERMONT]

I have yet to meet an offender who wanted to get caught. What has happened is one of the following. The perpetrator miscalculates after having gotten away with so much that he is certain he is invincible. Alternatively, because he has used a mind-altering substance prior to committing the crime, he becomes careless and less vigilant. The offender's slipup may appear so blatant that it suggests that he must have been asking for someone to stop him. However, the way it looks does not accurately reflect what actually occurred in the offender's mind.

People differ in their experience and expertise at crime just as they do in other endeavors. A neophyte at break-ins may bungle an attempt in a way that a seasoned burglar would not. An offender's lack of experience should not be interpreted later as a wish to be caught.

The origin for an erroneous interpretation that a person commits a crime while unconsciously seeking punishment is based on Freud's notion that some people feel guilty because of unconscious unresolved attractions toward the parent of the opposite sex. Because of this oedipal guilt, the person is impelled to do things that will result in the punishment that he unconsciously seeks for harboring forbidden desires. Freud was not writing about criminals, but his disciples have applied his theories to a category of people whom he neither studied nor treated.

> *Would you view shoplifting as a call for help by an adolescent who has a juvenile criminal record?*
> [PETERSBURG, VIRGINIA]

The fact that a juvenile is caught and may receive help or even be ordered by a court into counseling does not mean that the original motive for the crime was to seek that help.

More likely, I would regard the shoplifting as an act engaged in by a person who seeks a thrill. It is also a result of a sense of ownership that the thief has when he eyes the merchandise and considers it already his, just there for the taking. What he has to do is find a way to take possession of it. If he becomes accomplished at shoplifting, there is less of a thrill with each incident, but there still is a sense of being special as he outwits others and takes risks that others would not. I remember one young woman who prided herself on having become such a proficient thief that she would take orders from friends as to what they wanted her to bring them.

Because getting apprehended results in attention, I have heard people conjecture that attention seeking was the motive for the crime. This is a confusion of assuming that the effect was the cause. There are many ways, good and bad, to seek attention. Many children are neglected and crave more attention than they receive. How they attempt to satisfy this need conforms with their basic character and personality. One child may throw a temper tantrum. One may threaten to run away. One may work harder to please his parents. Many people prefer to attribute a child's stealing to circumstances, not to the child himself. It reinforces their ideal of childhood innocence to adhere to the belief that the environment is bad, not the child.

## The Criminal's Victims

> *How do criminals pick their victims?*
> [SANTA BARBARA, CALIFORNIA]

From childhood, the criminal becomes increasingly skilled at ferreting out vulnerability in others. He starts with parents, siblings, and peers. Anyone can become a victim, but he hones in particularly on people who are gullible, unsuspecting, greedy, careless, or timid.

The criminal takes advantage of the ordinary citizen's inclination to trust. I remember one 16-year-old who was brought to my office by his parents. This teenager had committed many petty crimes, but it was his incessant lying that the parents found most intolerable. Nonchalantly, the youth admitted that he lied because it was so easy to get people to believe him. This boy's main concern was that he had told so many different lies to friends at school that they might compare his stories and he would be found out. He saw nothing inherently wrong in lying. As a young con man, he was confident that he could persuade anyone to believe anything.

Trust is built into life. If we ask someone for directions, we trust that the individual will try to guide us correctly. If we lend someone money, we trust that he will pay it back. A person parks his car overnight in front of his home, expecting to find it intact the next morning. A jogger takes his accustomed route through a park on his daily run. The criminal preys upon this trusting attitude. One of the most far-reaching consequences of crime in our society is that we  cannot be as trusting of others as we want to be. We need to take reasonable precautions, yet not unreasonably limit our lives out of fear. A person paralyzed by fear may miss out on a lot because he refuses to come into the city. But a person oblivious to the threat of crime will offer an easy target because he does not take obvious precautions such as locking a car that contains valuables.

The criminal preys repeatedly upon the people who are closest to him, for they are the ones who are most at the mercy of his lies, his betrayal of their trust, and his anger when they do not do what he wants. The kinder they are to him, the more he takes advantage.

> *What kind of people are the least likely to be exploited by these criminals?* [DENVER, COLORADO]

No matter what precautions are taken, no one can render himself immune. Anyone, including the most careful, sensible, and responsible person can be a victim. In fact, a highly cautious person can pose the supreme challenge to a criminal. I know of a company founder and president who would have staked his life vouching for his long-time accountant's reliability and integrity. The employee had been so trusted that he was like a member of the executive's family and had unimpeded access to company money, the family's residence, and many of their personal belongings. Having patiently cultivated his position over several years, the accountant siphoned off hundreds of thousands of dollars through fraudulent bookkeeping practices. In another situation, a company's bookkeeper appropriated close to one million dollars and purchased a mansion and airplane. In both cases, the thief had deceived his employer for years and was the last person who would have been suspect.

Of course, taking ordinary precautions and using common sense do help. Making snap judgments to trust a stranger in important matters, especially without checking references, is an open invitation to the unscrupulous. This sounds obvious, but people sometimes are all too ready to place their confidence in a complete stranger who presents himself convincingly as a trustworthy person and then to grant that individual access to their property, investments, business interests, or even the care of family members.

## Is Lying by a Criminal Pathological?

> *My impression is that many pathological liars lie so*
> *much that they can't tell the difference between the truth*
> *and a lie anymore. That makes them just as delusional*
> *as a schizophrenic. Could you comment on this?*
>
> [PULLMAN, WASHINGTON]

Referring to anything as *pathological* suggests the presence of a disease. Even the most unprincipled offender can distinguish between the truth and a lie. However, he lies so frequently by making up stories or by leaving things out that it becomes habitual. He lies to get out of trouble, to cover his tracks, and he lies even when there seems to be no purpose. The senseless lie appears pathological because it seems to have no advantage for the individual and it is about the most incon-sequential of matters. The lie that seems to make no sense, in fact, makes a great deal of sense from the standpoint of the person telling the lie. By lying, the individual maintains a view of himself and the world.  There is power in lying for it means that the liar has pulled the wool over someone's eyes, even if the issue seems trivial. By claiming that he went to one store when he went to another or that he rode in one kind of car versus another, he has, in his estimation, outsmarted the listener.

Habitual lying does not constitute a psychopathological disorder as does a compulsion over which a person lacks control. The person with a criminal personality can tell the truth if it suits his purpose. In fact, being truthful at a critical time can help him establish a good reputation, which makes it easier to get away with lying in the future.

A *delusion* is a fixed belief that has no basis in reality. An example would be a person believing his behavior is being directed by a colony of Martians. A delusional person has no intention of deceiving others. In fact, he deceives himself by adhering to the delusion even in the face of contrary evidence. Delusions are indicators of a mental disorder. Unlike lies, they are not under rational control of the individual.

## Motivation to Rape

*What motivates a rapist?* [COLUMBIA, SOUTH CAROLINA]

Although rape is a sex offense, it is motivated by more than the seeking of sexual gratification. Rape is another outlet for criminals to pursue excitement by forcibly imposing their will upon another human being. It is about power and control. I have yet to interview a rapist who has not committed other types of crimes.

There is a theory that rape is a desperate way of seeking a sexual outlet, resorted to by men with low self-esteem. Convinced that no partner will find them attractive, they decide to take what they believe they can have in no other way. This theory bears no relationship to reality. Rapists whom I have interviewed have had consenting sexual partners. In fact, more than one has had sex with a spouse or girlfriend within twenty-four hours before committing a rape. Of course, there are individuals who are frustrated at not having a partner for sex, but they would not dream of forcing a person to have sex. The rapist's mentality is similar to that of the thief; it is more exciting to take something from someone than to obtain it legitimately.

Another theory is that men who rape harbor lingering resentment toward their mothers and are unconsciously expressing it toward their unsuspecting victim. I have found no truth to this. People may despise one or both parents, but they do not become criminals because of it. Furthermore, I have found that most rapists, when they are being truthful, report that they have the highest regard for their mothers. In short, rape has nothing to do with a man's relationship with his mother!

Still another erroneous theory is that men are driven to rape by impulses over which they have no control. Rape is a purposeful, deliberate act. The thought processes are similar to those of a bank robber, and there is excitement at every phase. The person identifies his target, cases it out, develops a particular modus operandi, executes the crime, and makes his getaway.

> *Do you see date/acquaintance rapists as the same as or*
> *different from other sexual offenders?* [TAMPA, FLORIDA]

I am not necessarily equating the victim's experience of being raped by a person who is known, such as a date or spouse, with being stalked and attacked by a stranger. However, I am equating the perpetrators in terms of their thinking processes. The date who intimidates or forces his partner into sex is doing exactly what the criminal does. Totally indifferent to the feelings of the victim, he uses her as an instrument of self-gratification. What he wants at the moment is all that counts. In forcing himself upon her, his mind-set is that he is irresistible and that his date really wants him. When held accountable, he attempts to justify his conduct by blaming his victim. He claims she initiated sex by acting seductively, or he asserts that she agreed to have sex. If you could watch this person in other situations, you would see that he would be equally unprincipled.

## Tastes and Preferences in Crime

> *Criminals make a choice in committing a crime. Do they*
> *also make a choice as to the type of crime?*
> [HAMILTON, OHIO]

> *Are all criminals capable of committing heinous crimes of*
> *torture or sadomasochistic acts? Why do some involve*
> *themselves in these sick crimes and others draw the line?*
> [STEAMBOAT SPRINGS, COLORADO]

> *Do you see a qualitative difference between a white-collar*
> *criminal and a serial killer?* [DENVER, COLORADO]

When it comes to particular crimes, criminals have their tastes and preferences. The white-collar offender may look down on a person who resorts to fists, guns, or other forms of violence. He may be an advocate of applying the stiffest penalties to violent offenders. The killer may regard the white-collar criminal as "weak," "lame," "a wimp," or "a sissy." One 16-year-old bragged to me about how he never let anyone mess with him. He asserted that he loved the cracking sound and oozing of blood when he broke the bones of his victims. The more they suffered, the more intense his excitement. Another boy who had committed dozens of crimes denounced violence completely. He told me that guys who physically attack others are nothing but savages. He was proud that he could talk his way out of any conflict and never had been in a fight.

Although criminals differ in the type, frequency, and gravity of the crimes they commit, they are alike in their view of themselves and the world. If you were to interview a rapist, an arsonist, a murderer, and a check forger, you might find that they come from a variety of backgrounds and that they differ in their educational and occupational accomplishments. Probing their psychology, you would discover more similarities than differences in terms of thinking patterns that, inevitably, give rise to criminal behavior. For example, each has a view of life in which he regards others as pawns on his own personal chessboard. In their attempts to control other people, one does it by deception, another through violence. All derive excitement and a self-buildup through their crimes. All offenders know right from wrong. All would be outraged if an immediate relative were a victim of a crime. All assert that, at heart, they are good people.

## Incest and Criminality

> *Could you address what the criminal mind elements are with the incest sex offender who appears to have few, if any, of the active antisocial behaviors?* [DENVER, COLORADO]

The person who commits incest leads a double life. The perpetrator and the child now have a secret to keep, and that affects relationships among all family members. Even if, as the offender may claim, the child consents to sexual activity, the perpetrator is pursuing his own self-gratification without the slightest consideration of the impact upon the child at the time or later in the youngster's life. The following case points out how incestuous fathers are similar to other offenders.

Frank engaged in various types of sexual contact with Diane, his 14-year-old daughter. Tearfully, he assured me that he had the most benevolent intentions. Because Diane was so beautiful and physically precocious, but still so naive and uninformed, he thought he should "educate" her. Frank showed her part of a pornographic tape so that she could see what sexual intercourse was. He told her that if she were ever accosted, she needed to remember that the most vulnerable part of a man was his scrotum and that this was the area she should kick. He had her touch him there so she would see how tender it was. Continuing with this "sex education," he had her masturbate him so she would learn about male orgasm and ejaculation. On subsequent occasions, more of the same occurred. Finally, Frank took it a step further and penetrated her anally. After that, Diane developed headaches and tried to avoid her father. Able to keep what happened to herself no longer, she confided in a girlfriend who informed a school counselor. Shortly thereafter, Frank was arrested.

Frank did not have to intimidate Diane into silence. She was deeply ashamed of what she had done, and she did not want her father to get into trouble. Of course, Frank's whole line about sex education was nothing but a self-serving rationalization for behavior that he knew was wrong. Frank's irresponsibility and criminality were not limited to incest. He was an uncompromising, moody individual with such a sharp temper that everyone in the family walked on eggshells. Frequently, Frank retreated into his bedroom where he smoked marijuana, watched pornographic movies, and masturbated.

When Frank was arrested for sexually assaulting Diane, he claimed that he was a "sick" person and attributed his illness to job-related stress. This after-the-fact explanation had nothing to do with the sexual episodes with Diane. Frank never considered the potentially serious ramifications of the incest upon his daughter. How could Diane ever trust him again? How did the incest affect her relationship with her mother from whom she concealed the events? How would her brothers react? What difficulty might she have trusting men in the future? How might she feel about her own body? How might the incest affect her future sexual experience? All that had mattered to Frank was his own self-indulgence and excitement.

## The Child Molester

*Is a child molester a different type of criminal? Some people talk about child molestation as an addiction. What is your opinion?* [EVANSVILLE, INDIANA]

I do not regard the child molester as different in terms of basic thinking patterns from other types of offenders. What I said above with respect to perpetrators of incest applies as well to pedophiles (people who prefer children as sexual partners).

I have heard pedophiles claim that they have done nothing wrong, that it is the laws that are wrong. They assert that they did not harm the child by becoming physically involved. Rather, the true victimizers are the criminal justice system and child protective services who they claim make the child feel afraid and ashamed for having sex with an adult with whom he has developed a special closeness. They cite other cultures and other times in history during which children and adults could have sex with impunity. Such statements have no bearing on a pedophile's true motives.

I am not speaking of a stranger who lures a child into his car and abducts him or her to have sex. There is no question about the criminal intent in such a situation. Instead, consider the adult male who befriends a boy, develops a bond with him and, eventually, has sex. The pedophile would contend that he has done an immeasurable amount to help the child, who is likely to come from a troubled home. He treats the boy to meals, helps him with school work, takes him on outings, and does a lot to boost his self-confidence. As the pedophile becomes friend, mentor, and counselor, he turns to sexual matters, perhaps at first by engaging in relatively benign discussions of physical development. The pedophile may approach this through initiating "sex education" by bringing out books and magazines or by showing videotapes. Providing assurances that a desire to experiment and learn is normal and enjoyable, he draws the child into sexual activity. If apprehended, the pedophile emphasizes the child's willingness, perhaps even eagerness, to participate. He asserts that sexual contact with the minor was as natural as physical intimacy between consenting adults who develop a close relationship.

There is no doubt as to who is in control of this situation. If the pedophile simply adored children and wanted to help them, he would stop short of sexual contact. All the criminal patterns discussed in this book come into play. The pedophile hides his activities from others and has the child convinced that to tell anyone would endanger both of them. When he tires of one youngster, he moves on to the next. The pedophile has betrayed the trust of the parents who, if they had known what he was up to, would have kept their child far away from him. The perpetrator has given no thought to the conflicts that the child may experience. Some youngsters develop a dependency and feel an obligation to please this adult. They fear doing anything to jeopardize him or themselves. What is the effect on the youngster of knowingly doing something illicit and concealing it from his parents? What if other children find out—a worry that torments him? How does he feel when the pedophile abandons him for someone else? What is the impact of all that has occurred on his later sexual experience?

---

*Please comment on the issue of pedophile priests. Is there a link between their celibacy and abuse of children?*
[DES PLANES, ILLINOIS]

---

I have little to add to the above characterization of pedophiles. A priest has tremendous authority and influence. Consider the position of the child who, most likely, is being drawn into behavior contrary to his conscience and to the teachings of his parents and his faith by a trusted person whom he regards almost as a deity. If the youngster were to inform on the priest, who would think he was telling the truth? If he were to be believed, what might happen to the priest? The child might later feel responsible for destroying the very person whom he had long been taught to revere. And what would the aftermath be for this youngster in terms of maintaining trust or faith in religious leaders or teachers?

Pedophilia in the clergy is not caused by celibacy. Many people are celibate, priests included, but they do not become sexually involved with children. For a priest to engage in sexual behavior with a child constitutes an intentional exploitation of his position for his own self-gratification.

---

*Are people with homosexual orientations more likely to abuse children?* [DES PLANES, ILLINOIS]

---

This is a myth. A person's orientation, whether heterosexual or homosexual, has nothing to do with the sexual abuse of children. Most homosexuals are not pedophiles. We do not know why some adults are sexually attracted to children rather than to adults. Even with a genetic determination to sexual orientation, a person still could choose whether actually to engage in behavior that he knows is illegal and harmful to children. Because of the severe social and legal sanctions for adult sexual involvement with children, I think few people would freely choose to become pedophiles.

## Romantic Involvement with a Criminal

---

*When dating a person, how can one tell if the individual has an antisocial personality since he is probably very charming, manipulative, and persuasive?*
[DENVER, COLORADO]

---

A person with a criminal personality does not quickly show himself for what he is. It is precisely because he is so gregarious and charming that he is able to insinuate himself into the lives of those who eventually will become his victims. A woman may become enamored of a man with a criminal personality because he is romantic and affectionate and appears eager to gratify her every wish. If she is reticent about the quick intimacy that he is pushing for, she may face her first major conflict with him. Not one to heed the word *no*, the criminal presses for what he wants, using any tactic or strategy that he thinks will work. He interprets indecision and hesitation as signals to press ahead. After appearing to be accommodating, he will attempt to make her feel guilty if she refuses to do what he wants. Or he will play upon her inexperience and insecurity, contending that something is wrong with her if she rejects physical intimacy.

The criminal has developed a knack for wearing others down until they capitulate. While professing to have his partner's interests at heart, he is focused on what he wants. In dating, one should be wary when faced with deciding whether to compromise one's principles or act contrary to one's better judgment.

The criminal is proficient in maneuvering so that his partner will distrust herself rather than him. If she is involved with a person who constantly blames others for whatever goes wrong, she must beware! When he does not get his way, sooner or later, he will blame her for problems in the relationship. Finally, this partner must pay close attention when hearing things that just do not seem plausible. Someone who is romantically involved may be inclined to minimize or ignore behavior that otherwise she would question or condemn. She must trust herself rather than this person whom she really does not know.

---

*She said to me, "He's like a chameleon. He acts sweet and loving, but I feel it's an act. He turns right around and says he doesn't love me because I won't have sex where people can see. He now is withdrawing, but he says he could make me like it. I see that it's not working. So he wants to find someone who will." What is your opinion?*

[WICHITA, KANSAS]

Without knowing more about the person, it is hard for me to respond in specific terms. He sounds like a self-centered, controlling individual because he withdraws or threatens to abandon his partner if she refuses to participate in what he finds sexually exciting. Rather than identifying him as the one with the problem, she is doubting herself. This is par for the course in a relationship between a person with a criminal personality and an insecure partner. He structures the relationship so that his love is conditional on her caving in to his every demand.

The person in this predicament would be well-advised to end the relationship, which clearly is not based on mutual respect and affection. It is evident that the relationship can continue only if the lady does whatever her partner demands. Undoubtedly, he will keep chipping away at her resistance until she accommodates him by having sex on his terms. Then it will be something else upon which he insists. Constantly, she will have to determine whether she can tolerate what amounts to emotional blackmail: either capitulate to his demand or face anger, withdrawal, and eventual abandonment.

## Predictability of Criminality

> *Psychiatrists often say human behavior cannot be predicted. Are you saying that people who frequently commit crimes are indeed predictable people?*
> [FAIRBANKS, ALASKA]

Although making specific predictions is problematic, it does not take a genius to predict that more damage will be done by an individual who already has shown an expanding pattern of criminal behavior and whose only regret is that he was caught. Innumerable times I have warned a repeat offender who was hostile to counseling, "I predict that, given the way you have been behaving and what you are telling me now, you will be in serious trouble within a year." Naturally, the response was an angry denial that any such thing would happen.

Months later, when I interviewed that individual in the detention center, he was surprised that I had accurately foreseen his future. I did not know exactly what crime he would commit or when he would do it, but I had an accurate understanding of how this person's mind was working. Because he saw no need to make changes, it was not difficult to predict that he would continue along the path he had chosen.

## Is Criminality a Disease?

> *Why is criminality not a disease?* [PORTLAND, OREGON]

Criminality is not a disease like a contagious illness; one does not catch it from someone else. One might question whether crime is freely chosen if genetic or biological factors were found to play important contributory roles. Although having a genetic predisposition toward criminality would be a handicap, it would not automatically condemn a person to a life of crime. As I shall point out in a later section of this book, children who show early signs of antisocial patterns can be helped to make responsible choices.

# 10

# Criminals, Not Drugs, Cause Crime

> *Is alcohol/drug use antisocial during teenage years, or is it
> social during those years? It appears to be a social norm
> in high school, even on to college.* [SPRINGFIELD, ILLINOIS]

Not every adolescent who drinks beer socially becomes an alcoholic, nor does every person who experiments with marijuana become a confirmed user of narcotics. Much like any other person, the individual with a criminal personality starts to use mind-altering substances out of curiosity and because there is excitement in doing something forbidden. Whether drug use becomes prominent in a teenager's life depends on what the individual is seeking. After trying marijuana, perhaps smoking it for a brief period in their lives, many young people never use it again. They find it has no strong attraction, especially in light of potentially disagreeable legal, health, and other consequences. There are others for whom marijuana, indeed, becomes a "gateway drug" to the use of other mind-altering substances.

Before drug use became a regular part of his life, the person with the criminal personality already was irresponsible, perhaps a law breaker. Drug use provided another avenue for seeking excitement. Reflecting on his social drug use, which began when he was a teenager, one man observed that he discovered, "Drugs added new rooms to my life." In addition to experiencing the mind-altering effects of the substances themselves, he immersed himself in a whole new world of exciting people, places, and activities. Thinking about drugs, hanging out with drug users, locating and paying for drugs, and using drugs became central to his life, so much so that obligations to family, school, and work were largely ignored.

There are adolescents and adults who tell others they are social users of mind-altering substances. They claim to have a few drinks or smoke marijuana recreationally with their friends on a regular basis. I have evaluated and counseled lawyers, doctors, businessmen, and other professionals who make such assertions usually, as it turns out, understating their consumption. Before using drugs, these individuals were self-centered, untruthful, controlling, and arrogant. They were willing to risk themselves, their families, and their jobs in order to pursue whatever excitement drugs offered. For some, activities related to drugs became increasingly important and consumed considerable time and money. Many of their friends and activities centered around drug use. To represent their use of mind-altering drugs as social is a gross minimization and distortion of the facts.

> *Is drug addiction or alcoholism a disease or willful misconduct?* [ERIE, PENNSYLVANIA]

The term *addiction* has been so used and overused that it almost has become devoid of meaning. If a person consumes a lot of chocolate, he is a "chocoholic." If he spends a great deal of time jogging, he is a "jogoholic." If sexual gratification becomes a high priority, he is a "sex addict." I testified in a court case in which a father was called a "pornography addict" because he liked to view sexually explicit magazines and films. And so it goes. Anything a person enjoys inordinately is considered an addiction.

Drug use is a matter of choice. The person who decides to use an illegal drug knows it is illegal and potentially harmful in other ways. He has been exposed to, if not bombarded by, messages from parents, teachers, and television informing him of the dangers of drugs. When he uses drugs, he chooses to ignore all these warnings.

Some regular users of mind-altering substances develop a physiological tolerance to them. To obtain the desired effect, they need increasing amounts of the drug. Their daily lives entail a scramble to obtain what they crave. However, the psychological aspects of drug and alcohol use are far more difficult to overcome than the physical dependence. I remember a teenager telling me, "I'm addicted to marijuana." When I questioned his using the word "addicted," he explained, "Yeah, I like it too much to quit. I know that there are kids who get something out of life without pot, but don't ask me what." He could not stomach a daily routine of getting up early to ride the school bus, attending classes and having to do what others told him, returning home to his family and homework, and repeating the same thing day after day. A 19-year-old commented that he expected life to be trouble-free once he stopped using drugs. Having abstained from drugs for eighteen months, he complained that he had more hassles than when he was using drugs every day. He had to contend with demanding customers at work, co-workers who did not show up, which meant more drudgery for him, his girlfriend's nagging about one thing or another, and having to find time to attend required Alcoholics Anonymous and counseling programs. This young man had been released from a jail sentence and had his freedom, good health, a job that paid well, and a devoted girlfriend. Perceiving his opportunities mainly as burdens, he commented, "If this is life, it's a hell of a life." He was complaining that living like a regular person hardly compared with his former life when he regularly used cocaine. And so he decided to return to a life that he knew well and preferred because it was far more exciting.

Users explain that their addiction enables them to escape. When I inquire into what it is that they aim to escape, it turns out to be ordinary demands of life: putting up with a job that, at times, is disagreeable, having to do what other people ask, paying bills, and enduring other mundane aspects of existence. Some users claim that drugs help them escape bleak circumstances in which they live. Yet others, living under similar or worse conditions, make different choices, some electing to work hard and overcome adversities around them.

It is more than the drug itself upon which the individual is hooked. The "addiction" is to an entire way of life that he finds intensely exciting. "Crime is like ice cream; it's delicious," asserted one user. Why would he voluntarily give up something he finds so enticing for a conventional existence that he has long regarded as bland and desultory?

Some users tire of the perils and uncertainties of the drug world and stop using drugs. They choose to do this on their own and go "cold turkey," withdrawing from what are considered highly addictive substances with no medical help. Others seek assistance and support. The element of choice is present from the first time the person has contact with a mind-altering substance. No one bends his arm or forces him to smoke, ingest, or inject a particular substance. Having made a series of choices to use drugs, he can make a series of choices to give them up.

One might argue that drug addiction is a disease because of a predisposition toward it in some families. If this is so, then all the more compelling the reason for a person entirely to avoid mind-altering substances. I have interviewed criminals who have committed many serious crimes, but they maintain that they never use illegal drugs, and some claim that they do not drink alcoholic beverages because they witnessed a family member destroy himself by using these substances.

> *What about drug- or alcohol-induced crime? Is there such a thing?* [COLORADO SPRINGS, COLORADO]

> *How do you explain the many cases of spouse abuse that occur only when alcohol is a factor? These people are normally law-abiding.* [BUTTE, MONTANA]

> *Does using drugs relieve the criminal of responsibility for the criminal act?* [WICHITA, KANSAS]

"I didn't kill him. That wasn't me. The drugs did it," explained an inmate talking with me in the penitentiary. He said that killing another person was morally reprehensible, alien to his character. He went on at some length to describe the circumstances of the homicide, claiming he was not himself because he was on drugs at the time.

Denying responsibility for behavior because of drugs is an after-the-fact excuse. In the first place, a person chooses to use drugs. Secondly, drugs bring out only what already resides in that individual's personality. If ten people become drunk at the same party, they do not all behave similarly. Their reactions might include becoming drowsy, acting silly, talking boisterously, bragging, telling off-color jokes, or becoming assaultive. The key factor is the personality of the individual before he took his first drink. Alcohol cannot bring out what is not there. A boy out with a girl may drink too much, and the couple has a boring evening. Another fellow becomes drunk, takes his date home, forces his way into her apartment, and rapes her.

A career government employee in his mid-fifties was referred to me because he had severely beaten his wife while he was intoxicated. Convicted of assault, the man was ordered into treatment because the judge attributed his drinking to depression. This man did not appear to fit my profile of the criminal personality. He had no prior criminal record and had worked for the same agency for two decades. He and his wife of thirty years had two grown sons and had lived what appeared to be a stable life in a quiet, suburban community. His assault seemed totally out of character. I was able to interview the wife, who was fortunate to have no permanent physical injury from the severe beating, and one of his sons. The assailant turned out to be a domineering, rigid person with a volatile temper. On numerous occasions, he would fly into a rage even when he was sober. He had thrown things, smacked his sons, belittled and intimidated his wife and, on more than one occasion, threatened and slapped her. During the episode that resulted in the conviction, the assault was especially brutal.

In this particular incident, one might conjecture that the alcohol use was critical. Possibly, at that particular time, had he been sober, his behavior might have been less drastic. However, this individual's characteristic response to conflict rarely had been to resolve it amicably unless others came crawling to appease him. This tyrannical husband and father had established his authority over the years so that family members rarely challenged him. Instead of concluding that the assault would not have occurred without alcohol involvement, a more accurate assessment is that there would have been no assault if this man had had a different personality. When any crime is committed by a person who is drinking, one must focus primarily on the personality of the individual, not on the alcohol, for an explanation.

> *How do you distinguish between the drug user you have been describing and someone who gets a drug dependency due to prescription drugs initially given for a medical problem?* [BUTTE, MONTANA]

One must look at the personality of the patient. I have known people who were prescribed pain medication and, long past the point of any medical need, they found sources to obtain it, even if it took stealing a prescription pad from a physician's office and forging their own prescription. In contrast, other patients are grateful to have medication offered for pain relief but, out of fear of becoming dependent, cease taking the drug as soon as possible. In addition, consider a situation in which a patient is prescribed a tranquilizer to help him through an intensely stressful period. Worried about dependency, he first attempts to manage on his own. Reluctantly, he fills the prescription, then splits each pill in half rather than consume the full dose. He takes the drug only because he has felt so overwhelmed by anxiety that he fears he is letting down others who depend upon him. Unlike the person with a criminal personality, the farthest things from his mind are avoiding responsibility or seeking a "high."

> *Is tobacco a drug that criminals should be free from during incarceration?* [DENVER, COLORADO]

If a criminal wants to poison himself with tobacco products, that is his choice. However, I do not think that others in an enclosed environment such as a prison should have to be victims of that choice. Nor do I think that a state or federal agency should condone the use of tobacco in its facilities. I, therefore, favor smoke-free environments in correctional institutions.

# 11

## Criminals Are Neither Mentally Ill Nor Victims of Addictions

> *How can one (or should one even try to) differentiate*
> *between mental illness and evil?* [HOUSTON, TEXAS]

Any behavior that is deviant or harmful can be considered symptomatic of a disorder or illness. No basis exists for equating mental illness and evil. The person with a criminal personality is not mentally ill unless we really want to torture the definition of mental illness.

There are many types of mental disorders, which range from the transient and mild to the severe and chronic. Some appear to have a biological basis. For others, we are not sure of their origin. Among the most severe are disorders in which a person loses ability to reason and cannot function outside an institution. Because of confusion, loss of reality, and intense fear, people suffering from certain types of mental illness may be difficult to manage. They do not choose to be this way. The mentally ill do not maliciously and calculatingly prey upon innocent people. The concept of "evil" is not at all applicable.

The criminal harms other people by his own choice. With alternatives constantly available, he deliberately chooses to engage in whatever enhances his sense of superiority, whatever will gain him momentary advantage. Maudlin sentiment and savage brutality exist in the criminal and, in a flash, he can switch from one to the other. He willfully shuts out conscience to pursue whatever he has in mind at the moment. Giving little thought to the rights of others, he can become the greatest constitutional lawyer when he concludes he has been wronged. He is a perpetrator of evil, not a victim of evil.

## Gambling

*Do you not see gambling as an addiction?* [BUTTE, MONTANA]

As I said in my earlier discussion of drug and alcohol "addiction," nearly anything a person likes to do and does to the extent that it dominates a major part of his life has been termed an addiction. Gambling involves choices from the first time the thought occurs. When a person drops a coin into a slot machine, he is making a choice. He knows that the odds of losing the coin are great but, with the tantalizing prospect of getting more back than he put in, he challenges the odds. People vary in how powerful they find the intermittent reinforcement of occasionally winning. Let us consider the motives and personalities of frequent gamblers.

Many people may have a passing thought in the middle of a work day: "It's a nice day to go to the racetrack." But how many keep thinking about it, then drop whatever they are doing, and invent an excuse to leave work and go to the track? Having made the decision to gamble, the individual will make a series of other choices. How much will he gamble on any one race? How many bets will he place? How long will he stay at the track? If he wins, how much will he wager on the next race? What will he tell his co-workers the next day about where he was? What will he tell his wife who knew nothing about his leaving work?

For example, a businessman attending a convention in Las Vegas decides that he will limit himself to wagering fifty dollars at a casino on one night of his stay. He plays the roulette wheel until his fifty dollars are exhausted, whereupon he leaves the casino, and it may be years until he gambles again. His co-worker not only gambles hundreds of dollars every night, but he also skips meetings for more of the same during the day. By the end of the trip, he has run up thousands of dollars of debt, betting with cash advances obtained by credit card. Both men at the Las Vegas convention make choices. One regards a few hours in the casino as an evening's entertainment. He walks into the casino with minimal expectations, and he spends a fixed sum that he can afford. His co-worker has an entirely different mentality. Gambling has become a major part of his life, not restricted to business trips. At home, this man creates opportunities to gamble: card games, lottery tickets, football pools, horse races. Whatever time he actually allots to gambling, he spends far more thinking about it.

Gambling involves choices. The gambler does not lose the ability to stop. It becomes more difficult as he develops a pattern of thinking and behavior that becomes repetitive. Because a person enjoys an activity and it becomes habitual does not mean that he has an illness or addiction. In analyzing this behavior, one must ask what kind of person ignores obligations, jeopardizes his family, and persists in doing something that is potentially ruinous.

Features of a criminal personality are at work. Gambling no longer is entertainment; the gambler is leading a double life. With his tunnel vision, he lives in expectation, shutting off considerations of consequences that he knows could befall him, then blaming others or bad luck when he loses. Once his family discovers that he is siphoning off their money, he concocts explanations. As he loses, he becomes irritable and depressed. His wife's protestations, missing out on his children's activities, absence from work, encumbering the family with debt—the superoptimism of the criminal overrides all.

## The Sex Addict as Criminal

> *What do you think of the term "sexual addict"?*
> [KANSAS CITY, MISSOURI]

My analysis of so-called sexual addiction is no different from that of other so-called addictions. The "sex addict" has characteristics similar to those of people with a criminal personality. Having a relationship with a consenting partner is not sufficiently satisfying to a sex addict because he finds the pursuit of sex far more exciting than the sex itself. The quest for sexual gratification is strongly tied to controlling other people and building up his ego. Every time the sex addict makes a conquest, it bolsters his perception that he is irresistible. In seeking numerous partners, the sex addict has his victims. To make a conquest, he says anything to be persuasive and, if he meets resistance, may resort to intimidation or violence. This individual may consider the pursuit of sex so urgent that he becomes increasingly indiscriminate in his choice of a partner. One man affirmed, "I don't care if she's deaf, dumb, and blind. All I want is her torso." Another commented, "I operate by the five F's—find 'em, fool 'em, feel 'em, fuck 'em, and forget 'em." And that is just what many do—gratify their own needs, then discard their partners like a used tissue.

Sometimes these liaisons do not end amicably. Partners feel used and betrayed after they have been lied to and mistreated. Families of sex addicts are devastated by their behavior. For her faithfulness and loyalty, a sex addict's wife has her own physical health jeopardized and her marriage destroyed. As he spends more and more time thinking about and pursuing sexual adventures, the sex addict is less attentive to other responsibilities. As with other self-indulgent, habitual behavior, change is possible usually only after the person suffers severe consequences.

## Compulsion versus Habit

> What is the difference between a compulsive act and a habitual act? [AUSTIN, TEXAS]

A habit is a pattern of behavior that a person repeats with regularity until it becomes automatic without the individual's having to think about the individual steps. Procrastination is a habit, not a compulsion. A student delays assembling materials for his science fair project because he prefers to do other things. There is no inner force beyond his control responsible for postponing this or other work. If he discovers that procrastination is costing him too much—low grades and his parents' restriction—he can choose to reorder his priorities.

If a person is unable to resist constantly repeating behavior that even he finds objectionable, he suffers from a compulsion. A doctor has  a patient who scrubs his hands with soap so many times a day that the skin is peeling off them. With embarrassment, he admits to the doctor that he is powerless to stop the handwashing so terrified is he of being contaminated by germs. This is an obsessive-compulsive disorder. The thoughts about germs constitute an obsession, for they unceasingly intrude into the patient's functioning throughout each day. The compulsion is the repetitive act of handwashing, which represents the patient's desperate attempt to cope with his fear of germs. His internal distress is so great that he is motivated for treatment with medication or psychotherapy. In contrast, the procrastinator experiences little internal distress about his bad habit. Paying lip service to its evils, he will continue procrastinating, untroubled unless the consequences become intolerable. Then, with enough willpower, he can change. The patient with the obsessive-compulsive disorder cannot so easily surmount his difficulties.

## Kleptomania

> *If kleptomania is not compulsive, would you say the individual becomes addicted to the excitement of stealing?*
> [MIAMI, FLORIDA]

Kleptomania, an irresistible impulse to steal, exists in the minds of some mental health professionals but, in my experience, there is no such clinical condition. Some people steal wherever they go, from schools, cars, houses, stores, any opportunity they have. The act appears to be compulsive because of its frequency and also because the thief may steal items that he neither needs nor values. He may discard or give away the proceeds, and he may steal even when he has money in his wallet to pay for the merchandise.

These individuals are not suffering from a compulsion. They are making choices calculated upon their earlier success at stealing and their assessment of present odds. The person who steals frequently and skillfully rejects the occasion to steal if he figures he will be caught. If a store clerk, security guard, or other potential witness is nearby, he can forego the opportunity and return another time or decide to go elsewhere. This is not a mental disorder over which he lacks control. Quite the contrary; he prides himself on his prowess. Only when he is caught does he offer a psychological excuse by claiming that he did not know what came over him and that he felt compelled to steal.

For the person who steals frequently, the excitement of outwitting others and getting something for nothing is paramount. The proficient thief may think of himself as a big shot as he tells his buddies how he stole something that no one, even in his wildest imagination, would consider taking. One man boasted that he could steal anything that was not bolted down, and he made off with a huge iron cross from a church just to prove he could do it. A person who does not understand the psychology of the habitual thief might mistakenly surmise that the offender was suffering from a compulsion because the behavior does not make sense in that the potential gain is minimal given the risk.

## Not Guilty by Reason of Insanity?

> *Which, if any, of the insanity defenses do you think is most consistent with available psychological data?*
> [SIOUX CITY, IOWA]

> *Can crimes be committed by psychotic people as an outgrowth of psychosis (e.g., stake through an infant's heart because he was the devil)?*
> [COLORADO SPRINGS, COLORADO]

Some people who are mentally ill also commit crimes. Having evaluated a number of these individuals, I have found that, despite their mental illness, they still could distinguish right from wrong. I have encountered defendants whom others would consider to be legally insane because they reported delusions, hallucinations, and experiences of dissociation.

Consider the defendant who asserts that he heard a voice commanding him to commit a crime and felt compelled to obey it. I asked one such person, "Did the voice ever direct you to do something but you did not do as it instructed?" He replied that he heard the voice command him to steal, but he chose to ignore it. I also inquired, "Did you ever hear the voice order you *not* to do something, but you did it anyway?" He observed that the voice told him to stay away from church, but he disobeyed it and went.

If one refrains from discussing the crime for which the defendant is being tried, the individual likely will scoff at the mere suggestion that he is controlled by anything or anyone, including a voice. Then one could reasonably reach one of two conclusions. Either he never heard a voice at all or, if he did, he was not controlled by it.

One man told me he was the son of an insect god who commanded him to rob a bank. Clinical records from a previous psychiatric hospitalization verified that he had delusions about being an insect. Analyzing the circumstances of the crime, I was not distracted by this insect story. I found that this fellow was very familiar with banks because he had worked at one before he was fired. It was significant that the holdup occurred only after he had become financially destitute, and he chose a bank, not some other target. He confided that he had purchased a gun and spent twenty-four hours deliberating about whether and when to use it. His beliefs about being an insect did not interfere with the deliberation necessary to commit the crime.

In another case, a young man shot and killed a drug dealer who came to his house to collect a debt that he could not pay. A psychologist hired by the defense found that the defendant suffered from a "bipolar (manic-depressive) disorder." He based the diagnosis largely on reports by the youth and his parents that the boy had exhibited intense mood swings and, on several occasions, had tried to kill himself by drug overdoses.

The psychologist overlooked one important factor in arriving at his diagnosis. The so-called mood swings were evident only *after* the teenager had become a frequent user of marijuana, alcohol, and LSD. His parents did not take their son for an evaluation and therapy until he became intensely irritable, his grades plummeted in school, and he was keeping irregular hours, all of which coincided with drug use and associating with peers who also were drug users. His doctors made a huge assumption in concluding that the mood swings preceded drug use. They mistakenly believed that he turned to drugs for "self-medication."

The mental health professionals in this case paid scant attention to antisocial features that were present before the defendant was immersed in the drug world. The fact was that he had many hallmarks of the criminal personality. His mother told a therapist that her son rarely showed remorse for anything and displayed little empathy for others. He was an uncompromising and untruthful boy who alienated others by his lies, temper tantrums, and threats. His pretensions outstripped his achievements. Despite having no remarkable musical talents, he fantasized that he would make his mark as a celebrated rock star who would be wealthy enough at a young age to retire to his mansion and yacht. In the first two of these cases, the defendants had symptoms of a mental illness, but they also had features of a criminal personality. One heard a voice; the other had a delusion about being an insect. In neither case did their mental condition impair their knowledge of right and wrong, nor did it cripple their capacity to deliberate and carry out a crime. In the third case, mental health professionals had formulated a theory that purported to explain mood swings and a homicide. It was an after-the-fact explanation that confused cause and effect.

Sometimes a perpetrator's psychological defenses crumble under stress so that he suffers a breakdown while incarcerated. When he is interviewed days, weeks, or months after he has committed a crime, the evaluator may erroneously assume that the defendant's mental state in jail is identical to that which existed before the crime occurred. Because a person becomes psychotic in a stressful set of circumstances does not mean that he also was psychotic months earlier when he was living his regular life.

It would be difficult for most of us to recall and reconstruct precisely what we were thinking a few days ago. How much more difficult it would be for a total stranger, like a psychologist, to interview us to retrieve our specific recollections weeks or months after we allegedly committed an offense. If our freedom were at stake, would we not have every reason to come up with recollections that would serve us best!

Having an established history of serious mental illness can support a person's claim to be insane at the time he committed a crime. A man who had been psychiatrically hospitalized held a "hypothetical" discussion with his therapist about what might transpire if a mentally ill person happened to kill someone. The discussion was so general that the therapist did not suspect that the man was talking about himself. The therapist replied that if a person committed a crime and had a record of chronic mental illness, he likely would be returned to the hospital. Several weeks later, his patient stalked and murdered a girlfriend who had rejected him. From the perpetrator's standpoint, his mental illness was his license for crime.

> *Are you suggesting that the insanity pleas be totally done away with?* [COLORADO SPRINGS, COLORADO]

> *What are your views on the "guilty but mentally ill" verdict/plea now available in some states?*
> [SALT LAKE CITY, UTAH]

If a person is acquitted by reason of insanity, he does not go to prison. He may walk out of the courtroom a free man or be confined in a psychiatric facility until he is considered sufficiently improved to be released. I believe that it makes more sense for a person to be tried based on the rules of evidence to determine his guilt or innocence. Once that determination is made, if he is in need of treatment, he should receive it at a secure facility. When he has sufficiently improved, the offender would serve the rest of his sentence in a correctional facility.

> *Have you been hired by the defense in insanity cases?*
> [PHOENIX, ARIZONA]

I have been retained by defense attorneys as well as prosecutors in both insanity and capital punishment cases.

## Depression and the Criminal

> *Is depression in this population different from depression in other patient populations?* [COLORADO SPRINGS, COLORADO]

There is a considerable difference between the person who is despondent about his own inadequacies and the criminal who believes he is fine but despairs because he thinks others constantly misunderstand and mistreat him.

A depressive disorder is the most frequent misdiagnosis applied to juvenile offenders by mental health professionals. I can see why. The boy or girl being evaluated seems morose, teary, and unresponsive. What an interviewer needs to bear in mind is the obvious: these individuals do not want to talk. Having much to conceal, they resist adults questioning them. These youths are more likely to be far more depressed about their circumstances than they are about themselves. After all, they have gotten into trouble and face their questioners at a police station, hospital, clinic, or some other place where they do not want to be. One boy in a detention center ruefully commented, "I've been messing up." I first thought that he had reached a point of such intense despondency and remorse that he realized he needed to change. When I inquired as to how he had messed up, he explained, "If I didn't get caught, I wouldn't call it messing up." Candidly, he voiced what he really wanted in the future. "I'd like to do stuff and not get caught."

When a criminal becomes so depressed that he considers suicide, he is certain that life has shortchanged him. One man who had been incarcerated for sexually molesting two boys received notice that he was being sued civilly for psychological damage. From his perspective, his victims were taking advantage of him. He reacted by snapping, "Those miserable little bastards!" Then he added that before he was confined, he should have shot himself to death, while he had a gun in his hand and could quickly have put an end to it all.

When the criminal considers suicide, he has concluded that the world has failed him, not that he has personally failed. The antidote to this suicidal state is to return to old patterns and convince others that he is someone to be reckoned with. Because this is more difficult to do when confined, the suicidal thinking may intensify, and he may attempt suicide.

## Is the Criminal Manic-Depressive (Bipolar)?

> *Would you comment on manic-depression (bipolar)*
> *disorder and its association to the antisocial personality?*
> [MIAMI, FLORIDA]

The criminal's mood changes often are frequent and extreme. Rather than being caused by a mental disorder, the emotional volatility occurs as a result of the criminal's pretensions and unrealistic expectations. As his mind works, just thinking something makes it so. Because he makes an assumption, others are expected to validate it.

A teenager is certain that he will ace a test. He brings home no books and spends no time studying. With enormous confidence, he strides into the classroom only to fail the exam. Confronted with the failure, he does not fault himself but blasts the teacher and the test itself as unfair. The emotional roller coaster from smugness to disappointment and anger results from the youngster's unrealistic assessment of himself and his expectations of the teacher, not a mood disorder.

A young man is living with his mother. He is extremely pleasant and agreeable so long as she provides comfortable quarters, cooks meals, and washes his clothes. Meanwhile, he offers her no help, interrupts her sleep by playing loud music, and turns her home into a flophouse for himself and his friends. After a fair amount of nagging, she reaches the end of her rope and tells him he must leave. Until that moment, in his eyes, she was a saint. Claiming she does not care what happens to him, he screams and curses, then smashes a hole in the wall. This extreme change in attitude is not a manifestation of a mood disorder. Rather, it is one of many emotional peaks and swamps resulting from the criminal's shifting attitude toward other people. He is a delight to be around as long as others fulfill his expectations. When they do not, he seems to become a different person.

The criminal is very different from the person who suffers from a bipolar disorder, although superficially the behavior of one may resemble that of the other. The bipolar individual suffers from difficult-to-control mood swings as he experiences expansive moods of elation and intense moods of despair. A bipolar condition is not a product of a person's intentional irresponsibility. It is a disorder that, in many cases, can be treated successfully with medication. No medicine has yet been produced that alters the thought process of the criminal.

## Post-Traumatic Stress and Criminality

> *Is there a correlation between post-traumatic stress disorder and criminal behavior?* [COLUMBUS, OHIO]

> *Much has been said about the number of Vietnam veterans incarcerated today, implying their predicament is due to war trauma. Do you believe that those veterans who are in jail would be there if there had never been a Vietnam War?* [AUSTIN, TEXAS]

There is no causal connection between post-traumatic stress disorder and criminal behavior. Victims of terrorism, tragic accidents, war injuries, and other traumas suffer afterward from a variety of problems as they struggle to come to terms with what happened to them. Their response is in keeping with the personality that existed before the trauma occurred. Some people are highly resilient and recover relatively quickly from traumatic events. Others spend the rest of their lives impaired by their experiences.

When former soldiers committed heinous crimes in civilian life after the Vietnam War, it was not because they were responsible men who were transformed into criminals by their military service. It is absurd to suggest that a man's killing enemy troops in battle turned him into a murderer back home. The more plausible explanation is that he had a criminal personality before he ever served in the military.

## Attention-Deficit Disorder

> *What is your view of attention-deficit disorder in*
> *relation to criminal activity?* [AUSTIN, TEXAS]

Because of their restlessness, high energy level, and failure to concentrate at tasks set before them, antisocial children and adults are sometimes erroneously diagnosed as having an attention-deficit disorder (ADD). There is a considerable difference between a person having difficulty concentrating despite a desire to do so and a person who refuses to pay attention because he abhors the requirements and tasks imposed upon him.

An antisocial child who despises school and rejects whatever is being asked of him may appear fidgety and irritable. However, if one involves him in a task in which he has interest, one is likely to see that he does not have an ADD condition. Consider a 16-year-old whom I counseled. His parents told me that he had an attention-deficit disorder. In school, he would get out of his seat, agitate other students, and fail to pay attention to teachers. Bored at school and at home, he hung out with boys who roamed around drinking beer, looking for girls, stealing, and getting into fights. When his parents gave him a complicated airplane model to assemble, he secluded himself in his room for several days during a winter vacation. Working with detailed instructions and small, delicate pieces, he completed the project. When he was interested in something, he was able to concentrate for hours at a time. His parents still thought it worthwhile to consult a doctor who eventually prescribed him medication for ADD.

Although medication does help some people who have this condition, it has no significant effect on the behavior of most people with a criminal personality and, in this boy's case, made no difference at all. He continued to be disruptive in school, associated with the same friends, and got into further legal difficulties.

A person could have a criminal personality and an attention-deficit disorder as well. It is important not to confuse cause and effect. The attention-deficit disorder does not cause the person to commit crimes. Most individuals who suffer from ADD are not criminals. They want to do well in school or at work and are receptive to help, including medication.

## Multiple Personality

> *Should a person diagnosed with "multiple personality disorder" committing criminal acts be held legally responsible?* [TAMPA, FLORIDA]

> *Are some individuals actually antisocial but diagnosed as having multiple personality disorder?* [HELENA, MONTANA]

Multiple personality disorder (MPD) is an extremely rare condition. I recall talking with the medical director of a hospital that housed hundreds of so-called "mentally disordered sex offenders." He commented that during two decades working at that institution, seldom had he ever encountered anyone with an MPD and, the few times he did, he thought that the diagnosis was wrong. During the early 1980s, he heard more offenders claim to have multiple personalities than he had during all his previous years of practice. He had no reason to believe that the incidence of the disorder had increased either in the general population or among offenders. He surmised that word had gotten out that faking a multiple personality disorder might be effective when pleading insanity.

Because the criminal appears so changeable in his moods and erratic in his behavior, others mistakenly may conclude that he actually has different personalities that reside within him. Baffled parents have told me that a child was like several different people rolled into one. A mother observed that it was as though she had two sons, one with a sunny disposition, the other with a brooding, stormy personality. This boy's changeable behavior was not due to having multiple personalities or any other mental disorder. He was like a dormant volcano. As long as others did not disturb him and people did what he wanted, he was calm and affable. At the slightest rebuff or criticism, he would take offense and erupt.

# 12

# Schools and Crime: Schools Must Combat Crime, Not Coddle Offenders

## Being Soft on Crime

> *Would you comment on school systems that are, by*
> *policy, soft on crime?* [LINCOLN, NEBRASKA]

It depends upon what one means by "soft on crime." Not every fight or theft need be reported to the police. However, there *are* criminals in our schools and, because of them, thousands of children who want an education are afraid.

School personnel should report to the police serious crimes that occur on the grounds, press charges, and encourage victims to do the same. Although many children fear for their lives on the streets of their communities, school should offer a sanctuary where they do not have to spend the day on guard for thieves and assailants. If boys and girls do not feel safe at school, the most gifted instructional staff and the most superb educational facilities will be of little value. Ignoring, excusing, or failing to prosecute students who commit crimes at school amounts to being soft on crime. Refusing to take definitive action gives criminals free rein to prey upon children who have a right to be safe on school grounds.

> *As a teacher in an alternative school, how should I deal with administrators who instruct me to overlook the very behavior of my students that puts them in our school: fighting, smoking, stealing, swearing at the teachers, and so forth?* [STATESBORO, GEORGIA]

It is important to point out tactfully several facts to the administrators. Once antisocial youngsters discover that they can violate rules and victimize others without major consequences, their crimes are likely to become more serious. A second point is that overlooking criminal behavior sends the wrong message to students who are better behaved. What do they conclude when they witness infractions being ignored? A third point is that faculty morale invariably drops when teachers realize that their supervisor does not support them when they address the very behavior for which the students were referred to the alternative school in the first place.

## Educational Mainstreaming or Alternative Schools?

> *American schools are being blamed for low academic standards. Should the public school systems expel the kinds of children you are talking about so they can concentrate more on educating and less on maintaining order?*
> [LINCOLN, NEBRASKA]

> *Should antisocial children be placed in a classroom with emotionally handicapped children?* [INDIANAPOLIS, INDIANA]

> *What is your recommendation for alternative programming in the school system for adolescents who are antisocial?* [WICHITA, KANSAS]

The chronically disruptive, violent student does not belong in the mainstream classroom. This is a fact that schools must face. It takes only one such individual to victimize an entire class of students who want to learn. Alternative programs must be provided so that predators can be removed.

In too many places, the public schools are becoming the repository for students with behavior problems and for those who lack the money to escape and seek better opportunities. At great sacrifice in dollars, time, and energy, parents who normally support public education are enrolling their sons and daughters in private and parochial schools. Waiting lists are growing for admission to these schools in suburban as well as in urban areas. To these desperate parents who want their children to learn in a safe environment, the fact that some private and parochial schools have inferior physical facilities or less experienced teachers than some of the public schools makes little difference. What private and parochial schools can do is deny admission to disruptive students or expel them.

In any school, it is no secret as to which students are constant troublemakers. Shifting the antisocial child into a program for the emotionally disturbed is a frequent practice, but it is unconscionable. Because he is then considered handicapped, teachers and administrators may be even more hamstrung as to the disciplinary steps they can take. The other serious problem is that the antisocial students will prey upon peers who suffer from serious psychological problems.

Most school systems do not offer special programming for youngsters who are regarded as socially maladjusted or as having conduct disorders. These students just churn their way through regular classes until they drop out or are expelled. In order to qualify them for special services, it is understandable, although regrettable, that a diagnostician would succumb to the temptation of evaluating them as falling into the very elastic category of suffering from a serious emotional disturbance.

I recall observing in a public school an alternative classroom populated by children classified as seriously emotionally disturbed. It was easy to spot the antisocial students who were making life miserable not only for the teacher, but also for children who wanted to learn but were handicapped by depression, anxiety, or other significant psychological disorders. The antisocial youngsters were victimizing these more timid and less confident classmates. Actually, no one was benefiting from this arrangement. The class had become an assemblage of children who had manifested serious impediments to learning, with virtually no differentiation as to the source of their problems.

Programs for students who are antisocial must be well planned and staffed so that they do not become dumping grounds where teachers are merely baby sitters or guards. Specially trained teachers in small classes should work intensively with these students who require help in controlling their behavior and mastering academic content.

Specialized training of teachers is vital to establishing these alternative programs. The educators who will spend hours every day with these students must have a thorough knowledge of their thinking patterns and interpersonal tactics. These students should not move from classroom to classroom. To minimize disruption, instructors should come to them. The teachers of these boys and girls will need to communicate clearly academic standards and behavioral expectations. They must have latitude to impose appropriate consequences when students require discipline.

## Role of Learning Disabilities

> *How is the primary handicapping condition determined if an adolescent qualifies as a learning disabled student but also exhibits antisocial behavior? Did the behavior cause the learning disability, or did the learning disability cause the behavior?* [KANSAS CITY, MISSOURI]

The conventional wisdom has been that children with learning disabilities suffer from low self-esteem because they fail to do well academically. Criminal behavior is one way in which some try to compensate and gain recognition. The learning disability is regarded as the primary problem.

This theory is completely absurd. It is true that, having failed often, some children with learning disabilities do not think highly of themselves. By no means do most turn to crime.  Some achieve recognition by becoming proficient in athletics, music, art, or in other endeavors. Some enroll in specialized vocational training programs and acquire confidence because they have learned a trade so that they can become self-supporting. And others cope with their disability by working extremely hard, so determined are they to succeed academically.

Most learning disabled people are not criminals, and many criminals who appear to be learning disabled actually are not. The principal reason for high illiteracy among prison inmates is that most of them did not want to learn to read and write. What is involved—attention, concentration, drill, repetition, persistence—are requirements that are rejected by many antisocial youngsters who have other interests. The illiterate criminal has rejected what the school offered; the school did not reject him.

Some children are both learning disabled and criminal. One does not cause the other. Being learning disabled can provide a convenient excuse to avoid work or not be held to a particular standard. Some criminals do not think that being learning disabled has hurt them at all. One boy told me he had not read a book since the first grade but bragged that, while preparing for his juvenile court hearing, he had managed to read a volume on the rights of minors.

If a school is educating a child who is both learning disabled and antisocial, it is the latter characteristic that will need to be addressed primarily. He will not injure innocent people and end up in detention because of a learning disability, but both outcomes will result from his having a criminal personality.

## Victimization of Other Students

> *Does an antisocial adolescent in school tend to victimize classmates at random or does he or she tend to single out certain classmates and victimize them time and time again?*
>
> [LINCOLN, NEBRASKA]

Wherever he is, the criminal habitually scrutinizes others to pinpoint their weaknesses, identifying targets to pick on and bully. This is true in school as elsewhere. By and large, the antisocial adolescent is unsparing of classmates who he determines are gullible or weak. Even the severely handicapped may not be spared his taunting. On the other hand, a far greater challenge may be to take on another person much like himself.

# 13

# Criminals Can Change

## *Rehabilitation* Defined

> *What is your definition of "rehabilitation"?*
> [DES PLAINES, ILLINOIS]

*R*ehabilitation is a misconception as applied to criminals. It means to restore someone or something to a former, constructive condition. One rehabilitates an old home by restoring it to its former elegance. A person who has had a stroke attends a rehabilitation clinic to regain functions he once had. The criminal cannot be restored to something he never was. The scope of the task is more extensive than rebuilding. It entails helping the individual identify and eliminate long-standing thought patterns, then learn and implement new ones.

The pendulum of American opinion has swung back and forth with respect to the feasibility and desirability of helping criminals change. Passionate advocates of rehabilitation long have contended that with enough money, opportunity, and therapy, virtually any offender can be helped. But disenchantment with rehabilitation set in as one effort after another seemed fruitless. Proclaiming that "nothing works," opponents of rehabilitation clamored for more severe penalties and increased prison construction.

Education, job opportunities, social skill training, and psycho-therapy comprised past rehabilitative efforts. The outcome of these programs all too often was a criminal who remained a criminal despite becoming more educated, acquiring new job or social skills, or gaining personal insight. Some utilized their skills to gain entry to new arenas where they committed additional crimes.

I support education, occupational training, and other programs that can provide offenders with better opportunities to make a living. Most criminals, however, do not find it difficult to get jobs if they really want them. Many are educated. You can train a man or woman to be highly proficient at a trade, but that worker will be of little value if he steals from the job site, becomes embroiled in conflict with fellow workers, leaves projects half finished, or fails to show up at all.

There has long been a search for quick ways to help offenders change. The idea that they could be "scared straight" was appealing. A trip to the penitentiary to frighten youthful offenders into becoming honest citizens was touted as offering powerful incentives to change. Although it may have had value, no systematic long-term research was conducted to identify with whom it might be effective. In any case, it was naive to believe that complex human motivations and long-standing patterns could be changed quickly by one very negative experience.

Behavior is largely a result of the way a person thinks. Many efforts to help criminals change seem to have ignored that fact. In a process of *habilitation*, criminals learn not only to think before they act, but also to develop an awareness of what they are thinking so that they can evaluate it immediately. Recognizing the danger even of harboring particular thoughts, criminals can deter them while, at the same time, they acquire and implement new corrective thinking patterns. Habilitation involves cooperation by an offender once he has reached a low point in his life. The process does not entail someone else attempting to dictate his decisions. Rather, it helps him learn *how* to make decisions in a responsible manner.

No quick method has yet been developed that succeeds in helping criminals change. The process of habilitation usually is long and tedious. However, for every criminal who makes a 180-degree habilitative turn, the savings to society are incalculable.

> *Is your primary goal total reform of the criminal or do*
> *you look for (and consider it a success) some change,*
> *that is, the criminal now commits less-serious crimes?*
> [SALT LAKE CITY, UTAH]

The goal of habilitation is a basic and enduring change in the criminal's thinking and behavior. Anything less offers no insurance for the future. I recall a criminal who vowed to commit only misdemeanor crimes. He reported that, for months, he did just that. However, his appetite for excitement was so voracious that he sought out the "heavy action" and started taking greater risks. Finally, he was arrested and charged with a string of bank robberies. Another offender claimed he had changed because he had stopped using illegal drugs. He had abstained because he was tired of the hassles and dangers of the street, and he was worried about his health. However, he insisted that consuming an alcoholic beverage or two was safe, for he had not had a drinking problem. A few months later, the occasional one or two beers expanded to daily drinking after work and heavier drinking on weekends after which he would drive home from a party or bar. Always something of a gambler, his gambling increased, and his financial reserves dwindled. His work attendance and performance became erratic. Eventually, he was fired and started depending upon others to support him.

Changing one pattern or committing crimes that are less serious may be better than no change at all. However, without fundamental changes in his thinking, the person will continue to function irresponsibly and eventually commit other crimes. One might contend that if one cannot eradicate the entire cancer, it is better to eliminate as much as possible rather than do nothing. Either way, the cancer will prove lethal. And so it is with criminal thinking patterns. There may be fewer victims if one type of crime is eliminated, but there will be victims nonetheless because the criminal thinking persists, and the offender will find other avenues to pursue excitement and enhance his own ego.

## Is the Person or the Behavior Bad?

> *What is wrong with making the distinction between who the person is and what he has done? Is such a distinction valid?* [RENO, NEVADA]

Human beings have the capacity to choose between good and evil. The potential for goodness should not be equated with *being* good. The criminal adheres to the notion that, no matter what horror he has perpetrated, he is a good human being. Does it make a lot of sense to tell someone that he is good at heart even though he has brutally raped and maimed a woman who was sleeping innocently in her own bed? Does it make sense to assure him that he is essentially a decent individual even though he has broken into a home and terrorized a family? Are not the good deeds and personal qualities of such people significantly overshadowed by the injury that they inflict?

Do you base a program for change on assuring a criminal that he is basically a good person and will always be if he just refrains from raping and robbing? We know otherwise! We know that the criminality resides in thought patterns that must be eliminated. Otherwise, even if he does not rape or rob, he will continue to victimize people in other ways. The jails are filled with criminals professing their goodness. To agree with their self-evaluation and have that serve as a base for helping them change is like constructing a fine house on a rotten foundation.

> *Can we punish and habilitate at the same time?*
> [PITTSBURGH, PENNSYLVANIA]

Punishment is not antithetical to habilitation; rather, punishment or the threat of punishment is essential to habilitation. Offenders generally do not walk in off the streets voluntarily asking to participate in a demanding program to change their thinking. Moreover, offenders do not change when they are absolved from consequences and are free to do as they please.

## Psychosis in Criminals

> *If an offender became psychotic, would you ignore the psychosis and deal with the antisocial elements or would you give precedence to the psychosis?*
> [KANSAS CITY, MISSOURI]

After receiving my doctorate, my first full-time job included treating a young woman hospitalized after threatening another person with a knife. She had a history of violence, sexual promiscuity, and alcohol abuse. In the hospital, she was floridly psychotic. She would shuffle around the ward with her hands held in a prayerful pose, her eyes gazing heavenward. She had delusions that she had been contaminated by semen. Treated medically by the unit psychiatrist, this woman showed rapid improvement. The psychosis abated, and she was discharged to a family-care community program. No sooner was she released than she started ignoring the rules of the family-care facility. Breaking the curfew, she frequented bars and became involved with one man after another. She had been cured of an acute psychotic reaction, but what emerged was her antisocial personality. While she was psychotic, she did not violate rules or injure anyone. The hospital staff had erroneously believed that her prior antisocial activity was merely symptomatic of an underlying psychotic condition. Their thinking was that once she was restored to rationality, she would function in a responsible manner. That did not happen because the antisocial features existed independent of the psychosis and were never addressed.

In cases similar to this, there is no question that one must give priority to treating the psychotic condition. You cannot help a person evaluate his thought patterns in a logical manner when that individual is not in contact with reality to begin with. If the psychosis is successfully treated, the pre-psychotic personality must be evaluated. If the individual has a criminal personality, those features will emerge. One must not assume, however, that the psychosis was the cause of the criminality.

## The Disease Model

> *The model for treatment in Minnesota is the disease concept of chemical dependency. The person is told he or she has a primary, progressive fatal disease from which all else flows. The disease model draws a careful line between sickness and sin. What do you think?*
> [MINNEAPOLIS, MINNESOTA]

I am pragmatic and do not draw such a line. If elements of the disease concept are helpful in counseling offenders, then one should make use of them. It is critical to emphasize to the offender that one does not catch chemical dependency in the way one contracts a contagious disease. The role of choice must be a core concept in substance abuse treatment programs. People choose to use drugs, and they can choose to abstain from them. The concept of *relapse* is a potentially useful aspect of the disease model. If the offender abstains totally but then permits himself to make exceptions, he opens the door to resuming his entire past pattern. I have had many discussions with offenders who insist that they can have a drink or two, so long as they do not use other drugs. They think I am being unusually rigid in telling them that abstention from all mind-altering substances is vital to prevent reversion to old patterns. Sometimes, years later, these people return to me with new difficulties, including use of illegal drugs. You can invariably trace the current problems back to the first drink, which was indicative of the person's cockiness that he could make exceptions.

I have often heard offenders assert that their only problem is their drug use. They claim, were it not for drugs, they would not be in jail, they would not have committed particular crimes, and they would be successful in life. My response is to agree that drug use is a serious problem and also to agree that it has contributed to or compounded other difficulties. However, I caution them that even if they were to abstain from all mind-altering substances (which they must do), this is only one aspect of what needs to be done. The offender was irresponsible *before* using drugs and irresponsible in his decision to use drugs. Being drug-free does not automatically eliminate errors in thinking that were present long before drugs became part of his life.

## Motivation to Change

> *What can be a positive motivation for change for a criminal?*
> [LAFAYETTE, INDIANA]

Motivation to change may arise from either external or internal sources. For the criminal, external leverage is essential. He must be frightened either because something terrible has happened or because something terrible is about to happen to him. An analogy to giving up smoking applies here. A person may continue to smoke unless he thinks that he is at imminent risk for disease or unless he has heard the grim diagnosis of a condition that threatens to kill him if he persists. For the criminal, a powerful external motivating condition may be the impending loss of his freedom. Having been arrested and incarcerated, he awaits his trial and sentencing.

Some of the most effective interviews that I have had with juvenile and adult offenders occur in detention centers. Under these circumstances, I may encounter a different attitude expressed by a person who formerly maintained he was extremely satisfied with himself and rejected advice from others. I remember one 16-year-old lamenting that he had taken so much for granted, but now he would give anything to wake up in his own bed, to take a bicycle ride, and to hang out with his buddy next door. He detested life in confinement and was frightened about what the judge would do at the sentencing hearing.

Another type of leverage exists when the offender is on the brink of losing something he cherishes. Weary family members who have suffered enough may threaten to withdraw their support unless he convinces them that he is truly changing.

For any of us to change, we must become convinced that it is necessary, but not just because others are threatening us with dire consequences. A person is more likely to lose twenty pounds and keep the weight off if he looks in the mirror and is repulsed by his appearance than if others nag or threaten him.

A person with a criminal personality is unlikely to believe that anything is wrong with him. His problem is his disagreeable situation, not himself. Counselors and other professionals who work with offenders must adopt a stance that is likely to be at odds with their training. They were trained to extend a helping hand to people who are suffering—to comfort the afflicted. With the criminal, their job is completely different—to afflict the comfortable. The counselor has to help a criminal do something that most of us find disagreeable: look in the mirror and recognize our worst features. I remember a teenage boy who declared he had no need of my services. After he assured me that he would be just fine, I warned him that it would only be a matter of time before he was in serious trouble and locked up. He scoffed at this prediction. Several months later, his mother called and asked if I would see him in the detention center. There I found the boy in tears saying to me, "You were right. How did you know? Do you think you can keep me fed up with myself?" Only after he had lost what was precious, his freedom, was he ready to talk seriously.

> *If the criminal mind needs to have power and control, why would the individual open himself or herself to evaluation?*
> [JACKSONVILLE, FLORIDA]

He would submit and be candid only under circumstances in which he is extremely frightened about his current predicament and the future.

> *What motivational techniques do you use with children*
> *who are brought in by parents and not bound by a*
> *probation officer to be there?* [BOULDER, COLORADO]

Legal leverage is extremely important to efforts at helping both juvenile and adult offenders change. Sometimes a child brought to a counselor by a parent never has had criminal charges filed against him even though he has violated the law innumerable times. In these situations, external leverage can be applied in the form of removing a valued privilege or opportunity. Restricting a child's movement is, in some instances, tantamount to incarcerating him. His freedom to socialize outside school hours or on the telephone can be curtailed. If he is eagerly anticipating some activity, permission to attend that event can be withdrawn. Adolescents want their parents to sign for them to obtain a driver's license. This can be held in abeyance. A more drastic form of leverage is to capitalize on the teenager's desire to remain at the school he has been attending. To change schools introduces a set of unknowns and a potential loss of friends. A parent can inform the child that, although he would like him to continue to attend his current school, it will not be feasible unless he makes particular changes. A more drastic form of external pressure is to warn a son or daughter that living at home no longer may be possible, that placement in a boarding school is being considered. This is certainly warranted when other possibilities have been exhausted, and the child constitutes a danger to his own family and community. Of course, if the youngster commits a crime at home, there is always the option of calling the police.

I am opposed to making idle threats or manipulating a child so a parent can get what he wants. The context for what I am saying is contending with a child who is harming others and himself to the extent that something drastic must occur. Hopefully, the punitive measure will jolt him into recognizing that he must make changes but, at the very least, it will reduce his opportunity to victimize others.

A parent may have another child whom the antisocial youngster is abusing. The entire family may be in turmoil from the constant disruption created by the one member. The parent must have the fortitude to follow through and actually impose the threatened consequences. This may be far more arduous for the parent than it is for the child. One lady told me that her idea of being a mother was not to be a policeman to her own son. She needed a lot of support to stop wavering and to follow through on imposing restrictions. Another mother grounded her son so that he had to stay in the house during his week-long school break. To enforce this punishment, she could not go anywhere either. Remaining inside and enduring the tension and anger that permeated the household seemed to her like being imprisoned. It was entirely understandable that she felt this way but, for her son, this was what she needed to do.

> *Is there any way to treat people in this way without their*
> *being under outside pressure to participate—that is, any*
> *way to hook onto a person's inner desire to change?*
> [RALEIGH, NORTH CAROLINA]

This question assumes that there already exists within the person a strong desire to change. With the criminal, this is not usually the case. For him to perceive that his life is crumbling generally requires strong outside pressures. The question may refer to a criminal being dissatisfied with an isolated aspect of his life. A man voluntarily consulted me because he was "depressed" about his habit of pilfering small items when he shopped, and he feared it would only be a matter of time until it got out of hand as it had once before when he had been arrested and placed on probation. We discussed his thinking processes when he entered stores, while he shopped, and after he left. He practiced deterring thoughts about stealing. When I directed the discussion to other aspects of his life, such as his infidelity and his misuse of sick leave from work (claiming depression), he wanted no part of it. He focused only on the stealing, not because he believed it was inherently wrong, but because he feared another arrest and a greater likelihood of going to jail. He wanted a change, but really so he could rid himself from worry about one criminal pattern, then be freer to do whatever else he wanted. His plan was to kick his elderly mother out of his apartment, to take additional sick leave from work, and to leave town to carouse with his friends at the beach. The basic criminal personality remained unaltered. Once his probation expired, he terminated his contact with me. This is typical of people who lack internal motivation to change. If the external pressure is off before new patterns have started to become entrenched, the criminal is likely to go his own way.

> *I was trained to look for a client's vulnerable issues and*
> *to take advantage of those issues. Is this a valid and*
> *useful technique?* [BOISE, IDAHO]

Finding what matters to a person is crucial to furthering change. People voluntarily contact therapists because they are hurting. There is no need to hunt for the vulnerability in these individuals, for they disclose it directly. When consulting a counselor, a criminal does so involuntarily or else with a self-serving agenda in mind.

Criminals do not readily confess to being vulnerable in the sense that they doubt themselves or believe they have flaws. Nevertheless, these outwardly tough people are sentimental and very fearful. Their soft side must be discovered and probed: their view of themselves as good people, their love for their parents, their affection for their children, and their fervent religious beliefs.

During a staff training demonstration interview, I encountered a very resistant inmate. He declared that no other human being mattered, that he looked out only for himself. When I asked if he ever had a pet, he replied that his dog was his best friend. I asserted that because of his nomadic existence, his "best friend" must have suffered for days without water, food, and companionship. This tough guy's eyes misted over; he swallowed hard, but said nothing. In front of several dozen staff members, he was not about to display any more emotion. Had I been interviewing him in private, I might have made further inroads by expanding on the theme of how he repeatedly had hurt his loyal, innocent canine companion. Focusing on vulnerable areas helps motivate the criminal to begin to look in the mirror. If he does this, he may eventually realize that he is less than the sterling individual that he purports to be. With that acknowledgment, the door to further disclosures may open.

## Twelve-Step Programs

> *How do you feel about twelve-step groups? They attack*
> *self-centeredness and demand amends and accountability.*
> *Do you see twelve-step groups as helping?* [BOISE, IDAHO]

Twelve-step programs, such as Alcoholics Anonymous, are extremely helpful and have saved lives. In many communities, meetings are available at different times every day at a variety of locations and with no cost. Twelve-step programs emphasize personal responsibility and have an ethos in which members are not permitted to indulge in blaming others for their problems or wallowing in self-pity. They benefit by learning from others who have had similar difficulties. The possibility of obtaining support at any time by contacting a sponsor can be a godsend to people during crises.

These programs do not provide the intense professional help that is essential for criminals to change lifelong thinking patterns, nor do they purport to take on that task. Twelve-step programs can be invaluable adjuncts to the habilitative process of identifying and correcting errors of thinking by reinforcing the offender's abstention from particular patterns of destructive behavior such as drug use.

I have seen criminals misuse twelve-step programs from which others benefit. I know of instances in which a person wanted to stop using drugs so that he could be a better criminal. These people attended twelve-step programs so that their judgment and coordination would be unimpaired when they committed crimes. Because criminals misuse a program does not invalidate its mission or limit its potential helpfulness to others.

> *Could a nonprofessional program based on your*
> *treatment, using Alcoholics Anonymous as a model, be*
> *viable (i.e., Offenders Anonymous)?* [DENVER, COLORADO]

I do not believe that a program run entirely by offenders for one another would be effective. A severe limitation is inherent in having people who are constantly making errors in thinking trying to teach one another how to be responsible. Not only is it essential that the agent of change be trained to work with offenders but also that he be impeccably responsible in his own personal life.

## Short-Term Programs

> *Do you have any suggestions for short-term treatment*
> *programs, something that might be appropriate for a*
> *county jail?* [DENVER, COLORADO]

A 180-degree habilitative turnaround is unlikely to occur while working with criminals for only a few weeks or months. However, inmates can be introduced to the concept that they have errors in their thinking that have resulted in their hurting others and landing in jail. Through educational classes, audiovisual materials, keeping journals of their thoughts, and meeting regularly in groups, they can learn to recognize specific thinking errors. It is advisable, upon their release, to refer incarcerated individuals to professionals in the community for followup work.

## Criminal's Frustration while Changing

> *What suggestions do you have for keeping these*
> *individuals involved in a responsible lifestyle when they*
> *get frustrated with the problems they face?*
>
> [HELENA, MONTANA]

Criminals have numerous misconceptions about what responsible living entails. One is that, if they give up crime, life will be free of problems. Naturally, they discover that the opposite is true. If they function responsibly, they have a brand new set of problems.

Frustration is part of life; so an agent of change must help the criminal identify exactly what the issue is. If frustration arises because the criminal has been irresponsible, he needs to recognize this and make changes. If the frustration stems from outer circumstances, he must learn to cope constructively with life when things do not go his way. The more responsible and realistic he is, the more effectively he will deal with situations not of his own making, and the less frustration he will experience.

One cannot persuade, seduce, entice, or coerce a person to become responsible. When a criminal becomes frustrated and angry, he has three choices. One is to return to old patterns with the inevitable consequences. Another is to press on and learn to cope with problems in a manner that is brand new to him but, eventually, will yield certain satisfactions. A third choice is not to live at all.

When, out of frustration, the criminal is tempted to take a short cut or quit, all I can do is discuss the alternatives. For example, a criminal reports he is furious because his boss criticized his job performance. The offender has options that include assaulting the boss, leaving the job, or evaluating whether he deserved the criticism. An assault probably means jail. Blaming others and quitting are part of an old pattern, and he has experienced the consequences, which he may not wish to repeat. What about trying a different approach—learning from the criticism, sticking with the task, and trying to improve? All we can do is discuss the options. The offender makes the decisions.

# 14

# Helping
# a Criminal Change

## Deterrence of Thoughts

*How do you respond to statements like, "How do I stop having thoughts like these"?* [PORTLAND, OREGON]

The criminal looks for a quick solution to any difficulty. He is not accustomed to making a prolonged effort to alter a long-standing habit because he has never seen a need to do so. I have witnessed criminals revert to a past pattern and, after the fact, whine that because the thoughts kept entering their minds, they just knew that change was impossible, and so they gave in to those thoughts.

We have to teach the criminal to recognize and attack the first indication of a destructive thought pattern. For example, as soon as the alcoholic glimpses the very beginning of a television beer commercial, a red warning light must flash in his mind. He has no control over the commercial, but he does have control over his thinking. He can divert his attention, shut off the ad, or leave the room. Alternatively, he can watch the commercial and savor the thought of how refreshing a beer would be. If he does this, he is more likely to reach into the refrigerator or go to the nearest liquor store. To maintain sobriety, he must tell himself as soon as the commercial starts that beer is "poison." The poison deterrent is shorthand for a long list of adverse consequences that he has experienced in the past and will experience all over again if he resumes drinking. The greater his disgust for how he has behaved in the past, the more conscientious he will be at detecting and deterring old patterns of thinking. After substantial effort and success at deterrence, the thoughts will diminish in frequency and intensity until deterrence becomes automatic.

> *A technique used in teaching people to control*
> *uncontrollable anger is to replace the actual assault with a*
> *fantasied one. It works. Your comment?* [PORTLAND, OREGON]

I question the word "people"—what people? I absolutely do not recommend this approach with criminals. The message in endorsing it would be that as long as you do not actually do something terrible, thinking about it is harmless. With the criminal, there is a short distance between thought and action. Fantasy has two dangers. One is that it is the acorn from which the oak tree grows. It serves as rehearsal in the mind for the act that the criminal eventually commits. As an example, I have found that during and after intense arguments, the perpetrator had fantasized assaulting his spouse many times before he actually did it. A particular combination of circumstances (e.g., an especially heated argument or drinking) permitted deterrence of these thoughts to break down so that an assault actually occurred. Another danger of fantasy

for the criminal is that, after engaging in fantasy, the real world is less acceptable. Whereas this may be true for anyone, a criminal may become bored and irritable, then seek relief for this state of mind by committing a crime.

A criminal fantasizes having sex with a striking, voluptuous woman whom he eyes on a balcony of his high-rise apartment complex. Mentally, he contrasts her to his "old hag wife" who is neither old nor a hag. As he repeatedly fantasizes about this female, he becomes increasingly dissatisfied with his spouse who loyally has stuck with him for years. Anyone might have a lustful thought. The danger in the criminal is that the thinking will metastasize like a cancer. He starts wondering what the number of her apartment is, whether she lives alone, and what her schedule is. To find answers to his questions, he stalks her. Eventually, a rape occurs. It all started with a seemingly innocuous fantasy. Even if a responsible person indulges in a fantasy from time to time, he has a line that he will not cross. Because the fantasy gets deterred, he does not pursue the fantasied objective, such as establishing a liaison with a stranger and betraying his wife.

## Feelings

> *How do you address "feelings"?* [SALT LAKE CITY, UTAH]

The criminal experiences intense emotional states: excitement, rage, despair, and boredom. He endeavors to persuade others that because he was at the mercy of his feelings, he could not help doing what he did. "I felt so bad, I didn't go to work"; "I was uptight so I had a few drinks"; "I got really mad, so I punched him." He presents himself as a victim of feelings as though they overwhelmed him. "I don't know what came over me"; "The anger came out of nowhere." He then expects the agent of change to alter his feelings, or he may try to engage a counselor in an expedition into his past to unearth causes for the feelings.

My approach to feelings is to explain to the criminal that his feelings will change if his thinking changes. The criminal's attitude has been, "If I feel like it, I'll do it; if not, the heck with it." We have all had to do things that we dreaded, but we overcame our trepidation by focusing our thoughts on what was required and then we discharged our obligation. Afterward, we generally experienced a sense of satisfaction even if the task had been disagreeable. The alternative is to allow our feelings to rule us, thereby creating difficulties for ourselves and others.

## Do Criminals Change?

> *Do you believe that "once a criminal, always a criminal" is true? Do criminals ever truly change their way of thinking?* [RACINE, WISCONSIN]

The research-treatment study that I conducted with Dr. Yochelson at Saint Elizabeths Hospital in Washington demonstrated that criminals can and do change both thinking and behavior. My subsequent clinical experience and that of others confirm this. In working with offenders, I take the position "once a criminal, always a criminal" in the same sense that one speaks of an alcoholic always being an alcoholic even if he has not had a drink in twenty years. It is dangerous for a criminal to adopt a complacent attitude and to believe that he has it made. The potential for reversion to old patterns must always be taken seriously. The same could be said of a person who has dieted to achieve his targeted weight and maintained that weight for years. If he were to lower his guard, he would gain additional pounds.

A constructively self-critical attitude is vital to maintaining change. A criminal either looks for ways to improve his functioning throughout his life or reverts to old patterns. In that sense, the change process never ends.

> *Are there legitimate religious conversions that offer the antisocial individual a new foundation for thinking?*
> [CHICAGO, ILLINOIS]

I differentiate authentic religious conversions from conversions of convenience. Even assuming that a conversion is genuine, how does the criminal respond in the aftermath? All too often, the converted criminal declares that all his flaws have vanished, that he has become a completely different person. Resenting my making even brief allusions to his past, he stubbornly asserts that the past has no relevance to the person he is now. Such a person refuses to consider the possibility that, to prevent a return to old patterns, he must always remember the injury he has inflicted.

Instead of the conversion being a force propelling him toward further change, the converted criminal may remain a self-righteous, rigid zealot. Experiencing an inflated sense of power from his newfound purity, he believes that he is the one to teach others, but he remains unreceptive to what others might suggest to him.

My point is that an authentic religious conversion can occur. The conversion can help establish a new foundation for continuing to work on self-improvement or it can offer yet another impediment and support the criminal's sanctimoniousness and arrogance.

### Is the Criminal Ever Credible?

> *When counseling a criminal, can you ever believe that*
> *person when, by definition, he is a chronic liar?*
> [LINCOLN, NEBRASKA]

I am often asked how I know when to believe a criminal. Usually there is no telltale clue at a given moment as to whether he is being truthful. I do not waste time playing detective. If I have specific evidence that the person is lying, I will bring it to his attention. Otherwise, I work with the individual for the long haul. Three key words are *time will tell.* An individual can say anything and sound sincere. Only in time will I find out whether the person was honest.

The more detailed one's knowledge of the criminal's thinking patterns and tactics, the more difficult it is for him to conceal who he is and to hide what he does. Faced with a person who knows him very well, the criminal may decide that deception is not worth trying.

## Censorship of Television with Juvenile Offenders

> *In working with violent juvenile offenders in a locked treatment program, is it therapeutic to censor violent television programs, or does it matter?* [DENVER, COLORADO]

Censorship of regular television programs may create more problems than it avoids. These youngsters are already violent, and they will not become more violent just because of what they watch on television. Furthermore, when they are released, they will look at whatever they want. Why not work with this issue in the program for change and probe how youngsters are responding to what they see. One issue is their decision to view violent programs rather than devote time to something more worthwhile. There are additional questions. Do they identify with the perpetrators of violence? What aspects of the violence do they find exciting? How do they regard the victims of violence? Does watching violence feed their own violent fantasies?

## Having a Criminal Read *Inside the Criminal Mind*

> *As a means of assisting a somewhat intellectually inclined criminal to gain insight, would it be reasonable to provide a copy of your book* Inside the Criminal Mind?
> [SANTA CLARA, CALIFORNIA]

> *Do you think that having an inmate read your book would put us teachers at a disadvantage?* [DENVER, COLORADO]

> *How can you prevent your own work from being learned and manipulated by an antisocial person who simply uses his or her knowledge of the concepts to gain freedom? They can buy or steal your book too!* [BOULDER, COLORADO]

I heard someone assert that having a criminal read *Inside the Criminal Mind* would be tantamount to giving him a guide so that he could become a "craftier crook." His point was that the criminal would fortify himself with knowledge so that he would be in a better position to deceive and overcome an agent of change as well as others.

Because a criminal can misuse a book does not mean he should be kept from reading it, especially if there is potential benefit. The person who assigns the book needs to be highly specific about the task. Criminals often select books about crime and criminals for "the good parts," the passages that provide vivid accounts of crimes or graphic descriptions of sexual exploits. The instructor or counselor should inform the criminal that, as he reads, he should pick out from the text what applies to him and also note what he thinks does not apply. Often it is the latter that stimulates the more fruitful discussion. Having the criminal read the book can help him look in a mirror. One offender commented that reading *Inside the Criminal Mind* was like "eating glass," an image descriptive of how disagreeable he found recognizing himself in the pages. Another said that he felt like "a rabbit in the cross hairs of a rifle" because the observations fit him precisely.

## Rechanneling Thinking?

> *Do you try to rechannel the thinking to other exciting,
> but legal, activities or change the thinking to not
> needing the excitement?* [LOUISVILLE, KENTUCKY]

> *The emotion of excitement seems important to the criminal.
> Please comment on channeling. Is life so boring? How do
> we get these people high on life?* [LIGONIER, INDIANA]

People have conjectured that if it is excitement the criminal wants, then he should be helped to experience it but with his behavior channeled into legitimate endeavors so others do not get hurt. Suggestions have been offered to involve offenders in rock climbing, sky diving, or other risky, but legal, activities. An alternative is to place criminals in positions where they can feel powerful but can use that power in a beneficial way—for example, assign delinquent youngsters to be school hall monitors or safety patrols where they can detect and report peers who commit infractions.

I wish the means of helping a criminal change were so easy. The drawback to the "channeling" idea is that these approaches fail to get inside the criminal mind. The outcome is a criminal who rock climbs rather than a criminal who is not a rock climber. Seeking thrills from legitimate high-risk activities does not eliminate the search for thrills from doing what is forbidden. Appointing a boy a hall monitor may give him an arena to misuse his authority by bullying and intimidating other students.

## Group Therapy with Criminals

> *What is your opinion of group counseling with juvenile offenders or, for that matter, with adults?* [AUSTIN, TEXAS]

> *How do you present your ideas or concepts in a group therapy session with delinquents?* [CHARLESTON, WEST VIRGINIA]

Group counseling can be a powerful method of helping offenders change. However, a group composed of unchanged criminals constitutes a gang, which is likely to interfere with, rather than promote, the process of change. The diversionary tactics multiply geometrically, and it is extremely difficult to address matters of substance.

A group will be more productive if formed over time with offenders who are at different points in their progress. Attendance at any group meeting of Alcoholics Anonymous, for example, will include people who vary in the length of their sobriety. There might be a person who has not been sober for ten days along with a member who has been sober for ten years. A new person can learn from those who are making changes, and a person who has been diligently maintaining his sobriety can visualize himself all over again in the new entrant. Because a format is being adhered to, meetings are not likely to be taken over by people who engage mainly in posturing and creating diversions.

Group meetings of criminals should not be devoted to members pouncing on one another's faults and mistakes. I have observed groups turn into a criminal enterprise as criminals launch scathing attacks in order to enhance their own sense of power and virtuousness. The program developed at St. Elizabeths Hospital had at its core working intensively with criminals in groups numbering between two and six people. If one were a fly on the wall, one would have witnessed an assemblage that more resembled a class with a teacher than it did a traditional therapy group. A criminal would present a "report" of thinking that occurred during a specific time period. The objective of identifying thinking errors was accomplished not by personal attack, but by commentary and instruction by the agent of change. The other members of the group were challenged to consider, then discuss how the thinking error made by the reporting member applied to themselves. The process was devoted to criminals learning from one another in a civil discourse, not through harsh confrontation and condemnation. A group can include criminals from different backgrounds who were arrested for different types of crimes. The focus is not on these differences but on the commonalities in thinking patterns that all group members share.

## Victim Empathy Programs

*There is a movement in Utah corrections to provide classes in criminal thinking and victim empathy for general population inmates. Is there value to that in reducing recidivism or will it create a more manipulative inmate?*

[SALT LAKE CITY, UTAH]

> *Do you see any benefit in the programs where the defendant meets the true victim?* [LINCOLN, NEBRASKA]

The question is who benefits when offender meets victim? I favor nearly any approach that is both legal and moral to help a victim of crime. To develop motivation to change, criminals must see themselves realistically. This includes becoming aware of the devastating impact they have had on their victims. A young offender may gain a new perspective by meeting his victim and hearing about this firsthand. If such an encounter transpires, a counselor, officer of the court, or other neutral party should monitor it. Repeat offenders are unlikely to benefit from such encounters. In fact, the criminal may pervert their very purpose. Sitting down face-to-face with his victim may further elevate his already high opinion of himself. He may come away from it proud that he has helped the victim, but not any more remorseful.

A beneficial measure can be perverted by a criminal, yet not preclude its being useful. Anyone overseeing a criminal/victim encounter program needs to understand that, whereas the victim may benefit, the offender may derive nothing but a boost to his already well-entrenched belief that he is a good human being.

## Boot Camps

> *What is your position on boot camps?* [CLEVELAND, OHIO]

I do not have a position on boot camps in terms of endorsing or not endorsing the concept. As with most measures designed to be corrective, we should evaluate outcomes to determine what works and with whom. Subjecting undisciplined people to a military-like, highly disciplined environment can be beneficial. The memory of a harsh regimen may endure as a deterrent for some offenders. However, once the criminal is back in society, he is able to shut off memories of boot camp as well as memories of other deterrents.

The inmate may change his behavior while he is in boot camp.

That is, he may conform to the regimen that is imposed. However, it is only the outer behavior that changes while the same thought patterns remain. It is like trying to kill a weed by snipping off the top but failing to pull it up by the roots. An offender may endure the rigors of boot camp, complete the program, and "graduate" in good standing. Nonetheless, if he returns to civilian life with no concept of injury to others, unrealistic expectations of others, and irresponsible decision-making processes, he invariably will resume old patterns.

Some boot camps have incorporated counseling and teaching particular skills. I recommend that these programs address the participant's thinking errors and refer him to more of the same once he returns to the community.

## Good Behavior in Confinement

> *How does the presence or lack of institutional misconduct*
> *predict future community criminal activity? Or is the*
> *"good con" mostly playing a game?*
> [COLORADO SPRINGS, COLORADO]

If a criminal does not live by the rules and regulations of institutional life, he is not likely to be responsible when he has greater freedom in the community. Making this prediction is easy. The more troubling issue is how to assess the inmate whose behavior in confinement is exemplary. By being responsible, he obtains more freedom, privileges, and accolades. What does this signify—compliance or real change? I know of a man who had been so highly regarded as an inmate that he helped direct some of the institutional programs. Paroled from prison, he later was convicted of a series of murders. Was his good behavior calculated solely to curry favor with others, or did he have sincere intentions to change and did he make whatever positive contributions he could while confined? There is no way to answer this conclusively.

Compliance and basic change may look identical, but they have very different motives. In a structured, closely monitored environment, behavior may change, but the thinking patterns of a lifetime may remain completely unaffected. Unless one works intensively to help criminals identify and correct thinking errors, change is likely to be superficial and temporary.

An incarcerated criminal can appear to have made major strides in his habilitation, having become completely conversant with the thinking errors approach. No one can be certain whether he has changed significantly until he is living in the community. If the inmate has a lengthy history of serious crimes, he will require extensive monitoring in the community, no matter how good his institutional progress appears. If that supervision cannot be provided, he should not be released.

## Unmotivated Offenders

> *How do you help a youngster who does not*
> *want your help?* [SIOUX CITY, IOWA]

> *When you cannot get anywhere with a child, do you advise*
> *parents to just put up with his or her behavior [so long as]*
> *there are no laws broken and the child cannot be locked*
> *up? If so, isn't that condoning the child's actions?*
> [SACRAMENTO, CALIFORNIA]

I wish I could say that I can involve any offender who walks in the door in a process of change. Clearly, that is not so. There are instances where the criminal rejects my assistance; I do not reject him. A frustrated, desperate parent may bring a son or daughter to me, but that child is unwilling to speak. He occupies a chair, maybe not even that, and says as little as possible. In such cases, I do most of the talking. The youngster sees no reason to speak to me. He has been able to get away with a great deal that he does not want to disclose. His objective is to get others, including me, off his back and to continue to do just as he pleases. Politely, I express my view and predict that I may see him in the future under different, but far less agreeable, circumstances. Disagreeing intensely, the youngster becomes even more emphatic about wanting nothing to do with me.

Usually, I am not dissuaded by his negativity. I suggest he think about what I said, then I schedule a time to meet with him again. I offer to meet with the parents to discuss their approach. Or I may recommend nothing further, but I invite the parents to call me in the future when circumstances are different.

Rarely do I send a family out the door without any help. I sometimes identify errors in thinking that parents make as they try to cope with this difficult youngster. Among these are accepting too readily the child's self-serving rationalizations, allowing the child to pit members of the family against one another, blaming themselves or others for the child's behavior, and continually rescuing the youngster by bailing him out of difficulties that he has created by his own behavior. In some cases, I am able to help parents become more realistic, firm, and consistent in their management of their offspring so they effect positive changes in his behavior.

Sometimes the child's antisocial patterns have become so entrenched that neither parents nor anyone else has much influence. Even then, I can help parents take steps to improve the quality of their lives and the lives of their other offspring. I encourage them not to permit the antisocial child to dominate their attention to the extent that their marriage or relationships with their other children suffer. I support parents invoking severe consequences if the child's misconduct threatens the physical safety and emotional well-being of the rest of the family. This may entail pressing charges if the child commits a crime at home, hospitalizing him, petitioning the court for assistance, or placing him in a residential facility.

> *What do you tell the parents to do when they have an adult child who will not work, uses drugs, sleeps in the day time, pressures them for money, and is on the fringes of crime? They love him.* [SALT LAKE CITY, UTAH]

The parents face an excruciating dilemma, fearing that if they do not support him, he will end up in a worse situation on the streets and that it will be their fault. On the other hand, by allowing him to live at home or assisting him in other ways, they are being used and are enabling him to perpetuate patterns that will cost him (and perhaps them) dearly in the future. While assuring their offspring of their love, they need to tell him that they no longer can live with and support what they find irresponsible and dangerous. My specific recommendations, of course, depend on the situation. My inclination is to advise the parents to give their adult son or daughter a deadline for taking particular steps: finding a job, enrolling in drug treatment, locating a place to live, or doing whatever else is necessary. As the deadline approaches with no sign of compliance, I advise the parents to help their offspring find a very modest place to live and, if they can afford it, pay the first month's rent directly to the landlord (but not co-sign a lease or any other document). They might also advance their son or daughter money for food and public transportation.

Parents often find themselves paralyzed and therefore require a great deal of encouragement as well as specific advice to take these steps. If a parent is emotionally too fragile to do as I advise, I help the person decide how to maintain his own stability. If it means that the young person remains at home, I will counsel the parent as to how to cope with that set of circumstances in the most constructive way.

> *What do you recommend to parents who are overwhelmed with guilt and self-blame to the degree that they absolve their child from all responsibility?* [CHICAGO, ILLINOIS]

Desperate to make sense out of what has happened in their family, parents of antisocial children blame themselves for what they did wrong or for what, in retrospect, they think they should have done. By faulting themselves, parents at least think they have an understanding of a situation that otherwise defies comprehension.

In working with guilt-ridden parents, I emphasize the following.

No matter what mistakes they made, and all of us as parents make mistakes, each child makes his own choices to deal with whatever his circumstances are. Unless they have just the one child, mothers and fathers need to look at what is staring them in the face: that they have been raising other children who are behaving far more responsibly.

Finally, it is important to shift the focus away from assigning blame in order to direct attention to understanding the day-to-day thinking and behavior of the antisocial child, regardless of the cause. Inform the parents that a search for what has caused all this is futile for two reasons. One is that identification of the causes remains elusive. Second, pinpointing a cause would not make the problem vanish. If the parents remain mired in guilt, they will be unable to help the child because, instead of holding their offspring accountable, they will continue to see themselves as the cause and then excuse his misconduct.

## A Moral Stance

*Since you have said that you take a "moral" stance, whose morals do you use? Who decides what is bad and rotten?*
[SALT LAKE CITY, UTAH]

Some moral standards are nearly universal across racial, ethnic, and cultural groups. Killing, stealing, lying, cheating, and other injurious behavior are proscribed in most societies. If you ask impoverished inner-city parents or affluent suburban parents what they desire for their offspring, I think the responses would be similar. I believe those mothers and fathers would aspire for their children to become educated, to be equipped and motivated to earn a living, and to make their way in the world without harming innocent people.

## Abuse of the Agent of Change

> *In interviewing your clients who do not want to be*
> *there, do they ever become verbally or physically*
> *abusive toward you and, if so, how do you handle this?*
> [ST. CLOUD, MINNESOTA]

I have not been physically assaulted. I have had offenders become angry but not threatening to the point that I feared for my safety. If I find that an offender remains angry, and therefore is unreceptive to rational discussion, I terminate the meeting. There is no virtue in allowing a person to build up a head of steam preparatory to an angry outburst.

I am a careful listener. Knowing the thinking patterns and tactics of the criminal, I have been able to gauge my responses to de-escalate a volatile situation rather than throw gasoline on an already ignited blaze. Trying to overcome the offender by meeting anger with anger is a recipe for trouble. I have learned not to take personally the harsh comments that offenders make, but instead I understand that these show how such individuals characteristically deal with situations when they do not have the control that they wish.

> *If a counselor has a sex offender who says, "I have*
> *fantasies of raping and strangling you,"*
> *what is a good response?* [BOISE, IDAHO]

My first warning is not to take this as imminent and panic. Why is the criminal disclosing this fantasy? Is it a ploy to make you afraid? Is he articulating it because he is frightened and seeks assistance in self-control? Is he saying this because it is exciting to watch your reaction? I would respond to it in terms of what the fantasy reveals about him. Tell him you know that this is probably not the first time that he has had such a fantasy about you or anyone else. Establish that this is standard thinking when he is in the presence of any woman whom he wants to dominate. The next question is how is the criminal going to deal with this fantasy? He can encourage it by thinking more about it, elaborating on it, and enjoying the excitement. Discuss with him the detrimental consequences to others and himself if he savors such thoughts. If he is receptive, you can teach him methods to deter this thinking. If you are convinced that you are in imminent danger, you need to end the conversation calmly or, if necessary, obtain assistance.

### "Untreatable" Offenders

> *Under what circumstances would you refuse to treat a*
> *criminal?* [COLORADO SPRINGS, COLORADO]

I am not likely to undertake working with a criminal who consistently protests his innocence and whose main purpose is to convince me that he has been unjustly convicted in court. I will not work with an offender who insists on directing the course of the counseling, dictating what he will and will not do. And, clearly, I cannot work with an offender who continues to engage in criminal activity while professing he wants to change. Offenders with these attitudes are not interested in changing and, in most cases, continue to pose a danger. They cannot be counseled effectively as outpatients. If any work is to be done with them, a trial phase must be initiated in an institutional setting.

> *Who are those criminals who are untreatable and what*
> *is society to do with them?* [SEATTLE, WASHINGTON]

Some criminals will repeatedly reject whatever opportunities they are offered to change. Spending time and money counseling them is futile and wasteful. No one can make them change against their will. The community must be protected from unremorseful predators by incarcerating them for long periods, then by providing intensive supervision when they return to society.

> *In juvenile corrections/detention, there is a perennial danger of suicide due to acute depression. Can or do you attempt to instill self-disgust at the risk of precipitating an incident, or are prospective clients screened for such possibilities?* [SACRAMENTO, CALIFORNIA]

A professional responsibly engaged in this work does not tear the criminal apart simply to let him psychologically bleed to death. When a patient enters surgery, his doctor explains the procedure in advance so that the patient knows precisely what to expect. During his recovery, he has continuing treatment and support. There is a parallel to working with the criminal in that he will have to suffer to achieve a beneficial result. The offender is informed that experiencing pain while recognizing his deficiencies is a necessary and positive development. The agent of change is available throughout the process to help him cope with his internal distress.

## Criteria of Success

> *How do you measure success?* [ATLANTIC BEACH, NORTH CAROLINA]

The two most frequently cited criteria for measuring success are whether an offender remains arrest-free and whether he holds a job. These are flawed measures because criminals continue to commit crimes without being arrested, and most work. There is far more to living responsibly. Is the person accountable for how he spends his time and money? If he holds a job, is he also competent, reliable, and cooperative? Is he drug-free as indicated by random urine screenings? While a change agent is working with him, is the channel of communication open so that he continues to disclose criminal thinking? Is the offender receptive to criticism? Has he developed the habit of being constructively self-critical so that he is constantly striving to improve? Or has he become boastful and so complacent about his progress that he does not see a need for further change? Finally, it is important for the agent of change to have access to a reliable source of information who knows the criminal well.

## Rewards of Change

> *What rewards does the criminal in treatment get? How does appreciation for the rewards of the straight life come about?* [COLORADO SPRINGS, COLORADO]

Initially, the criminal should not be expected to make a firm commitment to change. Motivation and knowledge are lacking. Besides, who would readily embrace a life he has never experienced and for which he has expressed little but contempt? As cited earlier, one offender reflected, "If you take my crime away, you take my life away." If he abandons the life he has known, he must start from scratch to live a life that is drab by comparison and that offers no guarantees of success. Even to consider such an undertaking, an offender must reach a point of desperation.

As the criminal makes changes, he finds himself in what may seem like a prison. There are so many things he cannot do, and so many other things he must do as he muddles through a daily routine of working, taking care of responsibilities at home, and attending required meetings. "What can you offer me that compares with cocaine?" one young man asked me. Released from jail to participate in an intensive community supervision program, he had worked hard and lived within the law for nearly a year. No matter how well others thought he was doing, he found his new life abysmally dull. Bored and discouraged, he returned to cocaine, abandoning his efforts before he had realized some of the satisfactions of living responsibly.

In contrast, another criminal commented that he used to live in "a tiny corner of the world" but, having made extensive changes, felt "clean." People at work respected him. Because he had provided superb service to customers, he had been promoted several times and had reached a managerial position. His girlfriend decided to stay with him, so heartened was she by his turnaround. His parents began to have faith in him for the first time in years. And he did not have to look over his shoulder and fear that, at any time, he might be hauled away and locked in a cage.

The rewards of change are both tangible and intangible. The former include job promotions, salary raises, and material possessions obtained legitimately with money earned. Eventually, the less tangible satisfactions are experienced: earning respect and trust, achieving stability in relationships, and developing self-respect that is based not on pretensions but on effort and accomplishment.

## Positive Peer Pressure

> *If peer pressure does not cause criminality, will positive pressure help reverse criminality?* [DALLAS, TEXAS]

A criminal is suggestible only in directions of his own choosing. If he wants excitement, he will try a new "designer" drug that his buddy suggests. There was plenty of positive peer pressure in the past, but the criminal shunned those influences. Positive pressure later in life will have no more impact than it did before on a criminal who is unmotivated to change. For an offender who has reached a crisis point in his life, positive pressure can be helpful in increasing and sustaining motivation to change.

## Are Individual Differences To Be Ignored?

> *What about treating each person as an individual versus
> grouping behaviors and thinking patterns? Is there a
> danger of missing the subtleties that may be the key in
> helping this person change his or her behavior?*
> [MINNEAPOLIS, MINNESOTA]

It depends on what is meant by treating each person "as an individual." Everyone is unique in some fashion. Whatever individual differences exist, I have observed that there are thinking patterns common to all offenders. One need not discount or ignore significant individual differences while focusing on these important commonalities that directly give rise to criminal behavior. For example, one offender may be an expert auto mechanic, whereas another may be a skilled carpenter. The important point is not what each is good at, but that both individuals have lacked the self-discipline to utilize their talents. They have quit jobs, have failed to work for weeks at a time, and have lived off others. The individual skills matter, but more important are the personality deficiencies that have stood in the way of utilizing those skills responsibly.

## Empathy and Praise by the Agent of Change

> *What use, if any, do you see for an empathic approach?
> Is it useful at any point?* [MANKATO, MINNESOTA]

> *Do you feel compassion is outdated, at least
> toward an offender?* [BOISE, IDAHO]

I have been asked, "Where is the compassion in your approach? Do you have any empathy for people with a criminal personality?" My response is that I do not display compassion by sympathizing with a criminal who has created his own problems and has injured others in the process. I or any other agent of change can show our compassion through a strong commitment to work with a person whom others totally avoid.

One develops empathy with a criminal by having a thorough understanding of how he thinks, thereby recognizing the enormity of the task of helping him change. A change agent understands that the offender is confronting an extremely agonizing dilemma: whether to make the leap of faith that is necessary to embark on building a life with which he has no personal experience. The only comparable situation I can conceive of is what it would be like for a person of integrity and accomplishment to abandon his life and become a gun-toting drug dealer.

The agent of change knows what it is to contend with undesirable features in himself. He is aware of the struggles to deal with his own self-centeredness, his desires to opt for the shortcut, and his failures to be sensitive even toward people whom he loves. The change agent has a personal appreciation of the scope of the task in helping others who are far more extreme than he in these and other characteristics.

> *You have talked about constantly confronting flaws but avoiding encouragement (lest they "puff up"). Is there room for an encouraging progress report?* [LARAMIE, WYOMING]

> *Do you ever praise after exposing an error in thought (in a situation where the person refrained from acting on that thought)?* [HOUSTON, TEXAS]

I have had criminals complain that I do not say much positive about them. Occasionally, family members voice the same opinion. My initial response is that the criminal is not in jail, on probation, or in my office because of his good points. I am seeing him because of the damage he has inflicted and the danger that he continues to represent.

Whatever positive features he has are greatly overshadowed by breaking into homes, destroying property, sexually abusing children, or committing other serious crimes.

I do agree that a criminal, working diligently to make changes but hearing only criticism, might become discouraged. However, for doing what is expected of any responsible person, the criminal thinks he merits lavish praise. That is not how life is. A person is not commended just for showing up at work, but he is likely to hear about it if he is absent without explanation. The criminal thinks if he does something right one time, he has taken care of the entire matter permanently. He fails to realize that a single instance of change does not constitute a pattern. Another problem is that if he receives approval for one accomplishment, he interprets the praise as global approval of him as a human being.

To place a positive development in perspective, the agent of change can note the improvement, then emphasize that it does not yet constitute a pattern and, finally, discuss with the criminal how the new behavior contrasts with past irresponsibility. I remember a man who proudly reported that he went to the library and actually spent the time studying rather than losing himself in sexual fantasy. I commented positively on the change, then reminded this individual that, not long ago, he had been in the library and, instead of reading, had spent nearly the entire time staring at female students and fantasizing about sexual contact with them. He had made a beginning to discipline his thinking, but that is all it was, a start.

### Need for Follow-Up

> *What types of follow-up are required to reinforce the thinking changes addressed in treatment?* [AUSTIN, TEXAS]

When a person is released from a restrictive setting, he faces greater temptations because external deterrence is less. Put simply, he leaves the world of bars and strict supervision to step into a life where no one guards him. In a less restrictive environment, the criminal is inundated with all sorts of temptations, and he has many decisions to make. Unfortunately, no follow-up help is available when offenders leave many residential programs. An effective institutional program can provide a criminal with a foundation for change, but it offers only a limited arena for him to implement what he has learned. The offender's accomplishments are likely to be short-lived if he does not have the monitoring and continued corrective teaching as he takes up residence in the community. With the abolition of parole in many jurisdictions, there is no means to ensure that the offender receives further help. Whether he continues to participate in a program for change will depend both on his motivation and on help being available and affordable.

Community corrections must involve more than seeing a probation or parole officer once or twice a month. Releasing into the community even a person who wants to change, without offering a continuing program, constitutes a prescription for failure.

## When to Give Up

> When do you give up on someone as being incorrigible?
> [EL DORADO, KANSAS]

The criminal generally rejects me before I give up on him. In various ways, he indicates that he no longer wants to participate. He may cease to attend meetings. He may show up but argue constantly while being unresponsive to criticism and advice. Another possibility is that, while he professes to be changing, there are sporadic surprises. He closes the channel of communication so that I learn about events long after their occurrence. For example, a criminal mentions he will miss the next meeting because of a court hearing. This is news, for he never reported being arrested. The decision to terminate such a person's participation in a program for change is subjective. Continuing violations of the law or of program requirements would, at the very least, call for a discussion of termination with the criminal and perhaps additional discussion with someone who has influence or leverage, such as a probation officer, a spouse, or a parent.

# 15

# Agents of Change

## Being "Soft"

> *Do you think that people in the mental health field enable criminal behavior because of their "soft" and understanding approach?* [ST. LOUIS, MISSOURI]

Among mental health professionals, good intentions abound, but many are ill-equipped to assess and treat antisocial individuals. There are several reasons for this.

One reason is the tendency among mental health professionals to focus on causes. Mistakenly, they believe that if they understand the origin of the behavior, they can better treat it. In the effort to understand, they seek to unearth causative factors by exploring childhood experiences. The criminal is all too ready to assist us in that endeavor. The search for reasons why and the treatment based on those alleged causes invariably result in criminals developing psychological "insight," but remaining criminals. My colleague at St. Elizabeths remarked that the type of insight developed by criminals when treated by well-meaning, but uninformed, counselors and therapists should be spelled "incite." The offender is incited to blame people and forces outside himself, most of which he never would have thought of on his own.

Mental health professionals who help patients suffering from depression and low self-esteem mistakenly believe that these are the key problems that plague offenders. Certain obvious facts attest to the antisocial person's failures throughout his life. He may be an outcast from his family, uneducated, a dropout from the workforce, and an individual who never has supported himself. Unless the antisocial person has a long record that is known to the mental health worker, he does not wear a badge proclaiming his criminality.

Meeting his new patient or client in a detention center, hospital, or clinic, the therapist is likely to encounter a deeply distressed human being. He is likely to see his mission as helping his patient develop insight, feel better, and regard himself positively. The therapist approaches this task with empathy and understanding. In working with a criminal, these objectives all are counterproductive because they are based on erroneous premises. The criminal is depressed about his circumstances, not about himself. No matter how he seems to others, he does not regard himself as a failure. Rather than being rejected, the offender is the one who has done the rejecting, by turning his back on family, school, work, and others who tried to exert a positive influence. He will regard the compassionate therapist as a sucker and take advantage of him. His overriding aim is to escape from his disagreeable situation of the moment, not to improve himself.

Applying psychological approaches that work with most patient populations results in criminals sophisticated in psychology rather than criminals without psychology. They remain criminals. So long as the change agent fails to recognize that, in the criminal, he is dealing with virtually a different breed of human being, he cannot be effective. As the question suggests, he may inadvertently "enable" the behavior to persist.

## Motives to Work with This Personality

> *Why do we become attracted to this specialized kind of work and personality?* [MIAMI, FLORIDA]

> *Do you find that people in the human services have*
> *similar personality traits to those they are treating?*
> [SAN FRANCISCO, CALIFORNIA]

I recall being asked at one presentation I made in California, "Dr. Samenow, doesn't a person have to be a psychopath himself to work with a criminal?" I replied that nothing could be further from the truth. It is essential that people who work with offenders be extremely responsible and straightforward in their interpersonal relationships.

There are, however, people who work with offenders because they are fascinated by crime and seek vicarious excitement. Greatly intrigued by this population, they would work with no other. When the novelty wears off and they discover that the job is tedious and difficult, many become disenchanted and leave.

Then, there are individuals who choose to work with criminals because they themselves have a criminal personality. From time to time, we read about a police officer who has accepted bribes, overstepped his authority by using excessive force, or been arrested while committing a crime off duty. We may hear about an employee of a detention center bringing in contraband, involving himself in sexual liaisons, or helping an inmate escape. Some employees with a criminal personality do not commit crimes on the job, but they abuse the authority that is entrusted to them by mistreating offenders in custody or harassing subordinate employees. If they are caught doing something out of line, they may be quick to claim that they are being unfairly targeted and victimized. And, of course, it is always convenient to try to absolve themselves of culpability by claiming that whatever a criminal reports should not be believed because criminals lie.

Having talked with hundreds of people throughout North America, I have no doubt that most professionals who choose a career in fields that deal directly with criminals do so because they sincerely desire to make a contribution to society. Given the wages that are paid, I doubt many people enter law enforcement, corrections, social work, and other occupations working with offenders because they seek great financial rewards.

## Therapists with a Criminal Personality

> *Can you discuss the dynamics of what happens when a psychotherapist with personal characteristics of the criminal meets up with a patient who presents the same profile?*
> [SAN FRANCISCO, CALIFORNIA]

I observed one such individual run a therapy group for offenders. He was a colorful, charismatic individual who knew the street lingo and seemed able to talk to offenders on their level. I observed him using his position of authority as a therapist to tear into his patients verbally. In the name of "confrontation," he warned he would force them to "eat shit in front of authority." I watched as he leaned back in his chair and gloated in the power that he was exercising over his captive group. Of all the men present, the therapist had the loudest voice and used the crudest language. Several among the group bowed their heads and appeared to submit just to shut him up. Others relished challenging him and confronting one another. It all amounted to an exercise in which therapist and patients were building themselves up by tearing others down.

## Most Common Counselor Error

> *What is the most common counselor error in dealing with criminals?* [LOUISVILLE, KENTUCKY]

I am dividing my answer into two parts. The first is to identify the most common and, potentially, most lethal error anyone can make in dealing with a criminal. The second has to do with a commonly encountered mistake that people make in the attitude they adopt while interacting with criminals over time.

In any contact with a criminal, a counselor must avoid verbally cornering and attacking him. No matter how tough the offender seems, he has a very thin skin and quickly becomes defensive. The criminal perceives even the slightest reproach as a devastating blow to his entire self-worth. One can be confrontative without being provocative. In all interactions, it is important to convey one's message in such a manner that the criminal does not feel personally threatened. Maintaining an even and respectful tone is far more effective than coming across as accusatory or hostile.

Gullibility and cynicism both are counselor errors. The person new to working with criminals wants to believe what his client or patient is telling him. The criminal adroitly feeds a gullible therapist what he thinks the therapist wants to hear. Speaking of his former therapist, one offender recalled, "When I satisfied her theory, I was cured." The therapist had concluded that the offender's cruel treatment of females stemmed from long festering anger toward his mother who, he claimed, had treated him abusively. However, the offender failed to disclose that his mother was harsh only with him; she was very lenient with his brother and sister because they were easy to raise. They had excelled academically, worked during summers and diligently saved money, then attended college and prepared for careers. In stark contrast, the criminal headed down a different path. His mother wanted to trust him, just as she had trusted her other children, but he betrayed her trust. She found clothes and cassette tapes in his room that she knew she had not purchased and that he could not have paid for by himself. She received calls from neighborhood parents and school teachers about his picking fights with other children. He told her he had no homework when some had been assigned, and he feigned illness so he could stay home from school. When things did not go his way at home, he became extremely belligerent, sometimes destroying property. His mother responded by imposing restrictions, taking away privileges, refusing to sign for him to get a driver's license, grounding him, and doing just about anything else she could think of to try to teach him to be more responsible, to keep him safe, and to prevent him from throwing opportunities away.

The story the therapist received was of a child who got a raw deal from a mother who was mean, arbitrary, and played favorites with his two siblings. In session after session, the offender emphasized what his mother "did" to him, but he revealed very little of his own misconduct. The therapist believed that his physical and emotional mistreatment of girlfriends and, later, his wife stemmed from his long suppressed rage toward an authoritarian, unsympathetic mother, which was being displaced onto all women in his adult life. The offender convinced the therapist that he had improved because he had gained this insight and therefore no longer harbored this buried anger. She was preparing to discharge him from treatment when, much to her shock and dismay, he again beat up his wife.

The criminal quickly marks the gullible agent of change as an easy target to manipulate. The therapist believes his patient is being truthful and progressing. When the offender reverts to old patterns, the therapist grows disillusioned and, if this happens frequently enough with clients, quite cynical.

Although the opposite of gullibility, unbridled cynicism also imposes a formidable obstacle to effective work with this population. One must think of it from the offender's point of view. Who would like to confide deeply personal matters in a counselor who never seems to believe one word? Such a relationship would deteriorate quickly.

For agents of change working with criminals, it is necessary to avoid both gullibility and cynicism. By adopting a "time will tell" attitude, the change agent does not feel impelled to make an on the spot judgment as to the offender's credibility when he has no way of knowing at the time what the truth actually is. Eventually, the facts will emerge.

---

*Can caseworkers and psychologists have sincere and truthful interviews if they perform custody tasks in lockup settings (i.e., prisons)?* [SALT LAKE CITY, UTAH]

The criminal will maneuver to gain advantage with a change agent who holds great power over him, more so than with someone who is not in such a position. Nevertheless, a person who exercises day-to-day authority over a criminal can be an effective counselor. If a criminal genuinely wants to change, he will obey laws and institutional rules. Then penalties and disciplinary measures will not have to be imposed. Counselor and inmate can focus on the central task of identifying and changing errors in thinking. If the criminal persists in subverting the counselor's authority or pressing for more privileges that are not merited, such tactics can be addressed as part of the program for change. The issues arising in this context are similar to those in the past when the criminal flouted the authority of parents, teachers, and others.

## Qualifications for Change Agents

> *How much does the attitude, charisma, humor, finesse, and so forth of the counselor have to do with a person changing for the better? Do only a few counselors have the God-given qualities that are necessary for the person to respond, or can this be learned?* [COLORADO SPRINGS, COLORADO]

> *Would you comment on the personality, style, background, and training of therapists who are successful with antisocial personalities?* [DENVER, COLORADO]

> *Can this work be done by people other than trained clinicians, such as counselors or corrections officers?*
> [LANSING, MICHIGAN]

It is a myth that only a small number of specially endowed people can be effective. Charisma and humor are assets in working with this difficult population. However, far more essential are integrity, knowledge, experience, belief in a person's capacity to make responsible choices, a willingness to be firm when necessary, as well as other characteristics, such as being a good listener, that are important whenever one human endeavors to help another.

Specific skills to work with criminals can be learned by people with a variety of backgrounds, and an M.D. or Ph.D. is not necessary.

> *Can a woman who lives with a man who has an antisocial personality be an agent of change, or is she too close to the situation to facilitate change?*
> [COLORADO SPRINGS, COLORADO]

If an antisocial individual desires to change, he will respond positively to anyone who is genuinely trying to be helpful. I do not think that it is realistic for a roommate, partner, or relative to assume full responsibility for the task in the way a professional would. Even if the woman in the above question were trained in understanding and working with thinking patterns, she would likely be much too close emotionally to function as a counselor to the person with whom she is living. She can be a sounding board and a provider of valuable advice if the offender is receptive. If invited, she could also point out old patterns so the offender can become aware of them on the spot. However, this is a lot, probably too much, to undertake in this situation.

**The Race of the Agent of Change**

> *What are your thoughts about yourself as the white male authority figure—"the man"? How are you seen by minority criminals/clients?* [COLORADO SPRINGS, COLORADO]

Racial differences are irrelevant to the change process. For a person to maintain that he cannot learn from a person of another race is absurd. Making race an issue is a tactic criminals resort to when they want to deflect attention from more pressing matters and when they want to place someone immediately on the defensive. It is a convenient way for offenders to divert attention from their resistance to examining their own conduct, considering someone else's advice, and instituting changes.

## Female Change Agents with Male Offenders

*Given these individuals' view of women, how does this affect their relationship (or effectiveness of therapy) with a female counselor or therapist?* [DENVER, COLORADO]

*What do you think are the benefits of female counselors working with criminals (especially violent sex offenders)? What are the drawbacks?* [BOISE, IDAHO]

The offender's relationship with a counselor of either sex offers within itself an important arena for making changes. Whether the counselor is male or female is unimportant. What matters is the knowledgeability, integrity, and competence of the professional. I do not think a counselor has a particular advantage or disadvantage because of gender. Male offenders, who treat women with contempt and try to control them, are likely to approach a female counselor in the same manner. If she is equipped by personality and training, she will not take personally or react emotionally to what the offender says or does. Instead, the counselor will respond as she would to any of his tactics and errors in thinking.

## Burnout

> *It is hard for me to work full-time with people who can be constantly critical or who try to be abusive toward me on a regular basis. What are your ideas on how to best cope with this and keep from burning out?* [SALT LAKE CITY, UTAH]

Work with offenders is not for the fainthearted. It is difficult to work each day with people who have done terrible things to others, and who then arrogantly resist our efforts, try our patience and, at times, abuse us. No matter how dedicated we are, a certain personal detachment is necessary to withstand the disagreeable aspects of working with this population. To avoid taking personally what the criminal says and does, we should never lose sight of the fact that he is behaving toward us no differently than he has toward many other people throughout his life.

 The best prevention against burnout is knowledge and realistic expectations. I once heard someone in corrections (one could include any profession that deals with offenders) define burnout in the following manner. He said, "The first year, the person new to corrections tries to do everything *for* the inmate. The second year, he does everything *to* the inmate. And the third year, he doesn't give a damn." A given in the situation is the difficulty inherent in dealing with  an angry, controlling person who unrelentingly finds fault with others while rarely acknowledging shortcomings in himself. If we are not prepared for that, we have chosen the wrong field.

I have often spoken and written about the criminal's unrealistic expectations of others, but we need to be certain that we are realistic as to what we expect of ourselves and of the criminal. I remember a young woman who was a federal probation officer. She feared she was not up to the job because she believed it was her fault that her clients did not respond as she thought they should. Later, she concluded that her clients were hopeless. She told me that as she was contemplating leaving the field, she discovered and read the first volume of *The*

*Criminal Personality.* She then recognized that it was not a matter of her incompetence or of her criminal clients all being hopeless. Once she understood how people with a criminal personality think and she became familiar with their tactics, she approached the job less cynically and a lot more realistically. As a result, she found that she was more positive toward her work and more effective.

## Ex-Offenders as Change Agents

> *Are there particular inmates who could benefit by counseling juveniles?* [DENVER, COLORADO]

> *What do you think about ex-offenders working with offenders?*
> [DENVER, COLORADO]

Offenders must have their own lives in order before advising others how to run theirs. It is not prudent to grant offenders authority over other people until newly learned patterns of responsible thought and conduct have become so well entrenched that they are automatic.

There is no such person as an ex-offender any more than there is an ex-alcoholic or ex-addict. No matter what changes they have made, offenders must continue to be aware of their own thinking, so that they are responsive to the appearance of old patterns. There is no "ex" to it; the work of change is never completed. A person who has not had a drink in twenty years cannot afford to be smug in the belief that he is "cured" forever. "Cured" is not in the vocabulary of Alcoholics Anonymous, which asserts, "Once an alcoholic, always an alcoholic." This refers to the possibility that a person conceivably could toss aside decades of sobriety and resume drinking. So it is with the criminal. Only if he remains vigilant for old patterns of thinking and constantly searches for ways to improve will he continue to live responsibly. If he is successful at this and can obtain intensive supervision from someone experienced, he might be effective as a change agent.

## Training Volunteers

> *Would you please comment on training volunteers in a detention facility?* [DENVER, COLORADO]

Volunteers need to be told explicitly what purpose they are to serve. Training will enable them to avoid potential pitfalls. Taking a course in criminal thinking errors and tactics may reduce their gullibility and vulnerability.

Volunteers need to maintain a friendly but reserved attitude. It is improper and potentially dangerous to become involved in the legal cases or emotionally entangled in the lives of offenders. Helping volunteers comprehend the magnitude of the change process will help them avoid assuming inappropriate roles, such as being turned into errand runners and messengers. Another mistake is for the volunteer to become involved in seemingly harmless but potentially compromising activities, such as betting on a card game.

# 16

## Potential Criminal Patterns Can Be Identified Early and Preventive Steps Taken

## False Positives

> *When is a difficult child an antisocial child in formation?*
> [SALT LAKE CITY, UTAH]

> *Would you address the risks of false positives (i.e., false identification)?* [JACKSONVILLE, FLORIDA]

Practically everyone is for prevention. It is like being for motherhood and the flag. Taking steps that are truly preventive demands identifying early warning signs. Critics and skeptics say that early identification is too risky because children may be irrevocably damaged if they are prematurely or erroneously labeled as criminals.

If one presupposes that the aim is to tag preschoolers as criminals, then opposition to early identification is understandable. However, we do try to detect early signs of physical, learning, and emotional handicaps. Why wouldn't we be similarly concerned about a young child's lying, bullying, hitting, and cheating? Because a child engages in such behavior does not necessarily mean he will be a criminal. Occasional behavioral difficulties may not predict lifelong patterns. We have two choices: either hope the troublesome behavior will vanish by itself or attend to it when it occurs.

The question of false positives is a red herring raised by those who completely misunderstand or misrepresent what prevention entails. I have never advocated labeling young children as criminals. The point is that we do know what the thinking and behavior patterns of anti-social people are. Why not sensitize those who care for and instruct children so that when they observe signs of such patterns, they will address them? Whether the child becomes a criminal in the future is not the point. We want to help children become responsible human beings.

Let me offer a couple of examples. It is common for a child to blame someone else for something he did wrong. The little girl says the milk spilled because the dog knocked into the table. One child blames the other for starting a fight. A boy complains to his mother about his mean teacher. All this is pretty typical of kids. (Adults do plenty of this too.) The issue is not whether blaming others is a harbinger of criminal behavior. Rather, we want to help children take responsibility for their own behavior, to own up to mistakes rather than portray themselves as victims. Was the teacher really mean? Or did the teacher seem mean to the child who acted up in class and then complained about his punishment of no recess? If it was the former, we should help the child cope with what may be unfair treatment and do so in a responsible way.

Egocentric behavior in young children is normal. The world does revolve around infants in the sense that they are not equipped to meet their own needs. As babies become toddlers, they remain self-centered. Toddlers push each other around and grab whatever they want. They have to be taught how to share and to consider one another's feelings. Most children learn to compromise and get along. If you have a child who is becoming increasingly domineering, sneaky, and uncompromising, all the while ignoring what others are teaching him, you have a potential problem.

We need to sensitize parents, teachers, and others to recognize early warning signs. Whether or not the child will become a criminal in the future, some of the behavior that is merely annoying today can become extremely destructive later. The concept of prevention requires intervening early, not delaying until a potentially dangerous pattern becomes so firmly entrenched that it is intensely resistant to change.

> *Is it normal for every child to show some antisocial behavior (e.g., shoplift once or twice, experiment with drugs, rebel against authority) at some point in his or her childhood and adolescence but eventually choose adult norms in life, job, family, and relationships?* [BOISE, IDAHO]

I cannot say that it is normal for every child to shoplift. Certainly, most children who steal a candy bar do not become criminals. To varying degrees, children and adults engage in the behaviors cited in the question. The key phrase is "varying degrees."

Like so much else in life, behavior patterns lie along a spectrum of continuum. Although it is illegal, teenagers drink. However, there is a wide range of behavior from the youth who is a teetotaler to the teenage alcoholic. Questioning authority not only is fairly normal, but it is often desirable. It is not healthy for a person to be completely cowed by authority, totally submissive, and never questioning. At the other extreme is the individual who refuses to do anything on someone else's terms. He bucks authority simply because it is authority, and he insists upon being in control.

People go through phases. Some teenagers experiment with drugs, hang out with a wild crowd, perform poorly in school and, after suffering the consequences, make a different set of choices and live more responsibly. Others fail to learn from their experiences and take greater risks.

We cannot know for sure at the time whether a teenager will "grow out of" a particular behavior. Do we ignore the drug use and declining school performance in the hope that the youth will turn around on his own? Or do we want to intervene and try to help that youngster make more responsible choices so that he does not harm himself or others and forego opportunities that may never be available again?

## Risk Factors

> *Are there any risk factors to help identify crime-prone children? If so, what are they?* [THOUSAND OAKS, CALIFORNIA]

The following behaviors, *if they persist and intensify over time,* are potential forerunners of criminal behavior.

- Lying: both lies that are concocted (lies of commission) and lies that are told because information has been left out (lies of omission);
- Blaming other people and refusing to take responsibility for one's own actions;
- Taking the easy way out: constantly looking for the shortcut and opting for the expedient way rather than exerting effort over time;
- Showing determination to control others by deception, intimidation, or physical force;
- Failing to develop a concept of injury to others and empathize.

## Choosing One's Behavior

> *You speak of making choices. Do you believe a 3-year-old chooses to pursue antisocial conduct?* [KANSAS CITY, MISSOURI]

A 3-year-old does not have the concept of "antisocial conduct." However, innumerable times each day, the child makes choices as to whether to obey a parent, how to act toward another youngster, how to treat his own and others' possessions, and so forth. A child who is taught not to steal makes choices every time he sees something that is available for the taking. A boy who is told that he must share toys makes decisions as to whether he will actually do so.

When I say that crime is a matter of choice, I do not suggest for a moment that a youngster decides one day that he is going to be a criminal. Practically from the time he is born, parents, teachers, neighbors, and others present him with rules, instructions, warnings, and directives. Over time, the child makes a series of choices as to what to internalize, what to ignore, and what to reject.

## Addressing Causation

> *If we do not address causation, what does that leave us*
> *to address by way of prevention?* [AUSTIN, TEXAS]

Many people believe that preventing a problem requires knowledge of its cause. This is not always the case, and certainly it is not true for antisocial behavior. We know that particular patterns of thinking, especially when taken to an extreme, result in injury to others. In many instances, we can identify early indicators of these patterns that could intensify to the point that they are extremely difficult to overcome in the future. If a child steals chewing gum, candy bars, and other small items, we could approach the problem by looking for reasons why. Is he seeking attention that he is not receiving in other ways? Is he feeling deprived of love and struggling to fill an inner emptiness? Is he stealing because he is depressed and wants to feel better? Is he stealing because he saw his brother steal? One could conjecture endlessly. Let us say that the child is stealing because he craves attention. Many children receive far less attention, but they do not steal. So what is it about this particular child that he chooses to seek attention in this manner?

There is the possibility, I would say the likelihood, that the child is stealing simply because he finds it highly exciting. Then what do we do with that? Ask *why* the child finds it exciting? Perhaps a genetic or biological factor underlies the behavior. Possibly there is something else. The "why" questions continue indefinitely. Do we really ever have an answer? And even if we did, identifying the cause might only serve as an excuse to perpetuate the behavior, not change it.

Instead of embarking on an archeological expedition to dig up reasons why, we need to identify the behavior in question and the thinking patterns that give rise to it. Without knowing the "root cause," as many call it, we can effectively intervene.

## Becoming Antisocial "Overnight"

> *Can a child who is fairly conforming and cooperative change and become an abuser at the time of puberty? If so, why? How?* [BUTTE, MONTANA]

> *What about adolescents who are compliant, loving children who appear to turn overnight to defiant behaviors and go from A and B grades to failing classes and skipping school, running away, using alcohol and drugs, and violently threatening parents? Are these kids prone to criminal behavior or are they going through a phase?* [WICHITA, KANSAS]

When a hypothetical question is posed as to whether something can occur, the answer almost invariably is yes. Without splitting hairs, I would need to know what is meant by "abuser." I think parents might say they felt abused by a teenage son or daughter during this tumultuous period of the youngster's life.

Parents feel abused when a teenager defies their authority and creates turmoil at home. I have yet to see a highly responsible boy or girl suddenly turn into a criminal in adolescence. That youngster might experiment with drinking, driving too fast, staying out late, or becoming less conscientious for a while about homework or other requirements. I do not know of a case where, without any precedent from his earlier years, a youngster suddenly developed an antisocial personality and repeatedly abused other people. When extreme patterns manifest themselves during adolescence, most likely earlier warnings were not recognized. A saint does not turn into a devil overnight.

## Age for Intervention

> *In working with children and adolescents, is there an*
> *optimal age at which to begin therapy?* [SIOUX CITY, IOWA]

I do not know of an optimal age. The type of preventive work that I advocate should begin with children of preschool age. By engaging in early identification and preventive efforts, we can, in some instances, avoid the need for later therapy or far more extreme measures.

I have often been asked whether adolescence is a desirable time to begin therapeutic work with antisocial individuals. Unfortunately, psychotherapy with an adolescent already knee-deep in crime is not likely to be successful, at least on an outpatient basis. Consider the 15-year-old who has gotten away with far more than anyone suspects. He believes that he has everyone where he wants them. His parents have tried everything they can think of to no avail—restriction, deprivation of privileges, elimination of allowance, and so forth. The school has thrown up its hands as every attempt to teach this youngster has met with rejection. From his vantage point, he is in control; no one can impede him. Enter the therapist to whom he is dragged. What possible impact can this person, no matter how skilled and experienced, have meeting once or twice a week with a teenager who has no desire to have contact with him and who has determined to disclose as little as possible about what is going on in his life?

Only when extremely unpalatable consequences have occurred is there a possibility that the therapist will get this youth's attention. I have visited nearly every correctional facility in the Washington, D.C. region, the area in which I reside and have my practice. This is not because I especially enjoy spending time at jails and juvenile detention centers. However, these are the places where an offender finally has to face very specific and distasteful consequences for his transgressions. I may have the individual's attention there, whereas no one could have gained his cooperation earlier.

In the St. Elizabeths project where this work originated, Dr.

Yochelson worked with offenders ranging from their late teens into their forties. Nearly all were individuals who had reached a low point in their lives during a bleak, indefinite period of confinement in a psychiatric hospital. All had lost their freedom. Some had jeopardized careers. Some had alienated their families to the point that they had no contact. It was not so much the age, but the circumstances and timing, that made a difference.

## Kids Who Go Straight

> *How does your theory account for those youths who do get in trouble once or twice (shoplifting, experimentation with drugs, etc.) and then straighten themselves out, that is, get jobs, function appropriately, and succeed in relationships?*
>
> [PORTLAND, OREGON]

These generally are not the people who are referred to me in my practice, but I know that this happens. Some people learn from the consequences that befall them, then are motivated to make more responsible choices. I have had experience with individuals who break the law, get arrested, enter counseling for a brief period, and then make a dramatic turnaround. I met Bob after he was arrested for selling the drug phencyclidine (PCP) to an undercover police officer. Bob had been a source of heartbreak to his highly accomplished parents who had raised him and four siblings. Bob's newfound friends were spending most of their time partying, not studying or working. Never a particularly ambitious student, Bob barely managed to graduate from high school and seemed unmotivated to do much with his life thereafter.

After his arrest, Bob's parents insisted that he be evaluated by me and receive counseling. The judge appeared to be weighing several factors when he sentenced Bob. Bob had no prior criminal record, and he had a favorable report for his participation in counseling. Nevertheless, the offense was quite serious. The judge asked Bob whether he had spent any time in jail after his arrest. When Bob replied that he had not, the judge recessed the hearing and had Bob handcuffed and escorted by a sheriff's deputy to a cell located in the court house. He wanted him to experience the door locking behind him. After Bob spent two hours incarcerated, the hearing continued. The judge ordered Bob placed on probation with the stipulation that he complete counseling. Several years later, I encountered Bob's mother who was pleased to relate that Bob had made a total turnaround. He had graduated from college, had been promoted at work, and had had nothing more to do with his former drug-using friends.

In this case, the shock of the arrest and its aftermath, the counseling, and continuing family support all contributed to Bob's making progress. I have seen the same factors play a significant role in many other cases.

# 17

## Directions
## for Social Policy

## Social Ills Do Not Create Criminals

> *Why does society want to blame everybody but the offender? Why won't society hold the offender responsible?*
> [AUSTIN, TEXAS]

> *When we as law-abiding adults discredit negative influences within the environment as causes for criminal behavior by individuals, are we really trying to relieve ourselves of the responsibility of creating those negative influences or allowing them to flourish?* [GRAYSLAKE, ILLINOIS]

The psychological and sociological determinists have had a profound influence on our thinking about crime. They are quick to ascribe an offender's behavior to his environment or to a mental illness.

People resist accepting the fact that there are individuals who regularly choose evil over good. It is easier to believe that the offender behaved as he did because of circumstances, not because he chose to. By their very nature, some crimes are so repugnant that we cannot conceive of a person committing them unless he was impelled to by circumstances outside his control or by a mental illness. Frequently, I have heard people insist that anyone who murders has to be "sick." This is because they themselves cannot imagine deliberately taking another person's life.

Some critics have suggested that by blaming the offender, I let society off the hook. The implication is that if crime truly is the result of the offender's exercising free choice, then no attention need be paid to the environment that surrounds him. I am not recommending ignoring social ills. My point is that people from all sorts of environments choose to commit crimes. Their surroundings may subject them to temptations and severe stress, but it is the individual who chooses how to deal with whatever circumstances life presents.

I recall being invited to debate on national television the findings of a commission that advocated spending tens of billions of dollars in the inner city to reduce crime, which the commissioners saw as resulting from the frustrations of "urban pathology." I hesitated to participate in the broadcast because I did not want to be seen as opposing spending money to benefit poor people. The point I made on the program was that improving economic and social conditions helps people who are responsible avail themselves of new opportunities, thereby improving their own lot in life. It does not change the mindset of a criminal. If you provide a criminal with education, job skills, or a better house, he remains a criminal. The scope of the task of change involves far more than improving an offender's environment, however desirable that may seem.

If we are to make headway with crime, we must help offenders change the way they think, not simply tinker with their social conditions. This turns out to be extremely demanding, time-consuming, and expensive work. It is easier to believe that changing the environment will change the criminal than it is to accept that, no matter how favorable the environment, criminals will persist in choosing evil over good.

Programs to improve the environment can make a difference in that criminals are driven out of certain areas. Neighborhoods can become safer, but criminals remain criminals. They just go somewhere else.

## Holding Parents Responsible

> *What is your opinion of the new laws in some states that*
> *hold parents legally and financially accountable for*
> *their child's criminal behavior?* [HUTCHINSON, KANSAS]

I know that judges in some jurisdictions do hold parents at least partially responsible for crimes their children commit. I see little merit to such a policy and think it is potentially harmful.

Granted, there are parents who are grossly neglectful or negligent when it comes to supervising their children. Most communities have ways to deal with these parents outside of the criminal justice system. For example, petitions for neglect can be filed with social service departments, and the matter can be dealt with in civil, rather than criminal, proceedings.

I have worked with hundreds of families with criminal offspring. The assumption that a child's criminality has been caused by something the parents did or did not do is belied by the facts. It seems easier for people to blame parents (just as it is easier to blame the larger social environment) than even to consider that a child, quite independently, could willfully choose to commit heinous acts. The parents of criminals, like all mothers and fathers, have shortcomings, but none so egregious as to account for their child's wanton destructiveness.

One father told me that he and his wife had ten children, nine of whom were trustworthy and responsible. His 20-year-old had just been released from jail. This young man had been a problem to his family since he was a little boy. Trying to make sense of all that had happened, the father tortured himself by ruminating about what had gone wrong and what he and his wife could have done. He commented that his son was treated no differently from his brothers and sisters, at least not until he became a serious discipline problem. Then this boy received more attention than any of the others. He surmised that having so many children might have adversely affected his son. Then he realized that delinquent children can come from much smaller families or may even be only children. This closely knit family never gave up trying to bring their wayward child back into the fold. Should these parents be blamed for their son's choices?

The forgotten victims of the criminal child are his own parents who for years have endured a nightmarish existence in a virtual state of siege. A presumption that a parent is blameworthy for a child's criminality is nearly always unsupported by the facts.

In so many families, conscientious, caring, and responsible mothers and fathers have tried everything they could conceive of to gain control of and help their criminal child, and they have been constantly thwarted. Will they have to prove in a court of law years later that they made an effort to intervene? And who is to judge whether they should have or could have done more? For a court to prosecute these parents for the conduct of their offspring would itself be a miscarriage of justice.

### Responsibility or Excuses?

> *Inasmuch as society as a whole blames or uses excuses for everything, does this contribute to young people in their developmental stages learning to use them criminally?*
> [HELENA, MONTANA]

On the one hand, we hear calls to hold people accountable and to help our children learn to take responsibility for their own actions. Simultaneously, there seems to be a widespread tendency (sometimes it seems to be a prevailing ethos) for people who do something wrong to successfully wiggle out of assuming responsibility by casting blame.

Whereas people no longer have to suffer harassment or abuse silently, the down side to this is that an unprincipled person can claim harassment or abuse in order to divert attention from his own shortcomings or failures. A person is fired for poor performance on the job. He sues, claiming discrimination. The focus then shifts to the employer who has to defend himself even though all he did was rid his company of an employee who was incompetent or unreliable. A person cold-bloodedly kills someone, then asserts that he should be treated leniently because he was physically mistreated as a child. A man sexually molests children, then claims it was because he was molested himself. Even if the person had been physically or sexually abused, what does this have to do with his committing a crime?

Millions of people truly are victims. Something tragic happens to them over which they have no control. I know a woman who suffered for years after she was terrorized at gunpoint during a holdup at work. Had she behaved violently toward another person, she could have claimed that it was due to the trauma she experienced. But hurting another innocent person was almost the last thing she would have been capable of.

The criminal is well versed at portraying himself as a victim. He does it as a way of life. Does society need to supply him with more excuses than he already has? Although it is not enough to turn a child into a criminal, it still is a bad lesson to teach youngsters that, by blaming others, they can exonerate themselves from consequences of their own misconduct.

## Treatment by Corrections or Mental Health?

> *Do you feel people with an antisocial personality are better treated under the Department of Mental Health or the Department of Corrections?* [SAN FRANCISCO, CALIFORNIA]

> *Should sex offenders be treated in hospitals or incarcerated in a correctional facility?* [ATASCADERO, CALIFORNIA]

> *What are your thoughts on the use of the mental health system versus the juvenile justice system to house these children?* [CHICAGO, ILLINOIS]

Whether an offender ends up in a correctional or mental health setting may be a result of the particular statutes of a jurisdiction, and these statutes may change with the times. There was an era when so-called mentally disordered sex offenders were remanded to California psychiatric facilities. When the law changed, offenders in that population were sentenced to prisons operated by the Department of Corrections.

I have visited outstanding programs operated either by corrections or by mental health departments dedicated to helping juvenile and adult offenders change. The question is not which department should run the program, but how well thought out and effective it is. With budget cutbacks in many states, fewer services are being offered. This means that programs to help offenders change exist on paper, sometimes as window dressing, but the commitment to work intensively with offenders is not there. Mental health agencies have as their mission the treatment of people with psychological problems. Yet, many of their programs are only short-term. Some longer-term programs are run by corrections agencies that employ both corrections and mental health professionals.

A critical issue beyond the mere existence and length of a program is what philosophy prevails. Mental health professionals may be well trained to provide services to various patient populations, but they often lack specialized training in evaluating and counseling offenders. Consequently, they apply to an offender population what they have used successfully with other types of patients—the theoretical framework, evaluation methods, and treatment approaches. Invariably, these fail. In my own experience, I had to set aside much of what I learned in my early training and gain new training to work effectively with offenders.

## What Does Not Work?

*What kinds of programs do not work?* [PHOENIX, ARIZONA]

In my experience the following approaches to offenders are likely to be ineffective.

- Helping the offender gain insight into his criminality by focusing on background and environmental factors;
- Focusing on changing overall behavior with little detailed attention to thinking (this fosters compliance, not change);
- Giving emphasis to eliminating a single behavior pattern while ignoring thinking patterns that give rise not only to this particular behavior but also to many other forms of irresponsible and destructive behavior;
- Encouraging confrontations during which criminals hostilely criticize one another to build themselves up, but are not encouraged to apply the criticism to themselves;
- Teaching particular skills (e.g., occupational or social), while paying scant attention to the thinking processes that are necessary to utilize the skills responsibly;
- Providing opportunities for raising self-esteem without identifying and correcting errors in thinking that are essential for self-respect based on responsible accomplishments.

## Incarceration of Juveniles

> *What is your philosophy/position on incarceration of juveniles?* [LARAMIE, WYOMING]

I want to see the least restrictive measures utilized that make sense for the situation. Providing that he does not pose a danger, the youthful offender should be supervised in the community while he makes restitution or has counseling. However, incarceration can serve several important functions with juvenile offenders. One is simply punishment that is well deserved for conviction of a serious crime. There need be no other rationale. A second purpose for incarceration is to incapacitate the repeat offender after less restrictive measures, such as probation, have failed. Finally, a judge can utilize brief incarceration for shock value in the hope that it will deter a youth in the future.

## Age for Personal Accountability

> *At what age/developmental stage can we hold children*
> *accountable for their actions?* [ATHENS, GEORGIA]

Anyone who has been a parent recalls informing, cajoling, warning, and punishing a child even before he is fully ambulatory. The process is gradual by which a child understands what is expected of him in terms of his grasping cause and effect. A toddler may comprehend, "Don't touch—hot!" But he may not understand a parent's admonition to share toys rather than grab them. Because there are vast developmental differences among children, it is impossible to single out a particular age at which they should be held accountable for their behavior.

I think the person posing the question may have in mind the following sort of situation. A young child walks off with his playmate's toy. When do we consider this an innocent act by an unaware child versus a deliberate theft by a child who greedily snatches what belongs to someone else? Does the parent gently say, "Now you give that back to your friend" and ensure that it happens? Or does the parent punish the child for an intentional act of theft? Either may be proper, depending upon the child's level of social understanding, his prior experience, and his overall maturity.

## Methadone Treatment

> *What is your view of using methadone as treatment for*
> *heroin addiction?* [ATLANTIC BEACH, NORTH CAROLINA]

The use of methadone amounts to the substitution of one drug for another. The philosophy behind legally dispensing methadone is that, because it blockades the heroin "high," the user no longer craves the illegal substance. In every case that I have dealt with, the methadone user has continued to use illegal drugs. Although he may use heroin less often and in smaller amounts, his consumption of alcohol, marijuana, and other substances increases. I have yet to meet a heroin user who, while remaining on methadone for any length of time, totally ceased using heroin.

Advocates of methadone maintenance point out that in order to obtain the substance, the drug user must visit a clinic, which otherwise he never would do. Then he may be more amenable to receiving services including medical attention. I agree that this is an advantage. To whatever extent the drug user abstains from illegal drugs and frequents a clinic, he may avoid some dangers of the street drug market with its adulterated substances and contaminated needles.

Make no mistake about it. To function as a responsible person, ultimately the drug user will have to abstain from *all* drugs except those legitimately prescribed for an illness or injury. As I have said earlier in this book, addiction is difficult to break not so much because of the physiological aspects but because the person refuses to give up an entire way of life.

## Compulsory Drug Treatment

> *Please address the issue of forced public chemical dependency treatment by the court and legal system.*
> [BUTTE, MONTANA]

I have seen two extreme positions taken on this issue. One is that no one should be forced into drug treatment. The other is that anyone who abuses drugs is a candidate for treatment. Neither position is viable.

Just because a person is a regular drug user does not mean that he should be referred to treatment. In many areas, users far outnumber treatment slots. Evaluations are necessary to determine whether a user is motivated and an appropriate treatment candidate.

A drug user may be amenable to treatment either because he

genuinely wants to change or because he prefers that option to experiencing the imposition of a harsher penalty. In either case, because motivation can be fleeting the court should use whatever leverage it has to mandate drug treatment. It is in both the individual user's and the community's best interest to help him become drug-free, whether his motivation emanates from compelling external circumstances or from within himself. If a user insists he has "no problem" with drugs and rejects the entire idea of drug treatment, it is most likely futile to force him into it. Then it is a matter of monitoring whether he adheres to conditions of probation or parole that mandate abstinence and imposing a penalty if he does not.

## Comfort in Confinement

> *Should jails and prisons be less comfortable?*
> [BELOIT, WISCONSIN]

Law breakers go to jail as punishment. Once they are incarcerated, they should be confined in sanitary and safe conditions. Many people believe that some penal institutions offer too many comforts. Making television, recreation, and reading materials available to inmates has little to do with a desire to coddle criminals. Keeping inmates occupied and engaged in productive activity greatly assists institutional staff in maintaining control so that facilities remain secure and safe. Having a group of prisoners sitting around idly in squalid or overcrowded conditions breeds nothing but trouble.

> *How do you feel about providing prisoners with*
> *body-building equipment? Are we creating a stronger,*
> *more aggressive offender?* [AUSTIN, TEXAS]

I see no reason to provide prisoners with body-building equipment, the use of which ensures more muscular and stronger criminals.

Other forms of recreation are more suitable and appropriate for achieving physical fitness.

## Public Identification of Juvenile Offenders

> *Do you believe that the names of delinquent children*
> *should be published?* [DENVER, COLORADO]

There needs to be some forgiveness in the criminal justice system for children who make errors in judgment and commit minor crimes. However, I think that juveniles should know that if they are convicted of a felony, they will be held accountable for what they did and will not be entitled to anonymity because of their age.

## Legalization of Drugs

> *Do you think marijuana should be legalized?*
> [AUSTIN, TEXAS]

> *Do you think legalization of drugs would significantly*
> *reduce the prison population?* [ANCHORAGE, ALASKA]

Having witnessed the devastation that the use of drugs has caused in the life of individual users, to their families, and to the community, I do not advocate legalizing marijuana or other illegal drugs.

I have interviewed hundreds of young men and women who have destroyed their lives with drugs. At whatever age I encounter them, chronic users of drugs are less equipped to live in this world than most young children. This is true whether the user's so-called drug of choice has been termed a soft drug, such as marijuana, or a hard drug, such as heroin. They have failed to develop much of their potential and are not equipped educationally or occupationally to support themselves. Many lack the most rudimentary concepts of how to get along with other people.

If drugs were legalized, the prison population would be reduced because use, possession, and distribution of these substances would no longer result in penalties. With legalization, the thrill of obtaining drugs would be gone. The risks and dangers of buying and selling drugs on the streets would be virtually eliminated. However, regardless of the laws, the psychological makeup of these users remains the same, and most will continue to use drugs. Crime does not reside within the drug itself. Rather, it is what drugs bring out in the user's personality that is critical. Drugs knock out deterrents to all sorts of behavior, depending upon the person. Some people with a criminal personality rely on drugs in order to commit more daring and more serious crimes. To make drugs more accessible to such individuals is likely to contribute to a significant increase in their criminal behavior. This is to say nothing of the resulting increase in health problems, irresponsible behavior, and deaths by people who were deterred earlier because they did not want to face the consequences of breaking the law. For such individuals, providing easy access to drugs may be like placing a gun in their hands.

## Research Regarding Causation

> *Should we abandon the search for why children and*
> *adults begin making antisocial choices?* [COLUMBUS, OHIO]

I remain as interested in the etiology of antisocial behavior now as I was when I first entered this field in 1970. In fact, I appeared before a United States Senate subcommittee and urged the members to support long-term research in this area. Such research would include investigation into genetic and biological factors that may play a role. I continue to be an advocate of long term research that may illuminate the murky area of causation.

## Mandatory Sentencing

> *One judge gives ten years. Another judge gives probation*
> *for similar cases. How do you feel about mandatory*
> *sentencing to eliminate disparity in sentencing?*
> [RENO, NEVADA]

I am opposed to mandatory sentencing because I think that the offender needs to be considered, not just the crime. Consider the person who is arrested for selling a small quantity of drugs to an undercover police officer. It makes sense for one defendant to receive probation while another receives a jail sentence if the former were an 18-year-old who was looking for a quick dollar while the latter was a person who had been selling drugs in the community for years.

Another example could be a woman who is charged with grand larceny. She has been stealing for a decade. From time to time, she has been arrested and convicted. Each time, the court has given her another chance and has placed her on probation, ordered her to make restitution, and required her to seek counseling. No matter what the court did, the woman has remained a thief. Should she receive the same sentence as a woman who has committed the same offense but who has no prior record and who has excelled in her career and is supporting two children?

The advent of sentencing guidelines represented an attempt to even out disparate sentences that were handed down for the same crime by different judges (or even by the same judge). Granted that the guidelines may reduce gross disparities, the disadvantage is that in equalizing punishment, there may be little consideration of the offender.

It is critical that judges retain the power to fashion sentences appropriate to the perpetrator in addition to making them commensurate with the seriousness of the crime. An offender has a powerful incentive to straighten out when a judge pronounces a sentence and then suspends imposition of part of it. Fearing the unpalatable consequences the court can impose if he violates the law again, the offender may have additional motivation to change.

## Is the Juvenile Justice System Too Lenient?

> *Is the juvenile justice system's approach of giving the youths slaps on the wrist and many chances with little or no consequences actually enabling the youths and inviting more criminality?* [HAMILTON, OHIO]

The juvenile justice system does not "invite" criminality. Compassionate judges try to take into account the crime, the circumstances, and the personality of the juvenile offender. Originally, the juvenile court was established at the end of the nineteenth century to deal with youngsters who were runaways, neglected, or delinquent. A combination of punishment and delivery of social services was administered by juvenile service agencies.

In some states, juvenile reformatories still are run by a department of human services, not a department of corrections. A century after its founding, the juvenile court must deal with a greater diversity of offenders, many of whom are more hardened at younger ages. Whereas sentencing guidelines in adult courts tend to result in a focus mainly on the offense, in the juvenile court perhaps too much time and effort are expended trying to figure out why the youngster did what he did.

Adult offenders have asserted to me that they believe they would not be in jail now if, earlier in their lives, the juvenile court had been more severe. They fault the juvenile court for giving them what they call a slap on the wrist. Some of these statements sound like more after-the-fact rationalizations in which the adult offender blames his current predicament on what occurred years ago. No matter what transpired in the past, as an adult he still made the choice to commit the crime for which he now is accountable.

## The Death Penalty—A Deterrent?

> *Is the death penalty a deterrent?*
> [COLORADO SPRINGS, COLORADO]

Undoubtedly, for some offenders the death penalty is a deterrent. Others commit capital crimes fully aware of the possible penalty. In executing a crime, they are certain they will get away with it and shut off from their thinking all deterrent considerations. We have no way of determining what crimes are not committed because the would-be perpetrator paused to consider that the crime was not worth paying for with his life. The effectiveness of any particular deterrent is difficult to assess because the people who are deterred do not come to our attention.

## Defense Attorneys

> *What is your opinion of criminal defense attorneys who knowingly get criminals off the hook?* [BEDFORD, TEXAS]

Every defendant is entitled to legal representation. He is innocent until proven otherwise. It is the legitimate role of the defense attorney to make the best case for his client as he represents him in court. There is nothing unseemly about getting the accused off on a legal technicality, finding loopholes, or doing one's best to decimate the case of the prosecutor. Any citizen accused of a crime would desire no less than the best representation possible. I have nothing but respect for the defense attorneys with whom I have worked. They are hardworking, conscientious, and ethical in what is usually an uphill battle to defend their clients.

## Drug Testing

> *We are spending thousands of dollars testing defendants*
> *for drug and alcohol use. Are we wasting our time?*
> [STEAMBOAT SPRINGS, COLORADO]

If anything, the administration of urine screens to test criminals for drug use should be more widespread. For many antisocial men and women whom I counsel, the knowledge that, without advance warning, they will be subject to drug tests is an effective deterrent to drug use. As these offenders function drug-free, often for the first time in years, some make other significant changes in their lives. They return to school, succeed at jobs, and participate in counseling programs. Off drugs, they are able to live with their families more harmoniously, manage money more responsibly, and enjoy better physical health. More than one person has told me that the knowledge he could be summoned at any time for a drug test reinforced his decision to abstain at times when his motivation to do so was faltering.

Drug tests are not foolproof, and they do not constitute a deterrent to everyone. The cost of administering these tests is small given the potential benefit. Urine tests should be supervised so offenders do not substitute a sample from another person.

## Raising Infants in Prison

> *Do you feel that women should be permitted to raise their*
> *infants in prison to avoid placing them in foster care?*
> [EL PASO, TEXAS]

This is a difficult question. One has to weigh the positive aspects of infants bonding with their mothers against the fact that most prisons do not offer an environment conducive to raising children. Another consideration is how well equipped these mothers are to be caretakers for their children. A foster home would probably provide, at least for the interim, a potentially more stable and enriching experience while the mothers serve their time and, hopefully, receive counseling and other assistance so that, upon release, they can be better parents to their children.

## Incorrigible Recidivists

> *What do you recommend we do with recidivists who*
> *are dangerous to society and who are not*
> *helped by therapy?* [BETTENDORF, IOWA]

Men and women who pose a danger to society and repeatedly have rejected opportunities to become responsible citizens should be confined for long periods. If they complete their prison terms, they should be intensively supervised in the community. Because many states and the United States federal government have abolished parole, there does not seem to be a means to do this. Thus, unchanged criminals are free to roam the streets.

## Mission for Juvenile Justice Facility

> *If you were going to dedicate a new secure juvenile*
> *justice facility designed to rehabilitate juvenile felony*
> *offenders next week, what would be your primary*
> *message on dedication day?* [TOLEDO, OHIO]

I would emphasize the opportunity to be of service both to individual youths and to the community. I would underscore the dual mission of the facility. While providing appropriate punishment to offenders and protecting the community, the facility has the challenge to powerfully affect the lives of the boys and girls in its charge by helping them learn new ways to think and behave responsibly.

In my message, I would stress that expectations for the facility and its staff must be reasonable. There are no quick fixes. The staff is required to control, manage, and habilitate boys and girls whom no one else has been able to reach. The new facility is virtually the end of the road for a heretofore incorrigible group of young people. Rather than being simply a lockup, this institution will provide intensive programming so that its residents will learn to identify and correct errors in their thinking, an undertaking vital to significant lasting change. It is unrealistic to expect that all boys and girls who leave the institution will remain crime-free. Perhaps only a minority will avail themselves of the opportunities provided. For each youth who makes such a turnaround, the savings to society are incalculable.

## Benefits: Offenders and Victims

> *Why should criminals be allowed paid attorneys, health care, counseling, and so forth when victims do not receive these benefits for being victimized? And doesn't this encourage crime as the benefits would seem better than living in the streets and having to work to obtain health care, counseling, and so forth?* [TOLEDO, OHIO]

I am opposed to taking away constitutionally guaranteed rights. Every individual charged with a crime is entitled to legal representation. If he cannot afford to pay for it, then he should receive the assistance of a competent court-appointed attorney or public defender. Incarcerated people should not lose the opportunity for basic health care. Neglecting health problems may be more costly to the public in the long run. And counseling, in some cases, can pay dividends not measurable in dollars alone.

I have yet to meet a criminal who prefers incarceration over freedom simply because in prison he can receive health care, counseling, or other services.

Until relatively recently, rights have often not been accorded to victims, nor have they received much-needed services. All too frequently, attention still is focused on the defendant—the living, breathing human being on trial in the courtroom—while the victim remains a nonentity. In 1982, I served on the President's Task Force on Victims of Crime. At task force hearings, witnesses asserted that they had been victimized twice, once by the criminal and then again by the system to which they had turned for help. Increasingly, participation by victims has been solicited during legal proceedings against criminals. Victims are invited to prepare written "victim impact statements" and to testify at the time of sentencing. Continuing efforts need to be made to bring the scales of justice into balance, so that the rights of both victims and criminals are addressed.

# 18

## Offbeat Questions

> *What do you think of the judge who allows the victim of*
> *a property crime to go into the home of a criminal and*
> *take an object he or she wants (under law enforcement*
> *supervision and court order)?* [TAMPA, FLORIDA]

I find no merit in this idea. What does it teach either the criminal or the victim? This is an exercise in court-approved retributive justice. Is this an effort to teach a thief something by allowing the victim to turn into a thief? I fail to see either the morality or the utilitarian aspect of it.

> *Do you think the fact that you actually challenged the*
> *disease model of addiction in Minnesota was the reason*
> *the sky began to fall?* [MINNEAPOLIS, MINNESOTA]

This is a reference to an event that occurred during a daylong workshop that I presented in Minneapolis. Early in the afternoon, I was citing shortcomings in the disease model of addiction. Among the points that I made were the following:

- People choose to use mind-altering substances;
- People do not catch "drug use" as they do a communicable disease;
- The addiction involves more than physical dependence—the addiction is to an entire way of life;
- The psychological dependence on drugs is far more of an obstacle to overcome than the physical dependence;
- The role of choice and exercise of free will must be core concepts in a drug treatment program.

During my presentation, part of a chandelier in the meeting room dropped to the floor and shattered. (No one was hurt.) Someone in the room quipped, "That's what happens when you attack the disease model of drug abuse in Minnesota."

---

*Do you believe that experts can determine a person's culpability by his or her mannerisms (body language)?*
[HOUSTON, TEXAS]

---

I do not know of a reliable means to determine a person's guilt by his body language. Body language may reveal clues to a person's degree of comfort with what he is saying. Law enforcement officers sometimes make use of this when interrogating suspects.

---

*Do you think that weekly public executions televised on all channels would reduce the crime rate?*
[EAU CLAIRE, WISCONSIN]

---

It is impossible to say who might be deterred, but I doubt that there ever would be serious consideration to broadcasting executions on all channels. If executions were to be made public, as some people advocate, certain issues would have to be thought through. If, as a society, we want to discourage exposure to and fascination with violence, do we want to import this sort of violence into our homes? Do we want to satisfy people's morbid curiosity by making executions into public spectacles? Do we want our children viewing executions? I see no benefit to broadcasting executions and believe there are serious drawbacks.

> *We have a staff secretary who is thin-skinned. She sounds like the criminal flawed thinker you describe. Any comment?* [DENVER, COLORADO]

> *Is there any danger in a little knowledge of your theory? Could it be misapplied with disastrous consequences?*
> [PORTLAND, OREGON]

One possible misapplication of the work in which I have been involved is for others to prematurely leap to a conclusion and render a judgment based on a single event in a person's life or one particular characteristic of his personality.

People are thin-skinned for a variety of reasons. Some, like the criminal, erupt in anger at anyone who does not fulfill even their most minor expectations. Many thin-skinned people are not in the least criminal. Lacking self-confidence, their feelings may be hurt by a comment that others shrug off. They may respond totally differently than a criminal. Rather than lash out, they may internalize the slight or insult and withdraw.

Aware that a little knowledge can be dangerous, I have taken pains in my writing, in speaking engagements, and in television and radio appearances to emphasize that one must look for *patterns*, and even  these must be evaluated within the context of an entire personality. Not every child who has shot a beebee gun becomes an armed robber. Not every teenager who has tried marijuana becomes a confirmed drug user. And certainly not every person who has lied to avoid embarrassment also lies at the expense of other people as a way of life.

People can hear what they want to and be selective in extracting only that which supports a personal agenda. I have been perceived as representing extreme ends of the political spectrum. Some seize upon my emphasis that crime resides within the individual, not in the environment. They may use this or other aspects of my work to buttress a political position that is "tough on crime," ignoring that I am a psychologist who repeatedly emphasizes that civilized societies cannot afford to give up looking for better ways to help criminals change. Those who know that I am an advocate for the habilitation of the offender may use this element of my work to support a position that some perceive as "soft" on crime, ignoring my strong emphasis on a person's being accountable for whatever he does. My work is apolitical and has nothing to do with being harsh or lenient toward criminals. Rather, it is a body of extensive research and clinical data with conclusions drawn during twenty-eight years of working with criminals.

# 19

## Personal Questions

*Why did you go into this field?* [CHICAGO, ILLINOIS]

I received my doctorate from the University of Michigan in clinical psychology. At the time, I had no interest in working with criminals. The closest I had come to this was during my internship encounters with adults and adolescents who had been in legal difficulty as a result of behavior that I had thought was symptomatic of underlying serious psychological problems.

My father saw an item in the newspaper one day that mentioned that Dr. Samuel Yochelson, a friend from college days in New Haven, Connecticut, had moved to Washington, D.C. to direct the Program for the Investigation of Criminal Behavior at St. Elizabeths Hospital. Dr. Yochelson and my father resumed their friendship, and that was how I met Sam.

Knowing of my interest in psychology, Dr. Yochelson would often talk about his "crooks" and his program at the hospital. He gave me invaluable advice throughout my graduate school education and advised me on my doctoral dissertation, "The College Dropout: A Study in Self-Definition." When he first mentioned my joining him at St. Elizabeths Hospital, I was less than enthusiastic. I had no desire to work with criminals and thought that perhaps I might go elsewhere to work with adolescents rather than return to my native Washington, D.C. Sam suggested that I interview several of the criminals in his study so that I could understand more about his program. He knew that I had encountered frustration in my efforts to treat teenagers who broke the law, used drugs, and then continued to assert that they did not need to change. He said that, by collaborating with him, I would learn concepts and a treatment approach that could be effective with the population that I ultimately wanted to work with. I realized that, whether or not I had an interest in criminals, Samuel Yochelson was a singular human being. He was brilliant, creative, practical, kind, and humorous. Recognizing that I had absolutely nothing to lose and a lot to gain, I assumed the position of clinical research psychologist early in 1970.

As with so many things in life, you don't know what you might be interested in until you are exposed to it. The work with Sam was absolutely fascinating. I had the daunting task of reading thousands of pages of his dictated and transcribed interview notes, then organizing and outlining them for the writing I would do. These notes came to life as I sat in on sessions that Sam had with his criminals.

I had a deeply personal as well as professional relationship with Sam Yochelson. He had suffered a heart attack at age 55, before I knew him, but afterward had become extremely vigorous and self-disciplined. Daily, rain or shine, he would take a long walk on the hospital grounds. Often I would join him, and we would talk about the work or about a variety of other, sometimes personal, subjects.

As I became familiar with the concepts and well versed in his approach, he assigned an offender to me to work with in the program for change that he had pioneered. I continued to outline the fifteen-year accumulation of transcribed notes. The tangible product of my eight and a half years at St. Elizabeths Hospital was the co-authorship with Sam of the three volumes *The Criminal Personality.* [See Appendix]

By November 1976, the first volume had been published. The second was at the printer, and we had outlined the third volume. Sam was leaving Washington to make his first out-of-town presentation of this work. En route to a conference on the mentally disordered offender at Southern Illinois University in Carbondale, he collapsed and died at the age of 70. His legacy to me and the world was the seminal work to which he had energetically and enthusiastically devoted himself during the last fifteen years of his life.

> *Do you believe people are basically good? What is your motivation for your work? Are you trying to help change the criminal or are you trying more to protect society? (Granted, society will benefit if these folks change, but what drives your work?)* [BOISE, IDAHO]

I do not believe people are born good or evil. Human beings are unique because they have the capacity to make choices and behave rationally. They therefore have enormous potential for good or evil in deciding how they want to live. If a person becomes a criminal through a series of choices, he is able to make a different series of choices to take a path in life that is not destructive to himself and others.

I try to help offenders become responsible human beings; that offers the best protection to society. Another objective is to assist the many devoted professionals who have continuing contact with juvenile and adult offenders. I want to enhance their understanding of this difficult population so that they can be more effective in their day-to-day work.

> *What do you have to say about the person who is taping even though the signs say clearly it is prohibited?*
> [SANTA BARBARA, CALIFORNIA]

This question refers to a sign posted at a workshop that I was presenting. There are any number of assumptions I could make. I could surmise that the brazen taping represents the mere tip of an iceberg of other violations by that individual. I could assume that the person taping is committing a crime in the sense that he aims to profit by reproducing and selling the tapes without permission. However, I could as well assume that the taper is extremely conscientious and so highly motivated to retain the information that he wants to be certain he has it all recorded so he can hear it again word by word. Or perhaps he desires to share the information with a colleague who could not attend. Since I know absolutely nothing about the individual taping the presentation, it is best to draw no inferences at all.

> *If you had been born into an impoverished, inner-city home, could you have chosen Yale?* [INDIANAPOLIS, INDIANA]

I see no reason to believe otherwise. Growing up in poverty does not preclude working hard, doing well, and attending an outstanding college. The environment may offer impediments or opportunities. What matters more is the talent, ability, resourcefulness, courage, and persistence of the individual.

> *Are you a Republican, and how can I keep you off my jury?* [RACINE, WISCONSIN]

I am an independent voter, not a party partisan. I think the question assumes that, if I served on a jury, I would be tough on any criminal. I have not been asked to serve on jury duty. However, I have testified at numerous sentencing hearings at the request of defense attorneys. These lawyers have referred their clients to me for evaluation for a couple of reasons. Some attorneys want to know more about the people they are representing, and a psychological evaluation will help. More frequently, the reason for the referral is they hope that, after I evaluate their client, I will support a sentence that will minimize time in confinement. Of course, I do not always come up with the findings that the attorney hopes for. And, when I testify in a sentencing hearing, I do not always give the answer the attorney desires when I am cross-examined by the prosecutor.

At professional presentations, people are often surprised when I mention that I receive referrals from defense attorneys because I sound "tough on crime." The person asking the above question, implying that I would be a liability to a defense attorney, might be surprised that I am more even-handed than he thinks. An attorney believes his client's defense has been helped if I support the offender's remaining in the community under some special condition, such as making restitution, participating in drug treatment, or receiving counseling. I base my recommendations on my findings from clinical evaluation of the individual, not on ideology or emotion.

---

*What gives you job satisfaction?* [ROCKFORD, ILLINOIS]

---

*How has working with criminals for more than twenty years affected you personally?* [SOUTH BEND, INDIANA]

---

*After all the studying and work you have done in the field of crime, do you feel more cynical about our society?*
[PORTLAND, MAINE]

---

*How have you changed philosophically since you started working with this population?* [FT. MYERS, FLORIDA]

---

I have been fortunate to have fascinating challenges and tremendous variety in my career. Although I have evaluated and worked with criminals in the change process since the early 1970s, I also have had the opportunity to write, speak, consult, and take on other types of cases (especially child custody) in my clinical practice. The variety has helped me maintain perspective.

I doubt that anyone who knows me would call me a cynic or a pessimist. Being a realist, I know that most criminals will continue to take a large toll on society as they persist in making the choices that they see as being in their self-interest. However, based on what I have personally witnessed, there are few limits to what determined people can accomplish. It is truly inspiring to witness the courage, the tenacity, and finally the visible results when a criminal makes a 180-degree change and, motivated by disgust for his past, he becomes a contributor to society instead of a predator.

> *Are you afraid of your clients? Have you had to take steps to protect yourself?* [MESA, ARIZONA]

Day to day, I do not fear my clients. I think the reason for this is that I know who I am dealing with, and that knowledge guides how I interact with them. Over the years, I have said many negative things to criminals during interviews, evaluations, and counseling sessions. This is to be expected, because usually there is not a great deal positive to say. I have never been physically assaulted or intimidated to the point that I was afraid. No matter what I say to an offender, I state it in a forthright manner that conveys respect. Sarcasm, belittling remarks, or yelling are totally counterproductive. Knowing that the criminal has a very thin skin, I deliver criticism in a manner that communicates that I have nothing but the best intentions in being totally honest with him. He may dislike intensely what I say, but he usually respects me for having the candor to say it without beating around the bush.

I recall one young man who was dressed in black with a sleeveless shirt and tattoos up and down his arms. He leaned forward in his chair and said irritably, "You don't like me, do you? On the street, you wouldn't be my friend." In an almost casual fashion, but still clearly taking him seriously, I replied, "Well, Rob, I don't think whether I like you is the issue. A lot of people think you should be locked up for what you did. I am here to help you help yourself change. As to whether we would be friends on the street, I think we probably have very different interests." This tough guy relaxed immediately. He realized that whether I liked him was not the main point, and he knew that I was correct when I told him that plenty of people would prefer for him to be behind bars.

The criminal evaluates me as I am evaluating him. I make his evaluation of me easier than he anticipates. I do most of the talking and calmly relate my view of him—what I think a videotape of his life would reveal. During all these years, fewer than a handful of offenders have responded by walking out. Some clam up. Most perceive that I respect them. My respect is based not on their personalities or their behavior, but on their capacity for making different choices than they have in the past.

I tailor my approach to the way that the offender is behaving at the time. If I have an angry person before me, I am not going to deliver a lecture about what a tape of his life would show. My point is that when an interviewer or agent of change knows with whom he is dealing, he will minimize personal risk by the way he conducts himself.

> *Have you given lectures to groups of offenders and survived?*
> [DES MOINES, IOWA]

Not only have I survived, but I have found these to be extremely stimulating forums. I met with very little disagreement both regarding my description of the makeup of the criminal personality and regarding what is required for change. What I do hear frequently is offenders expressing indignation that they are locked up while others get away with far worse.

My initial response to their point is to agree to the incontrovertible point that other people escape apprehension. I then remind them, "But you are here now. Granted that injustices in society occur, you still must decide how to live your life." I direct the conversation to the choices that they need to make regardless of what happens to others. I encounter very little resistance to this approach.

> *Have you ever yelled at a client or displayed anger?*
> [SAN FRANCISCO, CALIFORNIA]

Because I understand the makeup of the criminal, I generally remain composed and rarely lose my temper. It has happened, however. One 16-year-old was extremely bright and quick in his responses, sometimes too quick, because he often did not listen. He had spent some time in a correctional facility and was required by his probation officer to see me for counseling. He announced he was attending his sister's wedding in a few weeks. I inquired as to whether alcoholic beverages would be served at the reception. He replied that of course they would and wondered why I had asked. I thought it reasonable to suggest that he think in advance about the temptation that he would face, because this teenager was an alcoholic. He looked at me incredulously and imperiously demanded to know why I would even think he might be tempted. I pointed out that not long ago he had removed the hinges of his parents' cabinet and consumed their liquor. With righteous indignation, he declared that he would not discuss the wedding, that it was pointless. He had learned his lesson and would not drink and that was that. As he ranted on, he became increasingly nasty. I lost it! I told him that if he knew it all, surely he had nothing to learn from me. Then I ordered him to leave. He was stunned. As he departed, I asked him to call to discuss further appointments. He did call, probably not because he wanted my counseling but because he had a probation requirement. Over the phone, I immediately apologized. I said I would have contacted him if I had not heard anything. I went on to say that I had overreacted, which I clearly had, but noted that he too could have handled the discussion better. When he showed up for the next meeting, I again apologized but pointed out that I was pretty sure that he had provoked comparable reactions from others in the past. He agreed that I was not the first person to become frustrated with his snide attitude. Fortunately, I was able to convert this situation into another opportunity for him to look in the mirror.

When the agent of change misjudges or overreacts, as I did, it is often possible to use the situation to benefit the offender. It is essential that the change agent admit it if he makes a mistake. Perhaps then, the offender will be more receptive so he can learn something about himself.

I have encountered innumerable situations far more trying than this and have remained calm. As to why I got angry in this case, I believe that my expectations were not realistic. I had surmised that the teenager had made considerably more progress than he had. My overestimation of his self-awareness had determined my response. Fortunately, some good came out of the incident.

> *How do you personally respond when a client makes the comment that you have broken laws too (speeding, for instance)?* [HOUSTON, TEXAS]

I acknowledge that I have received tickets for exceeding the speed limit. I point out the flaw in a criminal equating that offense with his living a life in which he victimizes others to advance his own objectives. If he continues to make my traffic ticket the subject of the discussion, I point out that this is a defensive tactic so that he can avoid self-disclosure. I note that this is not new in that he has a history of provoking confrontations with others about what they have done when he wants to divert discussion about himself.

> *What sense do you have about the acceptance of your views across the country?* [SAN FRANCISCO, CALIFORNIA]

After the original St. Elizabeths study was aired in 1977 on a segment of CBS News's "60 Minutes," I received calls and letters from across the country and was asked to speak at a number of conferences. Only one of the volumes of *The Criminal Personality* had been published at that time, so people had not been exposed to what this work was all about. There were unintentional misinterpretations and distortions and some not so unintentional by people who flat-out disagreed with and therefore discounted this work. The work was most controversial at St. Elizabeths Hospital where publication was delayed and, initially, the first volume was banned from the hospital library.

Over time, the serious interest in this work has increased, primarily among people who work daily with juvenile and adult offenders. Publication of the other two volumes of the original series helped, as well as later publication of *Inside the Criminal Mind* and *Before It's Too Late*. Publicity through the media has contributed enormously to making people aware of the work.

Although I have given individual lectures and delivered keynote speeches at conferences, most of my speaking engagements have involved presenting professional workshops and seminars lasting anywhere from one to three days. The individuals attending these presentations have been eager to understand the perspective, learn the concepts, and become familiar with specific approaches that they can use to work with offenders on a daily basis. A growing number of institutions, clinics, hospitals, and individual practitioners are utilizing the "thinking errors" approach that I have described in my writings and workshops.

> *How has your current position on criminal thinking,*
> *behavior, and motivation shifted in the past ten years?*
> [BOISE, IDAHO]

My fundamental understanding of the criminal personality has not changed. (Over the years, I have acquired additional information about mental processes and have refined aspects of the change process.) Overall, my experiences have been confirmatory of earlier findings. During consultations and informal discussions throughout North America, I continue to learn how to help professionals adapt the concepts to their own work in a variety of settings.

> *What do you feel is the biggest barrier to society*
> *embracing your theory and practices and implementing*
> *them? And do you feel your emphasis on moral values is*
> *one of those barriers?* [BOISE, IDAHO]

The greatest barrier is that many people simply refuse to accept that there are individuals who freely choose evil over good. They want to believe that everyone is basically good and that only because criminals are victims of their environment or of a mental illness do they commit crimes. These are the same people who contend that all human beings are alike in that, under certain circumstances, anyone could be a criminal.

By emphasizing environment, they ignore how people choose to deal with life. They regard human behavior as determined by circumstances or by inner forces not within the individual's control, thereby giving short shrift to a person's character and his ability to choose.

I was once asked at a presentation in Kansas, "Well, Dr. Samenow, what would it take for you to kill a person?" The assumption behind the question is that any human would kill, given the proper circumstances. I said that I am one of these people who, even as a child, never had been in a physical fight. I would run or talk my way out of a confrontation that threatened to become physical. I cannot conceive of killing someone unless it were in self-defense or in defense of a member of my family who was being immediately endangered. Most of my friends are the same way—a far cry from the criminal I have dealt with over the years whose aim in life is to overcome any adversary by whatever means it takes.

# A Final Note

In presenting the concept of the criminal personality and my approach to habilitation, I have made three points. First, much conventional wisdom regarding the causes of crime is not only unwise but is misleading, wrong, and even dangerous because adhering to it has resulted in wasting billions of dollars and incurring additional costs that cannot be measured in monetary terms. A belief that crime is caused by forces outside the individual continues to guide policies, laws, and programs. Criminality resides within the individual, not the environment, which only provides greater or lesser opportunity for it to be expressed. Whatever the reason, some people from a very early age reveal their inclinations toward criminality. If we are not sure why this is, let us admit it rather than continue adhering to a set of ideas about causes that will only provide criminals with more excuses and will make no inroads in reducing crime.

Second, we must know who the criminal is. An analogy of a scratched table is applicable. One does not need to know how or why the table got scratched. It is necessary to ascertain the current state of the table, its makeup, and condition. Then it is possible to make a well-informed decision as to what to do about the table. With the criminal, however he got to be the way he is, we should still understand his makeup—how his mind works, how he perceives himself and the world.

Finally, if we know the person with whom we are dealing, we are in a better position to make informed decisions as to what to do. Some people with a criminal personality are not willing to change. Society must be protected from these predators. The ray of light in a dark corner is that some criminals are amenable to habilitation. By knowing how their minds work and approaching them at a time when they are vulnerable, we can help some become responsible individuals.

As a society, we cannot afford to shift in attitude about criminals from one extreme to another. We must not underestimate the scope of the task of change and embrace fads and seek quick fixes. Nor must we take a stance that change is impossible and that building more prisons is the only answer. While protecting society, we must undertake the process of habilitation with those who are amenable. For every offender who changes, the savings to society are incalculable.

# Appendix:
# An Overview of
# *The Criminal Personality*

## by Samuel Yochelson and
## Stanton E. Samenow

# VOLUME 1: *A PROFILE FOR CHANGE*

## The Work in Perspective

When this study began, we were aware that whatever knowledge society had about the criminal had not been applied successfully to changing him. Our objective has been to learn about the criminal's thinking and action patterns and to utilize that knowledge effectively in the change process. We have had the advantage of retaining privileged communication in a hospital setting, being well-versed in eclectic approaches, and not being bound by a diagnosis.

We started with criminals found not guilty by reason of insanity at Saint Elizabeths Hospital, but gradually expanded the population to study (just as intensively) criminals not confined at that institution. Criminals do not willingly give themselves up to an invasion of their thinking processes. However, questionnaires, statistical studies, and routine examinations have proved futile in acquiring valid information. To study the criminal in depth, we had to offer him the opportunity for "therapy," which he wanted because he thought that it might be conducive to an earlier release from confinement or from the court's jurisdiction. Thus we began our study of criminals, realizing that they were not interested in change, that they scorned what we thought and did, and that they looked on us as people whom they could take in hand to achieve their purpose. During this time, we were acquiring an enormous amount of information about the thinking processes of criminals. By persistence we were able to interest some criminals in the substance of the material that we were gathering. But our efforts at treatment were failing, despite the expenditure of much energy and time.

Our period of "re-search" ended when we realized that criminal thinking and action patterns were not explained by the sociologic or psychologic molds into which the material was being forced. We saw that providing the criminal with an opportunity to present excuses diverted him and us further and further from change. In fact, the criminal is far more skillful at elaborating sociologic and psychologic material than many experts.

A period of "search" began when we dropped these excuses and bowed to the overwhelming evidence that the criminals were not mentally ill. The application of a mental illness diagnosis to this population was a consequence of the tortuous extension of psychologic concepts by mental health professionals. Most diagnoses of mental illness resulted from the criminal's fabrications. By his accountability statements, he misled many examiners into believing that he was mentally ill. In addition, many diagnoses of mental illness were made by examiners who simply did not understand the situation.

We also had to deal with the emotional aspects of the criminal's experience. Neither emotional insight nor catharsis helped in the change process, because the criminal resorted to feelings to justify any heinous crime or irresponsibility. We studied the thinking processes concurrent with feelings, as well as those operative when there was no noteworthy emotional state. For the criminal, a crime or any other act is the consequence of thinking processes. The more we understood what those processes were, the clearer it became that crimes do not occur out of impulse, compulsion, or passion.

This volume has presented a detailed description of the criminal's thinking patterns from the point of view of their being erroneous. Of course, the criminal does not regard them as erroneous, but society does with respect to responsible living.

Procedural alterations were made as we learned more about the criminal's thinking processes. The data, derived phenomenologically, reflected the importance of choice and will. The enterprise of altering thinking processes, when successful, invariably led to the criminal's leading a moral life. To describe this process of change is the major objective of Volume 2. In addition, we shall present a critique of one of the better-regarded institutions for treating the criminal and offer a proposal for a way of achieving successful results that is more effective than current methods. We have achieved such results in criminals whom we followed for more than ten years. To have written Volume 1 without Volume 2 would have been only to engage in an academic enterprise for the classroom. The concepts in Volume 1 are validated by the results achieved in the change process described in Volume 2.

We have reserved discussing the drug-using criminal until Volume 3, where the focus is not on drugs, but on his personality. However, Volume 1's description of the structural components of the criminal personality also applies to the criminal drug-user. The procedures for change described in Volume 2 are also applied to him, with some minor modifications.

### Establishing Individual Responsibility:
### The Elimination of Social and Psychologic Excuses

We came to Saint Elizabeths Hospital with many years of experience in group psychotherapy with noncriminals. During our group work with criminals, we had held sessions to assist in history-taking, to serve as forums for complaints, and to discuss traits. After these experiences, from which we were primarily learning, we decided to make treatment our major objective.

We established new guidelines, of which the most important was that the group members were to know that we did not regard them as mentally ill. Our operating within a mental-illness framework, whatever form it had taken, had resulted only in an illusion of accomplishment. Finding what we thought were the root causes of a man's criminality had not resulted in the elimination of criminal patterns. In our study, we had come to realize that these men did not regard themselves as "mentally ill." They were "sick" only for the purpose of getting admitted to the hospital and avoiding jail. Once admitted, they were eager to get out and sought to convince the authorities that they had recovered. Now we recognized the element of choice in criminal behavior. These men had control over what they did. The concept of "choice," rather than "illness," was essential in emphasizing personal responsibility. If we operated from the premise that a criminal was sick, a victim of mental illness, then we could not consider him responsible, and it would be up to someone else to cure him of his sickness. What an absurdity—to have a man await a cure of an illness he did not believe he had! Not only did we eliminate the concepts of "mental illness" and "sick choices," but we also discarded the word *therapist,* for two reasons. First, a therapist is one who administers therapy for an illness; if one is not ill, he does not need a therapist. Second, to a criminal, "therapist" means a person who can be easily influenced and led.

We had avoided calling our patients "criminals" because we had believed that we were dealing with mentally ill people. No longer did we hesitate to use this term. However, our definition of "criminality" was not contingent on arrestability or on the seriousness of an offense. We had been establishing that a criminal act was the end product of specific thinking processes and personality characteristics; thus, with our concept of a continuum the term "criminal" was broadened to encompass a wide range of thinking processes, as well as criminal acts.

The permissive attitude that we had taken earlier had not worked. These men had approved of us as therapists and even thrown parties for us out of appreciation and affection. But the most significant testimonial was not forthcoming—a change in their criminal patterns of thought and action. Now, we were changing our approach. We did not court the criminals' favor or appear at all sympathetic. We believed that their evasion could be broken down only by vigorous invasion of the inner man. We were uncertain as to how these men would react to an intense, direct approach; perhaps they would become upset and discouraged and leave the group. But our other methods had led to failure, and we had nothing to lose. We were convinced that we had to be firm, consistent, and evocative without being provocative. We had to afflict the comfortable, rather than comfort the afflicted. Of course, this shift from relative permissiveness to firmness did not occur overnight, but was gradual.

The changes in procedure gave us access to new material. In turn, the new material led to still further changes in procedure. For example, when we dispensed with mental illness and established personal responsibility, much of what the criminals had told us earlier became open to a far different interpretation. Instead of being viewed as the exploited, they were the exploiters. Instead of suffering from past traumas, they were the ones who had traumatized others. Instead of focusing on what others had done to them, we examined what they had done to others. Instead of subscribing to post facto justification, we were pursuing current thinking.

Analytic concepts were insufficient as explanation, and analytic techniques were unsatisfactory in producing change. The reenacting and analyzing of a parent–child relation that an analysis of transference entails would have been counterproductive. We realized that it would only reinforce a criminal's blame of others and his victim position. We had taken that path earlier and had seen "insight" become "incite," as a criminal, in righteous indignation, railed against others so as to absolve himself of responsibility.

Nevertheless, our objective was to clarify earlier concepts and to probe further, to improve our understanding of the fabric of the criminal mind. To this end, we initiated thematic discussions, so that each member of the group would examine how he had dealt with various aspects of life. Then we elaborated on the need for patterns of thought and action to change. We had regular three-hour meetings about family, work, school, social patterns, and women. It was hard to maintain continuity, because we were often confronted with day-to-day crises. For example, our men still were violating and receiving restrictions. Our approach was not to come to their aid or preach, but to help them learn. Many themes evolved from a single incident that could be generalized to other situations. Here is where we tried to teach these concrete thinkers to think conceptually. We discussed control, sexual competence, suggestibility, and so on. These discussions brought out new characteristics and thinking errors. They also enabled us to study their tactics and decision-making, as well as their thinking before, during, and after a crime.

We found the criminals' compartmentalization of life almost beyond comprehension. We have referred to the simultaneous presence of extreme sentimentality and extreme brutality within a given man. What seemed paradoxical to us did not seem so to the criminals. From our point of view, a criminal was living in a state of anarchy. From his point of view, he was not. Although he was not psychotic, he appeared to be creating his own reality. Yet he was oriented, his memory was intact, and he was intelligent and shrewd in his dealings with the world. His different reality did not make him psychotic. We were learning that, from a criminal's view of *his* reality, it was we (the noncriminals) who were stupid, crazy, or both. We began to recognize that, to understand what constitutes reality for a criminal, we would have to know his premises of life, his desires, his experiences. Once we discarded "mental illness" as a factor, we began to understand more about a criminal's reality. The concept of mental illness had been the greatest barrier to acquiring this fundamental knowledge.

Recognizing that our understanding of criminal characteristics was far from complete, we made what use we could of our observations. Their sentimentality was so striking that we thought that we could make an inroad with the criminals by appealing to the "good" in them, and somehow dipping into this well of sentimentality. There is a part of a criminal that is "noble"—a part that he himself often cannot tolerate. We were thinking in terms of an "index of reachability" based on how strong the sentimentality was. We considered drug-users to be more reachable, because, in our experience, they seemed to show more sentimentality than non–drug-users. We knew that criminals had consciences, but we also saw them fail to function. We thought that we could make conscience operable by appealing to sentimentality.

As we looked into the operation of conscience, we spent some time in considering guilt. Some men who earlier had psychotherapy talked about guilt related to oedipal desires. It is true that many of these men had had not only incestuous desires, but also some actual incestuous experiences. To the extent that this was true, they may have had some basis for talking about guilt. However, their insight into the basis of their guilt did not seem to keep them from harming others. Thus, we tended to disregard the significance of such insight in these men who mugged, raped, and murdered. Instead of trying to alleviate a feeling of guilt in the criminals, we wanted to increase it. If a criminal experienced any guilt about his criminality, it apparently did not stay with him long; and he could turn it, like other deterrents, off. Instead of viewing guilt as disabling, as it may be in noncriminals, we stressed the benefits of guilt and encouraged the criminals to keep in mind the many injurious things that they had done to others.

We learned that many of the psychiatric concepts and techniques that we had found effective with noncriminals were not applicable to criminals. Their depressions, anxieties, and tensions were different phenomena. We were dealing with a different breed of person, so different was the mental makeup.

The criminals also used language differently, so we became students of semantics. Sometimes, we thought we grasped what a criminal was saying, and later found out that he had meant something quite different. He had a different frame of reference. If he said he was "lonely," it did not refer to a lack of companionship—he knew nothing of companionship based on a community of interest and experiences. "Lonely" meant having no one to control and exploit. In addition, much of our descriptive terminology was inadequate or meaningless when applied to criminals. Saying that a man was "manipulative" reflected his effect on us more than it indicated how his mind worked; the criminals did not view themselves as manipulative, but we thought that we were being manipulated by their tactics. Furthermore, we began to understand the criminals' view that society was manipulating them, which in some cases was true. Our words did not contribute to an understanding of the world *as the criminals viewed it*. Psychiatric parlance was also inadequate when applied to this population. For example, we could have termed many of the criminals' traits "defenses," but using the word so broadly would have rendered it meaningless. Superimposing a traditional theoretical framework hindered our understanding of the people with whom we were dealing. Although we sought to understand the criminals' language, we did not adopt it ourselves. We did not have to say, "Where did you get the bread?" for them to see that we were referring to money.

We encountered the problem others have had of establishing an open channel of communication. Although we were maintaining privileged communication, the criminals still did not disclose fully. The channel was closed by self-serving stories and rationalizations in which they were either victors or victims. Sometimes a criminal lied merely for the pleasure of putting one over on us. On other occasions, we thought the channel was open when it was not. It was common for a criminal to disclose a small part of the truth and give us the impression that he was telling everything. When he informed on others, we thought that this breaking of the criminal code of "no snitching" was an advance; instead of opening the channel, what he was doing by informing was building himself up and improving his image. Similarly, we thought that full disclosure was occurring when he confessed to crimes and violations; this, too, was often done solely for impact. He was feeding us what he thought we wanted, and the reporting was usually shot through with distortion and minimization.

Another major impediment was the criminals' insistence that change be brought about by their own rules; our program was to be a "do it yourself" procedure. Basically, each of them wanted to control us and convince us of his point of view. The group resembled a football team in which each member considered himself the quarterback. Every criminal wanted to be the big shot and determine what would happen. He confronted others, but responded angrily when he was confronted. When we firmly opposed his point of view, he accused us of being "inflexible" and disregarded what he did not want to hear. Thus, what we thought had been absorbed was not implemented. In fact, it sometimes seemed as though the criminals had not been present at the preceding meetings. The criminals shut us out just as they turned off deterrents so that they could execute crimes. The mechanism was the same. In fact, it operated so rapidly that we termed it a "cutoff": With almost surgical knifelike precision, a criminal in an instant would turn from tears to ice. He could pray devoutly at 9:00, and be involved in a holdup at 10:00. He could participate avidly in a group discussion on anger and show considerable insight, and assault someone an hour later.

These men were not only fighting change, but asserting that they were incapable of it. They did not necessarily blame others for this; they knew that we would not accept it. Instead, they declared simply that "I can't do it." Exploring what this meant, we found that "I can't" signified that they were not putting sufficient effort into living responsibly. Behind this was a refusal: "I won't" or "I don't want to." There was no issue of "can't" in terms of capacity to change. After all, these were men who in their criminal lives rarely said "I can't" to anything. However, they were now whining "I can't" with respect to having to give up their criminal excitement.

With increased knowledge, we began to tell the criminals immediately that we knew how their minds worked and what their tactics were. We were no longer fishermen, dangling our lines in the water, casting about to catch something. Instead, we knew exactly where the fish were and went to hook them. Thus, we were able to extract more information and reduce the criminals' game-playing. They found our candor refreshing, something they had not previously experienced. Consequently, they believed that, inasmuch as we knew so much to begin with, there was less point to their trying to put on a front and hide things.

We had come to believe that these men had to be "won" early in our contact with them, or they would be "lost." We controlled the interviews and did not wait for a criminal to bring things out or to direct the conversation. Our men had to recognize that we were knowledgeable and firm. We assumed the initiative to bring out important material, probing beyond surface reports. We disallowed the criminals' numerous excuses, their blaming of others, and the victim stance in its various forms.

Every such obstacle introduced by a criminal said something about the kind of person he was. We encountered the same obstacle in many forms. For example, if a criminal did not tell us he was a victim of environmental circumstances, he said he was a victim of his own character structure, but put it in terms of "feelings." A man might try to explain away his violations by saying that he had been depressed, tense, or upset. He also used his feelings as an excuse not to change. Here, again, we took a firm position. We told the men that sitting around waiting for feelings to change was futile. Feelings do not change in a vacuum, but as a result of thinking processes. Emerging was the beginning of a concept (developed later) that feelings were an epiphenomenon of thought. They could be changed by substituting different thinking processes.

We had found that the thinking that gave rise to feelings was the most important unit for dissection. If thinking processes changed, feelings would change. Whatever the tactics, we showed the error in thinking, in much the same manner as when we met the countless permutations of the victim stance. This reduced the obstacles. One consequence was that the same men who had provided us originally with self-serving stories when we had taken histories now volunteered to review that material and correct it. In some cases, if one were to compare the two accounts, he would not know they were from the same man.

We were still not making the progress we desired. Just as we thought some of our people were doing well, things started going awry. Some criminals showed old behavior patterns precisely when they were about to advance in status, such as by obtaining ground privileges or a conditional release. When a man gained more privileges, he had less supervision, and thus a greater arena for "action." Then he began to stay away from the group, or, if he came, to attend in body only. He told us that there was nothing more to learn and that he did not need us, because he was ready to handle things on his own. All the "insights" that we thought he had gained seemed to vanish. The familiar patterns at first took a nonarrestable form, such as lying, irresponsible handling of money, and exploitation of women. Soon, they were reflected in more serious offenses: elopements, coming to group meetings on drugs or intoxicated, and engaging in a variety of criminal activities both on and off the grounds.

The failures were disappointing, but they prompted us to reexamine our idea and techniques. Clearly, we had placed too much faith in the efficacy of talk. To a considerable extent, we had been judging a criminal's progress by his verbalization. Here was the treachery in relying too much on the value of insight; it was not the insight of psychoanalysis, but the insight into characteristics. As used by a criminal, the whole insight procedure was itself a "criminal enterprise." A criminal assented and conned just as he had done with others in the past. He used psychiatric formulations as excuses. One criminal commented tersely: "If I didn't have enough excuses for crime before I had psychiatry, psychiatry gave me more." The end product of insight therapy was a criminal with psychiatric sophistication. He was still a criminal. Thus, we heard our terms and concepts coming back to us as a defense of indefensible patterns.

We did not totally discount the value of insight or self-understanding. Indeed, we recognized that it was necessary, but only as a part of the change process. In addition, a criminal needed to be educated about the responsible world, which was so foreign to him. So we began to stress our role as teachers, rather than therapists. We knew that words alone were insufficient to accomplish change. New knowledge had to be implemented. Old patterns had to be destroyed, and new habits established. Our task now was to develop the substance of a program, so that we could achieve a "metamorphosis."

## The Continuum of Criminality

A continuum can be established in terms of something specific and easily measurable, such as height and hue; and less tangible entities, such as personality features, can also be conceived of as lying along a continuum, although they cannot be quantified. For example, it has been said that there is larceny in every soul. If this is true, we would say that a person with the feeblest desires to commit larceny is at one end of the continuum, and a person for whom larceny is virtually a way of life is at the other end.

The term "criminal" evokes stereotypes and strong emotional responses that confuse or mislead more than they inform. It is essential for the reader to understand that we do not use "criminal" in a legal sense. Our emphasis is on *thinking processes* that the irresponsible but nonarrestable person, the petty thief, and the "professional" criminal all manifest, but to different degrees and with different consequences. A person who lies frequently may be cut of the same mental fabric as the arrestable criminal. A responsible person may also lie, but infrequently. In his case, lying is not a way of life. Lying may be just a piece of ice floating in the sea, or it may be the tip of an iceberg that contains the entire spectrum of criminal patterns, untruthfulness being only one element. The criminal continuum allows a more precise description and analysis and guides us in our work to effect change. We may diagram this continuum with the basically responsible person at one end and the extreme criminal at the other.

| RESPONSIBLE | IRRESPONSIBLE | |
| --- | --- | --- |
| Nonarrestable | Arrestable Criminal | Extreme Criminal |

The basically responsible person has a life-style of hard work, fulfillment of obligations, and consideration for others. He derives self-respect and the respect of others from his achievements. Desires to violate do occur, but they disappear, usually without the person's having to make a conscious choice. A thought about violating is discarded because it does not fit his view of life; no effort is needed to eliminate it. When a deviation does happen, it does not become a way of life. For example, he has moments of extreme anger, but anger and vindictiveness are not automatic responses to things that do not go his way, as they are for the criminal. The basically responsible person has a pattern of being conscientious in occupational, domestic, and social affairs. He works productively and contributes toward the good of others while trying to advance himself. If he is a recluse and is unconcerned with other people, he does not infringe on their rights and property.

In referring to people as "irresponsible," there is room for misunderstanding. Some people do not violate the law, but can be considered irresponsible. These are the defaulters, liars, excuse-offerers—people who are generally unreliable. They are chronically late, perform poorly at work, or fail to fulfill promises and obligations at home. They cannot be arrested for any of these shortcomings. They may show irresponsibility in some ways and be conscientious otherwise. We do not call such people "criminal." Their irresponsibility does not result in criminal acts.

People referred to on the continuum as "arrestable criminal" have all the thinking patterns of the extreme, or hard-core, criminal, but their crime patterns are less extensive and serious. They are minor violators who rarely get caught, such as employees who take items from their jobs that do not belong to them and people who may steal merchandise from a store whenever surveillance is not too tight. Many of these people are failures in life, as judged by societal standards. Some do advance, despite their violations, which go undetected. People in this group have recurrent strong desires to violate, but are deterred. Occasionally, someone in this group who had always seemed responsible surprises everyone by getting caught at something fairly serious. In a situation where restraints are not great, he might indeed implement the violations that he has previously only thought about. A criminal might move from a small rural community to a large city. In a small town, it is harder to get away with infractions; but when such a person moves to an area where he experiences greater freedom and anonymity, the criminal components emerge. His basic personality has not changed, but now the violation will occur, because external restraints are fewer.

At the opposite end of the continuum from those basically responsible are the "extreme criminals." The thinking processes described in this chapter are operative in this group from an early age. The outcome of such mental processes is inevitably crime. This is not to say that these people are in crime every moment. They have a succession of mental states that range from active criminality to an intense striving for purity. Although the extreme criminals constitute only a small fraction of the population, they pose the greatest problem because of the heavy injuries they inflict. When people use the term "criminal," it is usually with reference to the extreme criminal. It is primarily the extreme criminal who is the subject of our writing.

The reader should keep the continuum concept always in mind for the sake of perspective. Otherwise, he will think that we are indiscriminately calling everyone, including him, a criminal. It must be understood that our work is with a population that is at the extreme end of the continuum. Just as severe backward schizophrenics were often the subjects of early efforts to understand thinking processes of schizophrenia and to effect change, so we have chosen to work intensively with the severe criminal in an attempt to comprehend his mental processes and to develop procedures for change. Only by this method can one understand those who are less extreme on the criminal continuum so that they too can be changed.

A pitfall in presenting this material is that the reader might be offended or worried by finding that, to a degree, he has some of the characteristics attributed to the extreme criminal. The reader may think of times he has lied or misrepresented a situation. He may recall with some embarrassment an occasion when he has let temper get the best of him or an isolated instance of taking something that did not belong to him. Such behavior does not automatically place him on the criminal end of the continuum. We warn the reader against "medical student's disease," in which one wholeheartedly applies everything to himself. Every characteristic of the criminal is present to some degree in the noncriminal. But, for example, although everyone has fear, what is at issue is the nature of the fear and how one copes with it.

# VOLUME 2: *THE CHANGE PROCESS*

## A New Horizon for Total Change of the Criminal

The dimensions of the task of changing a criminal to a responsible person are poorly understood. The procedures that have been used with criminals have not been effective. Crime is still very much with us and, indeed, according to statistics, is a more formidable problem today than ever before. Previous efforts at rehabilitation have failed for two main reasons: there has been insufficient knowledge of what the criminal is—his thinking processes and behavior patterns—and the techniques used have almost all been adaptations of techniques used with noncriminals. In Volume 1, we presented a detailed picture of the criminal's thinking and action. Utilizing this knowledge, it was possible to develop new procedures necessary to achieve basic change and, with them, to succeed in changing some criminals into responsible citizens.

In setting before the reader the dimensions of the change process, it is necessary to review the profile of the criminal. To do so, we draw selectively from the material presented in much greater detail in Volume 1.

At an early age, the criminal-to-be makes a series of choices that involve going counter to the responsible forces that prevail in all socio-economic levels. Even in the high-crime areas, most of his contemporaries do not choose a criminal path. However, as a youngster, the criminal finds the restraints of responsible living unacceptable and even contemptible. He rejects the requirements and way of life of parents, siblings, teachers, employers, and others in his environment who are responsible.

Although he may manage to convince others that he is responsible and, through a facade of conformity, keep society at bay while pursuing his criminal objectives, he scorns such social institutions as the school, the church, and the law.

To be like the responsible children in his neighborhood and at school is to be a "nothing." The criminal child wants something different. He usually begins his violating patterns at home. Then if he cannot find the excitement that he wants in his own surroundings, he goes where he can find it. Crime does not come to the criminal-to-be; he goes to it.

Whatever his background, the criminal youngster views himself as different from others, as one of a kind. In whatever he undertakes, he has to be not only number one but a unique number one. To be like anyone else is to be a failure. If something appeals to him, this exceedingly energetic youngster works to be the best; when he tires of the endeavor, he quits. Throughout his life, the criminal is a sprinter, never a long-distance runner. Even when he does enough to rank first in a particular activity, it may mean little to him, because he wants to be a big shot for doing what others will not do, not for doing what is expected or acceptable. Thus success at school or work does not satisfy him. The things that an elementary school pupil learns do not interest him. Indeed, the criminal never develops an accurate concept of what family life is, what an education is, what a sense of community is, or what a vocation is.

Patterns of deception are established very early. Lying is a way of life. Lying patterns are habitual; the criminal needs only to change the details to accommodate a particular situation. Lies of omission are more frequent than lies of commission.

The criminal disregards other people's right to live safely, but demands that others show him the utmost respect and consideration. He breaks promises; in fact, he never regards a promise as a promise unless it is part of a larger operation to secure something for himself. It does not bother him to injure others; he rarely sees anything from another's point of view. Although society considers him harmful, the criminal believes that he is exercising a right to live as he chooses. In the pursuit of what is important to him, the criminal puts his family, teachers, employers, and other people concerned about him through worry and expense. As his violating patterns expand, they inflict a toll on society that is incalculable—not only monetarily but in terms of pervasive fear and broken hearts.

The hard-core criminal commits thousands of arrestable crimes and violates countless ethical and moral standards but he is rarely apprehended. If apprehended, he is likely to escape conviction. If convicted, he is likely to be given a light sentence or be returned to society immediately. If he is held accountable for a violation, he believes that he is the one who is violated, because being caught is an injustice and being interfered with makes him a victim, not a victim-izer. He blames forces outside himself for his crime or for making him the way he is: others are responsible, not he. This position is usually reinforced by current concepts and practices and often by the judicial attitudes and decisions of those who deal with criminals.

We have described the criminal population as a different breed— a group of humans with the same physical needs as the rest of us but with an entirely different view of life and an entirely different set of thinking patterns. The criminal is oriented; i.e., he knows what he is doing and what others are doing. But he has his own reality, in which society's values and rules are absurd or unimportant. He chooses *his* reality, not ours.*

---

*The psychotic has his own reality, too, but his reality is one in which his orientation is very different. He deals with constructs of the mind that have no basis in fact. He may respond to voices. He may believe that people are after him. None of this has a factual basis. In contrast with the psychotic, the criminal is sharp, alert, and in touch with the facts of life. For example, if he thinks that people are after him, this is based on the fact that he is being sought, even though he may err with respect to the particular person seeking him.

The criminal lives in a world where there is no loyalty or trust, even in relation to others like him. Untrustworthy himself, he demands that others trust him. If he happens to earn others' trust, he exploits it. He depends on others but does not see his own dependence. To him, this exhibits weakness and places him in jeopardy. He claims he can live without interdependence but demands that others provide him with whatever he wants. The criminal does not know how to get along with responsible people from day to day; he generally occupies the extremes of total withdrawal or inappropriate intimacy. He is intolerant of others' shortcomings but reacts angrily when anyone finds fault with him. Instead of friendships, the criminal seeks avenues of triumph. People are to be used, conquered, controlled like pawns, exploited, and then discarded when they can no longer serve a purpose useful to him. Only rarely does the criminal genuinely "like" another person. His liking is based on someone's agreeing with him, building him up, assisting him in his plans, or at least not interfering with him. He also "likes" someone he can exploit. His very characteristics preclude his genuinely loving anyone. He regards kindness as weakness. Although he expresses fragments of sentimentality, the criminal cold-bloodedly uses the very people he professes to love.

Criminals seem tough, but they are actually extremely fearful. The criminal child, who scorns responsible youngsters as "chicken," has fears that are more numerous and intense than theirs. Criminal youngsters fear darkness, water, heights, and many other things. Some of these fears persist into adulthood. The criminal must also deal with recurrent fears of getting caught for his violations. And he does have conscience fears; that is, there are some things he claims to hold inviolate. However, he does not tolerate continuing in a fearful state. In fact, he avoids even speaking of his fears, because it is "sissy," "lame," and "weak" to do so. The criminal has a remarkable capacity for eliminating fear, at least for long enough to do as he wants. The mental processes of corrosion and cutoff allow him to turn rapidly from trembling and uncertainty to composure and confidence.

Most of all, the criminal fears being put down by other people. A putdown occurs when someone fails to gratify his every desire or fulfill his every expectation. Any inconvenience is regarded as a personal affront. What a noncriminal habitually shrugs off reduces the power-thrusting, controlling criminal to a zero. The zero state, which is far more encompassing than the noncriminal's inferiority feelings, reflects the criminal's extremes in thinking and his misconception of himself and the outside world. He is either a colossus or a nothing. He regards himself as a zero when the world does not accord him the status that he thinks he deserves and things are not going according to plan. On such occasions, the criminal believes that everyone looks upon him as a nothing and that this state is permanent. The seeming finality and futility of such a state are intolerable to him, and he usually responds with criminal acts, as well as with anger and with determination to reassert his status as "somebody" rather than continue to be (by his definition) a "nobody." Life for the criminal is a series of anger reactions to surmount his fear of being a nothing. The antidote to the zero state is not constructive activity but a cutoff of fear, an angry reaction, and a search for excitement (crime). Anger is a basic component of the criminal's personality; it is pervasive, although not always apparent to others.

The pursuit of power and control pervades the criminal's thinking, conversation, and action. Power and control are sought in irresponsible ways purely for self-aggrandizement. The criminal approaches life pursuing personal triumphs, conquests, and build-ups. To achieve these, he promotes himself at the expense of others. He recognizes no limit to his personal power and control; the world is his to do with as he pleases. Whatever he does, whomever he deals with, he expects the world to adapt immediately to his wants, even when he is apprehended and confined.

The criminal expects to be an overnight success. A goal to him is an instant triumph achieved criminally, not a responsible objective achieved by hard work or talent. He disregards the future, does not plan long range (except when scheming a crime), and ignores the past (except for profiting from some mistakes in crime). He is a concrete thinker who lacks a time perspective.

When the criminal embarks on an enterprise (criminal or not), he either abandons it or develops a state of near certainty or "superoptimism." For the criminal, possibilities become accomplished facts. There are no imponderables; thinking something makes it so.

If necessary, the criminal endures some hardships and overcomes some obstacles in crime, but he refuses to endure the slightest adversities of responsible living. He refuses to do anything disagreeable unless he can envision its furthering his criminal objectives. Throughout his life, others have asked and pleaded with him to change, but he has put the burden on them to persuade him he should make the effort. The criminal lacks the thinking patterns needed to make prudent decisions. His decisions are determined largely by his pretensions, unrealistic expectations, prejudgments, and assumptions. He reads others according to his own premises and attributes to them qualities and motives they do not have. When he miscalculates, he blames others. He does not admit to or tolerate uncertainty. He is not a fact-finder (except with respect to a crime and not always then). Even when he wants more information, he is reluctant to search for it because an admission of ignorance runs counter to his self-image and the image that he wants to convey to others. His lack of foresight and his failure to consider different options result in poor decision-making and in injury to others.

To even the most astute observer, the criminal looks like a mass of contradictions. He is fragmented in his thinking, having fluctuating attitudes that appear to oppose one another. He seems to be both fearless and cowardly, religious and blatant in his sinning, sexually a "King Kong" and sexually incompetent. In general, criminals lack a consistent and cohesive set of attitudes toward their place in the world.

One of the most striking features of the criminal is his view of himself as a good person. Despite all the injuries he has inflicted on others, he does not consider himself a criminal. His idea of "right" is subjective in the extreme: whatever he wants to do at a given moment is right. If at that time he considered an act wrong for him and regarded himself as an evil person, he would not act as he does. What society calls crime, the criminal regards as his work. When he is required to defend himself, he strives to convince others that they are wrong and that he is right. The criminal's view of himself as a good person constitutes an enormous obstacle to those who seek to rehabilitate him, and an examiner or agent of change encounters a formidable array of tactics that are designed in part to support this view but are actually further expressions of criminal thinking patterns.

A change agent or interviewer encounters in the criminal a person who does not tell the truth, does not listen, and does not take stock of himself. Telling the truth puts the criminal in jeopardy and makes him face unpleasant facts about himself. When he does talk, others think that they understand him but often do not. The criminal has such a different frame of reference that even simple words like *friend*, *love*, and *trust* have meanings radically different from conventional usage. The criminal hears but does not listen. His silence often conveys the impression that he is listening when actually he is inwardly disputatious or has his mind on something totally apart from the issue at hand. He is so busy proving he is in control and knows it all that he dismisses what others say, unless it pertains to a criminal scheme. As far as he is concerned, even listening to someone else is tantamount to being managed by that person. Another reason for not listening is to avoid considering points of view that oppose what he wants. Sometimes, the criminal assents to make others think that he is listening and agreeing; this is a convenient way to end a conversation and to get people to leave him alone without alienating them in the process. The third major obstacle to an open channel of communication is the criminal's lack of interest in the process of self-examination. He finds fault with the world but is unaccustomed to evaluating his own role in it. It is others who constitute the problem, not he.

As the criminal approaches a program for change, he brings to it the mental processes of a lifetime. He treats an agent of change as he has treated others, sizing him up and then trying to manage him. His tactic may entail a naked display of power or, more likely, ingratiating strategies that are subtle and difficult to detect. A problem that constantly besets an agent of change is knowing whether a criminal believes what he says or is only trying to score points; it is impossible to determine this at any given moment. Because of the criminal's fragmentation, he may be sincere one day and completely insincere the next.

If he participates in a program for change, the criminal expects to change now—instantly and totally—and do it better than anyone else.

Again, thinking makes it so. He also expects the change agent to do the work. Moreover, the criminal attempts to dictate the terms of the program and manage the personnel administering it. When told that he has to do things that he dislikes, he reverts to a variety of excuses. All in all, the criminal approaches a program for change as he does a criminal enterprise. He is there to convince others of his point of view rather than to learn a new one. Criminals usually enter change programs to extricate themselves from trouble and less often because of genuine (although transient) self-disgust.

This capsule description shows what kind of a person a change agent is dealing with when he undertakes to change a criminal. Society's ways of dealing with such a person are based on inadequate knowledge. The criminal's fragmentation and seeming contradictions have made it difficult for others to formulate coherent programs.

Society has dealt with criminals in four basic ways: retribution (punishment), confinement (to protect society), deterrence (new statutes and stricter enforcement), and rehabilitation. Retribution has been increasingly rejected because of the belief that a criminal should be helped to change, not condemned and punished. Confinement has been described as mere "warehousing" and viewed as destructive, and it outrages moral sensibilities because it is not constructive. A high rate of recidivism (which is underestimated according to our findings) indicates that efforts at deterrence have not worked well. The current  trend is toward rehabilitation. Many different approaches have been tried, but the professionals, and therefore society, have failed to grasp the magnitude and complexity of the task. Some efforts have focused on criminal behavior as the problem and used arrest and job records as criteria of successful rehabilitation. (We have found as many employed as unemployed criminals who are still engaged in crime.) Others have focused on isolated aspects of the criminal's functioning, using the same methods that have been used with noncriminals; it has been assumed that the application of intensive individual therapy, family counseling, group therapy, the therapeutic community, and other procedures to change specific features of the criminal would cause him to straighten out, much as noncriminal patients have straightened out. For example, in treating neurotics, the objective has been to leave the person intact psychologically but to alter features that are maladaptive. The criminal has been approached in the same way in an attempt to make selective alterations while keeping the basic personality intact. We have found that the scope of the change process must be far greater.

We shall review in detail the efforts made by others to change the criminal. Organic treatments (psychosurgery, medication, etc.) have been unsuccessful. The numerous programs for altering an environment that is thought to produce crime have resulted in the expenditure of manpower, money, and energy but have left crime a domestic problem of top priority. Criminals have taken advantage of these programs and demanded more benefits and services, typically selecting what they want and contributing nothing productive to society. Criminals have been given more and more opportunities to change instead of long terms in confinement. Because of a trend toward community-based corrections, criminals have participated in community education and vocational training programs and have lived in community facilities, such as halfway houses, rather than in prisons. These opportunities have not resulted in change from criminal to responsible citizen. Job skills and education that criminals have acquired either have been utilized in the promotion of further crime or have been abandoned altogether. With the return of criminals to the community, the number of crimes committed is extremely high. Criminals have exploited psychotherapeutic work, especially efforts to reconstruct their past to find out why they are the way they are. If a criminal did not have enough excuses for crime before psychotherapy, he has many more after it. As we pointed out in Volume 1, the search for causes leads criminals to blame others for what they themselves have done and for their current situations. Other psychotherapeutic techniques that have been successful with noncriminals have been tried with criminals. Advocates of a more present-oriented, rational approach have used their techniques with criminals. Rewards and punishments of various types have been administered to criminals, through the legal process (confinement and deterrence) or through behavior modification therapy. These efforts have failed to change the thinking processes of criminals and have had, at best, only a short-lived effect on their behavior. The threat of punishment at the hands of the law has deterred only people less extreme on the continuum of crime and has had a temporary effect on chronic offenders weary of the revolving door of penal institutions. In general, criminals have used the programs to curry favor with others in order to get out of difficulty. In almost all correctional programs, criminals have been expected to identify with change agents who serve as models of responsibility. Except for lip service and some transient sentimental attachments, criminals have exploited the change agents and continued to scorn responsible living. Because of the necessity to do something rather than nothing, society persists with procedures that have failed.

For several years, we failed as others did. To succeed, we gradually developed a process of change that is extreme in its objectives and in its attention to detail. (The method of original investigation that provided so much substantive material was itself the product of extreme attention to detail.) We know that every one of the criminal's thinking processes described in Volume 1 must be eliminated by choice and will and replaced. We know of no other task in human behavior as vast as this.

There are three broad prerequisites of the change process. First, the change agent must make an effective presentation to the criminal at a time when he is vulnerable and therefore wants to change. Second, the change agent must have a detailed knowledge of the criminal's thinking processes (the material presented in Volume 1): he must know with whom he is dealing. Third, this knowledge must be made operational through the set of procedures to be described at length in this volume. We begin with a thumbnail sketch of our program, which has been successful in changing some criminals into responsible citizens. The details of how the program operates are then presented in greater detail.

The agent of change must deal with the "inner man," not with his environment. A change agent must begin by capitalizing on periods in which a criminal is vulnerable. The criminal has never had a firm conviction about wanting to change. At most, he has made some token efforts during brief periods in which there has been a sense of futility with his chosen life. It is during one of these periods in which the criminal is dissatisfied with himself that the agent of change must make his approach. The criminal may be vulnerable owing to an arrest or confinement. On occasion, conscience may be operative, so that momentarily the criminal is fed up with himself and his way of life: he may be offended by some feature of his own crime pattern, or he may be in a state of mind in which he does not want to harm his family anymore. The criminal must be reached when his opinion of himself as a good person is at an ebb and when he recognizes that he has failed even at being a criminal.

Not every criminal is suitable for this program. At the very beginning, a series of meetings are necessary in which the criminal has a chance to experience our procedures and learn of our program's requirements. We can assess his mental state with respect to change, and he can make his decision as to whether he wants to participate.

In the initial approach, we strive to have the criminal see himself as he is. Rather than ask him who he is, we present him with a profile of who he is. Our objective is to establish valid facts rather than listen to his self-serving reports. We let him know right away that we know how his mind works. We point out the apparent paradoxes in his thinking and actions (which at times have puzzled him as well as society) and show how they are not paradoxes but a natural outcome of the mental processes required to live the kind of life that he has chosen. We anticipate what tactics the criminal will use with us and enlighten him on these. We are aware of the misinterpretations resulting from the semantics of his speech. Our approach helps to elicit a great deal of information in a short time and works as a process of "de-lying," since we do not give him the occasion to direct the transaction with his self-serving accounts. With statements rather than open-ended questions, we present facts with which he is familiar but that he has cut off time and again. We face him with disagreeable but accurate statements about himself. Our accumulated knowledge of the criminal baffles him, impresses him, and occasionally shocks him, even to the extent that some say, "It takes one to know one," meaning that we must be criminals ourselves. In this initial contact, we establish that he is in fact a criminal, something that he does not want to consider, much less believe. Unpalatable as our approach is, it permits us to win his respect and usually his confidence in the fact that we know what we are talking about. In some, we elicit an initial willingness to strive for change.

In these early meetings, we make it clear that from our point of view nothing of the criminal's way of life is to be preserved. Putting on new clothes over old and stained ones is not enough; the old clothes must be regarded as contaminated and diseased and then discarded and destroyed. The criminal must eliminate his old patterns and become responsible in every way. We present him with the severity of the requirements of our program and with the austere life that will be his. We describe in detail what is necessary for the 180-degree shift from total irresponsibility to total integrity. Instead of the amoral stance, we have adopted a moral position and have made it the very cornerstone of our change program. In short, we give the criminal in these early meetings our view of him and of the kind of life that he will lead as a responsible person. The criminal is then faced with a decision as to whether to choose this program. Some select themselves out. If a criminal is willing to participate, we accept him whether or not he agrees entirely with our point of view.

We take the position that man has the capacity to choose. The criminal made choices early in life and continues to do so in the present. Now, he is in a position in which he has three options: more crime with all its risks (which may seem less appealing from behind bars), suicide, or total change as we define and practice it. We do not try to persuade him to change. It is his choice; it is his life. To succeed in our program, the criminal must reach a position of "no choice but to change." He must desire change for its own sake and regard this program as the only possible course for him. Change requires effort (restraining himself from what he wants to do and doing what he does not want to do) and the development of endurance, if he is to eliminate old thought and action patterns and replace them with responsible ones. The criminal needs a head, a heart, and a gut. He needs a head to evaluate himself self-critically, to learn, and to solve problems rationally and construc- tively. He needs a heart to give him sensitivity to other people and compassion. He needs a gut to endure the hardships of a way of life that he has heretofore scorned. These are hardships only from the unchanged criminal's point of view, such as being deprived of his preferred excitements and having to cope with daily problems of life with which he has had little concern and no experience.

This approach is totally new to most criminals and, as one man put it, as foreign as "the dark side of the moon." Those who have been exposed to psychiatry previously have had their behavior explained in terms of psychologic mechanisms and external events that they have used to justify their irresponsibility. *We do not attempt to derive causation.* We meet issues with facts, pointing out what patterns are operative. Going into how it all began takes us too far afield. In our early meetings, we eliminate sociologic and psychologic excuses. From our point of view, any criminal who clings to a victim stance indicates his lack of commitment to change.

In general, we avoid setting up causal connections between events. Establishing such sequences may sound impressive, but it does not contribute to change. Instead we take a situation for what it is, point out the thinking errors, and teach correctives. We dissect the criminal's thinking patterns rather than focus on his behavior; although behavior as observed may be outwardly responsible, his thinking is invariably irresponsible. We are not interested in the crime for which a criminal is originally arrested. We do not address ourselves to a specific manifestation of criminality, such as check-forging, or to an isolated problem, such as impotence. We spend almost no time on such things but instead dissect all the criminal's thinking patterns that have resulted in difficulties for him and injury to society.

 The topics of each session are not arbitrarily chosen. To reach the substantive material (the thinking processes), we developed a procedure to elicit without bias, interpretation, prejudgment, or explanation the total contents of mind for a prescribed period. This is the technique of phenomenologic reporting by the criminal. Thinking processes are probed down to the last detail to prevent later criminal acts. Otherwise, days, weeks, or months later, an incipient criminal idea will result in a crime. We have found stray thoughts to be of considerable significance, although they often seem inconsequential to the criminal. Dreams are treated like any other thinking. We do not unravel unconscious determinants or analyze symbols. Instead, we view them as indicators of the persistence of old patterns and the presence of new ones. The phenomenologic report is totally different from free association. Instead of saying whatever comes to mind, the criminal presents a well-ordered report of his thinking and actions over the preceding twenty-four hours. To capture as much of the thinking as possible, we ask that the criminal write notes between meetings. The phenomenologic report provides the material for which we offer corrections, in the form of both specific deterrent considerations and new concepts that constitute the substance of new thinking patterns.

In the phenomenologic report, we elicit both thinking and feelings. We have not regarded emotions as the primary cause of behavior and therefore of crime. Emotions, of course, are always present, but we emphasize concomitant thinking. In dealing with a criminal, to make feelings the focus results in multiplying his excuses, rationalizations, and self-deceptions. We probe thinking processes and regard the accompanying feelings as epiphenomena of thought. When criminal thinking processes are replaced by responsible ones, the emotions change correspondingly. (Despite current views, repeated and prolonged efforts at altering emotions have not changed thinking processes.) By altering thinking processes, we have totally eliminated both outward and inward anger in the criminal. Furthermore, the emotional experiences of fear and self-disgust have enhanced responsible functioning *after* the criminal makes responsible thinking patterns habitual.

We begin our work with the criminal on an individual basis. Groups are not advisable in the beginning because a group of unchanged criminals presents so many tactical problems that our concentrated approach is considerably diluted and the process prolonged. After learning what our view of him is and what our program requires, if a criminal decides to participate, he is asked to join a group of three or four other criminals. We have found the group method not only more economical in time but advantageous, in that one member learns from another. The group is a microcosm in the sense that each individual learns to absorb severe criticism—an ability necessary in the macrocosm of society.

A criminal must be educated in two respects. First, he must develop self-understanding. This is not achieved through deriving "insight" into what caused him to be as he is. Some self-understanding results from our careful dissection of his thinking processes, but the bulk of it *follows* change, rather than precedes it. A man comes to understand much more about himself and other people *after* he has changed his behavior than he does sitting around waiting for insight to propel him toward change. Second, the criminal requires a fundamental education about the outside world. He is beginning to function, much as an infant does, in a world foreign to him, and a whole new set of thinking processes has to be developed. Every old thinking pattern is replaced with a new way of thinking. The instruction is in many areas of living. All educating occurs in the context of life situations; it is not didactic. What seems self-evident to responsible people is new to the criminal. Education includes attention to the smallest details of daily living. The criminal learns what the restraints in life are and what initiatives are necessary. He practices those restraints and actually takes those initiatives. This very concrete thinker is trained to think conceptually both about himself and about the world. He learns to view the world as a responsible person does and to *implement* this view. His pretensions and expectations are scaled down. Above all, he comes to the recognition that life is a series of problems he has to meet and struggle with responsibly. With more and more education, the criminal develops genuine self-disgust and views himself as having been very  stupid in the past. He sees how irresponsibly he has functioned, how he has inflicted injuries, and he gains a realization of all that he has yet to learn. Mounting self-disgust and a sense of stupidity are necessary to reaffirm continually the initial choice to change.

Learning to deter criminal activity is critically important, and deterring criminal *thinking* is basic to this. The possibility of apprehension has always had some deterrent value, but it is insufficient in building a new life. We instruct the criminal in a new sophisticated set of mental processes that constitute deterrents. In addition, all the new concepts of responsibility that the criminal learns and practices constitute deterrence. In time, the criminal is able to anticipate the types of situations that will stimulate criminal thinking and to preempt them. The ultimate objective is the total elimination of criminal thinking and its replacement by responsible thinking.

Office meetings are for instruction and clarification, but the criminal learns through life experiences. Words spoken in the office are meaningless, if there is no implementation outside. Declarations of intent must be substantiated by deeds. Thus, there must be what we term the *calisthenics of change*, i.e., implementation of new thinking processes with attention to even the most minute details of living. Instruction begins with a thought fragment or a small incident. We point out and correct the error of thinking and thus go from the concrete incident to a concept that can be applied elsewhere. The criminal must learn from the present event, so that he will recognize a similar situation in the future and cope with it effectively. Finally, we become more abstract and show how the concept fits into an overall view of life. Actually, the end result is that we deal with what may be properly termed existential issues. What kind of person is the criminal? What kind of life does he want to lead? How does he expect to relate to his fellow man, and how does he expect his fellow man to relate to him? These existential questions can be considered only *after* substantial change has occurred. These issues call for choices that the criminal cannot make until he has experienced enough change to make choices.

The process of instruction requires a tremendous amount of repetition. The criminal's habitual practice of cutting off what is disagreeable or uninteresting is so automatic that hearing something once or twice never suffices. Criminals often react to an idea as though it is a brand-new revelation when, in fact, they have discussed it previously. The reason is that it has been office talk. Since the ideas do not have impact if they are not part of life experiences outside the office, repetition also is necessary to establish habits. Each time we go over what we think should be familiar ground, additional material and new considerations emerge.

In our instruction, we do not solve problems for the criminal, give advice, or direct his decision-making. The *process* of decision-making is far more important than an actual decision reached. We help the criminal understand the value of fact-finding and consider a wide range of options (which he had no need of previously). In no way do we direct him toward a particular conclusion. All that is of ultimate concern to us is whether the criminal has thought and acted responsibly. If he makes a mistake, it is carefully evaluated and he is expected to learn from it and apply it to the next experience.

The criminal has to learn and practice habits that are ordinary and routine for the noncriminal. Part of the calisthenics or selfdiscipline involves learning to deal constructively with adversity—paraphrasing Alcoholics Anonymous, to surmount what can be surmounted, to live with what cannot be changed, and to be able to tell the difference. We emphasize to the criminal the comprehensiveness of the effort that is necessary. The door must be closed all the way on old patterns of excitement-seeking. Specifically, this means no more violations and no more relationships with other criminals.

Far more important than crimelessness is the continuous implementation of new responsible patterns of thought. This program is extremely demanding in that the criminal must always strive to attack every difficulty responsibly. There can be no respite from this. Complacency is the greatest barrier to change, because in its wake comes inertia; soon after inertia, old patterns of thinking emerge, and crime is not far behind. Permanent crimelessness does not exist. Criminality must be replaced by responsibility. At no time does the criminal have it made. A self-critical implementing attitude must constantly be maintained, because there is always room for improvement. In fact, we have not yet learned the limits of the extent of change that a man can produce from within himself. It has been striking to watch extreme criminals change, in a matter of a few months, patterns that have been entrenched for decades.

As we embark on the process of effecting change, it is a case of a midget versus a monster—the midget being the program for change and the monster, the criminal's years of experiences and lifetime patterns of thinking. We work so that the midget will prevail. The criminal finds responsibility boring; it is antithetic to his whole life style. However, the amount of suffering that he experiences is inversely proportional to the degree of his commitment. A criminal who views the program as a "lifeline" does not suffer in it but approaches change with zest. A criminal who is reluctant to give up the excitements of the past and who disputes the requirements of the program suffers, being torn by the mandates of two opposing life styles.

We tell the criminal that no one knows the limits of choice and will. However, if he looks around, he sees or hears about people who, on their own or with help, have overcome tremendous obstacles and made remarkable achievements through choice and will. (Attributing such success to a strong ego or failure to a weak ego does not contribute to change.)

A fairly reliable indicator of change is the recognition that the criminal himself can see what he has accomplished by hard work and does not want to imperil it by reverting to old patterns. Moral values develop when a person acquires something honestly and prizes it. This occurs when the criminal has plugged away for an indefinite period (usually at least a year) and has built up something for himself in the responsible world that he is afraid to lose. It is a time in the criminal's life when he is developing some respect for his achievements as a consequence of how he is living. He is no longer living in one tiny corner of the world; as a responsible person, he has expanded his interests and activities and can deal more effectively with people than he ever did as a criminal. He is no longer looking over his shoulder to see whether a policeman is there because he is not getting into trouble. Furthermore, he does not miss the old excitements. Even the *thought* of how he used to be fills him with loathing. His gains are precious; he does not want to jeopardize them. And so he strives to preserve what he has worked hard to build.

An important aspect of our work with the criminal, indeed a precondition for work with him, is that we have contact with people who are important in his life. It may be a single meeting with a criminal and a girl friend or a series of regular sessions with the criminal and another person, such as his wife. These meetings take the same general format as our regular meetings with the criminal, in that there are specific problems to tackle. Sometimes, an agenda is prepared in advance. Because criminals often marry irresponsible women, we often have to instruct a wife in some of the same concepts that her husband is acquiring. If the other party is responsible, less time is devoted in the meetings to the fundamentals of responsibility, and there is more of a focus on the relationship. These meetings serve two purposes: they are a check on the integrity and completeness of the criminal's reporting, and they help in promoting a more harmonious, interdependent relationship.

One might think that as the criminal progresses in change, the material would dry up. However, more and more material emerges, even though crime is eliminated and deterrence of criminal thinking is developed. There are abundant new considerations as the criminal encounters new problems inherent in responsible living. The greatest increase in material occurs when a criminal moves from the restricted arena of confinement into the community, where there are both fewer restraints and more problems to solve. Criminals participate on a daily basis for a year after release from confinement. Some men have wanted to extend their daily contact beyond a year because they have found themselves still insecure in their new life. They are constantly faced with new decisions to make and are still developing new ways of relating to people. Those who want to and whose work schedules permit it continue to attend daily. Most, however, have daytime jobs and meet with us once a week and eventually less often.

A monitoring process is necessary. Long after all legal holds have expired, our changing people still meet with us. They seek assistance, much as noncriminals approach a therapist, with a self-critical attitude, trying to improve their functioning as responsible people. We emphasize continually that there is no room for complacency, there is always room for self-improvement. We take the view, Once a criminal, always a criminal, in the sense that unless a criminal continues to attack new problems thoughtfully, there is always a possibility that he may make irresponsible choices. In other words, change is always in process. With implementation over time, there is, of course less and less likelihood that old patterns will emerge. The criminal values his new way of life too highly.

Our subject has been a lifelong liar who cannot be believed or trusted, a practiced and secret violator in a variety of areas, an intolerant and insensitive pursuer of conquests who imposes his views and desires on others, a self-righteous believer that he is a unique number one, an exploiter of everyone, a blamer of others, a person guided by pretentions and prejudgments instead of facts, a person whose fragmentation is so pervasive that he cannot rely even on himself, a skillful strategist who devises tactics to achieve his criminal objectives, a scorner of responsibility and a ridiculer of those who are responsible, and a person whose entire thinking apparatus is designed to achieve his antisocial objectives. In addition, he has always been contemptuous of those who would attempt to counsel or change him. It is no wonder that others who have contended with such a person have failed, as we did at the start. The criminal has posed a challenge to all. With a new body of knowledge, with an emphasis on dissecting and rebuilding thinking processes, and with new procedures, we have met the challenge.

We do not view change solely in terms of such specific accomplishments as release from confinement, graduation from school, promotion on a job, or money saved in a bank. Instead, we view change as a total alteration of existing thinking patterns and implementation of new thinking patterns of responsibility.

## VOLUME 3: *THE DRUG USER*

### The Mental Makeup of the Drug-Using Criminal

Our objectives have been the same in working with drug users and nonusers—to understand the makeup of the criminal and to help him to change. In the course of our early work, criminals were providing us with excuses for committing crimes. The drug-using criminals presented the very same reasons for using drugs that they offered to justify other crimes. Because we promised all participants in our study privileged communication and played no administrative role in their lives, we naively believed that they would have no reason to lie to us. Accordingly, we considered their reports valid and recorded what they said. The statements they made were totally compatible with current theories of crime causation.

The reason for crime most frequently cited was that the drug user was beset by intolerable burdens of life; drugs were part of his desperate attempt to cope with stress. The sources of such stress varied from person to person. Many drug users poignantly described their struggles to cope with poverty, family disorganization, lack of opportunity, and racial discrimination. Those from upper-income homes discussed family turmoil and a variety of overwhelming pressures in the community, school, or at work. All drug users described life as being an unrelenting series of "hassles" with parents, teachers, employers, and sex partners. If the world was not treating them badly at a particular time, they complained of intolerable boredom and of a life that seemed meaningless. Invariably, the drug user and nonuser described the same phenomena. And we found their explanations credible. Drug use was simply one other way, and a relatively effortless one, to cope with disadvantage and distress. It seemed logical to us that environmental factors were directly related to drug use, just as we believed they were to other forms of crime. In fact, drug-using inmates of the hospital's forensic division convinced us that conditions at the hospital were having a corrosive effect on them, virtually driving them to use drugs to make life in confinement tolerable. Although we opposed their drug use, we were sympathetic to their plight.

Our drug users asserted that their irresponsibility and frank criminality were, in part, efforts to gain a sense of belonging and acceptance that had eluded them at home, at school, and in the community at large. Those from neighborhoods where drugs were easily available contended that the drug-using crowd offered what they were looking for. Using drugs was one way to be "in." To turn down drugs was to become an outcast. Others from different kinds of neighborhoods admitted that it was by their own choice and initiative that they traveled to other areas to seek excitement and found drugs available there. All participants in our study, drug users and nonusers alike, found companionship with those who, like themselves, were violators. From our study of criminals' thinking patterns, we believed that they all, but particularly the drug users, were easily influenced by others. After an early interview, we wrote: "He's in the role of a little boy, anxious to please, wanting to be accepted. The underlying weakness, the suggestibility, the starvation for a friend comes into play."*

Only retrospectively did we recognize our naiveté in the early days of our study when we believed what the criminal told us about his

---

*In this section, all passages in quotation marks are from our early notes that were dictated and transcribed.

motivation for doing the things that he had done. We were looking for
the *roots* of crime and in this quest spent countless hours probing for
psychological conflict and unconscious motivation. It seemed obvious
to us that criminality was a way in which our participants had tried to
cope with intrapsychic conflict. The drug user, in particular, had found
instant relief through drugs. Drugs offered an antidote to depression
and relief from a sense of despair about one's own worthlessness. We
described one man as follows: "Barbiturates don't make him feel big,
great, or important, but they make him feel a little less acutely about his
being a nothing." Drug users averred that they used drugs to cope with
anxiety. Drugs had a calming influence, offering serenity and allevia-
tion of tension. High on drugs, the criminal replaced anxiety with
optimism. We noted: "It's only when you see the effect of the drug in
producing calmness that you can understand the mixed up, lonely,
confused state prior to drugs."

Drug users contended that drugs helped them to cope with a
variety of other unpleasant states, including anger, disappointment,
psychosomatic symptoms, and dependency. Indeed, when a man used
drugs in the course of treatment, it sometimes seemed as though he did
so because he was threatened by his dependence on us as therapists. In
the conventional wisdom, drugs were said to offer a quick escape from
painful mental states and to allow the user to function more comfort-
ably. In fact, some claimed that drugs facilitated their acting responsibly. Again, we absorbed what the criminal told us, believing that he
demonstrated insight when he stated that he had acted irresponsibly by
using drugs to ward off anxiety or depression. By valuing such insight,
we tended to overlook the drug use itself. Of course, we did not
approve of drug use, but by accepting the user's excuses, we appeared
to condone it.

We believed then, as we worked with criminals, that they were
ultimately defeating themselves. This was especially true of the drug
user who, in addition to running all the usual risks by engaging in
crime, was jeopardizing his freedom and health by drug use. The
vicious circle was obvious. A man used drugs to escape a painful
mental state or to remove himself from a disagreeable environment. As
drugs became a more frequent solution, he developed a "habit," at least

in the case of the opiate user. To support that habit, he committed more and more crimes, placing himself almost constantly in danger of arrest. The drug became a "monkey on my back." The user increased his criminal output so that he could buy more drugs, thus increasing the risk of apprehension. Furthermore, every time he obtained, possessed, or used a drug, he committed another criminal offense. Finally he was faced with staving off withdrawal symptoms and other physical difficulties consequent to drug use. To us, the whole business of using drugs appeared overwhelmingly self-defeating because it caused the criminal's life to become even more unstable and stressful than it would have been without drugs.

Because we had imposed our framework on his statements, we believed that the criminal was unconsciously defeating himself. At the time, we perceived all criminal behavior to be self-defeating and, in other ways, pathological. As stated in the first chapter of Volume 1, we initially believed that the criminal was mentally ill, whether or not he used drugs. In fact, we regarded drugs as simply another manifestation of his psychopathology.

From the outset, drug use was not our focus. The criminals' rationale for drug use emerged with the rest of the material about why they committed crimes. Even when a criminal emphasized the importance of drugs in his life, we tended to overlook this because we were focusing on other issues. However, as we continued to take careful histories and to offer individual and group treatment to criminals, significant information about drug use began to accummulate. There was much to suggest that the drug user did more than escape from unpleasantness; drugs facilitated objectives that were difficult for him  to achieve otherwise. Some users talked about the courage that drugs gave them to stand up to a fight. Others mentioned having greater sexual prowess with drugs. Some indicated that drugs helped them to summon the courage to commit acts that they had been afraid to commit in the past. At the time, we did not seek elaboration on such observations but simply noted them. Our interest was centered on crime patterns, not on drugs. To us, a theft was a theft and a rape was a rape; whether a criminal used drugs while committing a crime was of secondary significance.

It was our probing of criminal thinking patterns that eventually obliged us to examine more closely what drugs did for the criminal. Drug-using criminals averred that crime was a consequence of drug use. Like the nonusers, they maintained that they were decent people, not criminals. Illegal acts were committed only to support a habit to which they had hopelessly fallen victim. Users asserted that they were caught in a cycle of drugs, crime, more drugs, more crime. Indeed, some bewailed the "daily grind" that was necessary to support their habits. And another vicious cycle emerged, but this time of a different nature. They maintained that they had to commit crimes to support their habits. However, they often were afraid to commit those crimes.  Drugs eliminated fear. Consequently, they used more and more drugs to commit increasingly serious crimes. That is what drug users told us, one after the other, and that is what we believed. It appeared to make sense that most crime committed by the drug user was directed solely to supporting a habit that had passed beyond the point of his control.

However, as the hours we were spending with these people accumulated, our belief that most of the drug user's crime was aimed at supporting his habit was shaken. We were finding that, *in every case*,  the criminal had embarked on his life of crime very early. He was fighting, stealing, lying, and intimidating others as a child, long before he had direct experience with drugs. Our first major objection to what the criminal was telling us was based on the discovery that, although most had not been apprehended, all criminals who had used drugs had  a long history of crime that antedated their use of drugs.

As already stated, material about drug use was emerging that we noted but did not pursue. One observation was that some people needed drugs to commit crimes that others could commit without drugs.* The major breakthrough that facilitated our studying this phenomenon was our gradual rejection of sociologic and psychologic excuses for criminality. It was becoming increasingly apparent that we, and traditional psychiatry, were only offering criminals more excuses for their criminality. We abandoned the search for causation gradually

---

*In 1963 we had noted, "The effects of drugs are only to do things with less caution and more abandon."

as we saw that no condition or set of conditions could account adequately for an individual's turning to crime. We saw as crucial the role of individual choice (actually a series of choices). Disposing of sociologic and psychologic excuses permitted us to focus on the criminal's thinking, so that we could eventually evaluate how drugs affect thinking processes.

A simultaneous development in our work was the gradual alteration of our interviewing procedure. As we learned more about our subjects and increasingly were dismissing sociologic and psychologic excuses, we stopped asking open-ended questions.* Before questioning our subjects, we told them what we knew about their thinking and acting patterns. This new format of "you know that I know" helped us to probe more effectively and eliminated some of the obstructive tactics deployed by the person being interviewed. Consequently, we were in an even better position to study thinking patterns and, more specifically, thinking patterns related to drugs.

We learned how the criminal began to use drugs after criminal patterns were firmly entrenched. As youngsters, criminals sought others like themselves and engaged in doing whatever was forbidden. Even in early adolescence, they knew of the potential dangers of drugs but disregarded this information. Some criminals, however, regarded using drugs as a sign of weakness and were reluctant to use them at all, even if legitimately prescribed. To use a drug was a putdown because it signified that they had to rely on something other than themselves, and thus they were not in control. Furthermore, they did not need drugs to accomplish their objectives. Drugs would only impair their effectiveness in crime and render them more vulnerable to arrest. In fact, they looked down on drug users. Another group of criminals experimented with drugs but rarely used them thereafter because they did not find their effects exciting. Furthermore, they concluded, the possible physical harm and the increased risk of apprehension were not worth it. Members of a third group were sporadic users of drugs. Finally, there were those who became regular users. When the criminal decided

---

*For example, we did not ask them to tell us about their home life or query them as to why they committed crimes.

to use drugs, it was not with naiveté or in ignorance. He was not seduced into drug use but was a willing customer.

The role of choice in crime and, in particular, drug use was becoming increasingly apparent to us. However, we were still viewing many criminals from the standpoint of having a mental illness. To us, crime (including drug use) was a choice, but we called it a "sick choice." Increasingly, drug users chose to immerse themselves deeply in the drug world. They were resourceful in obtaining drugs by purchase or theft—at school, on the street, from medical facilities, from wherever they could be found.

Because we were meeting daily with drug users and nonusers together, we were in a favorable position to compare them. Had we worked only with drug-using criminals, it would have been more difficult for us to derive information about drug use. We learned much about the drug user directly from the criminal who was a nonuser. Both were on the street together and had had many associations with one another. Having the two groups together made it possible to focus upon common features. Every feature that we found in the nonuser was even more prominent in the user. Both were suggestible, but the drug user was extremely so. Both were fearful, but the drug user was especially fear-ridden. Both had a limited concept of injury to others, but the drug user's ideas on this subject were even more concrete and narrow than the nonuser's. Meeting together with both groups enabled us to make comparisons, and gave us leads to pursue further. So it was fortunate that when we began our work, we conceived of it as a study of criminals and did not focus on drug use.

Focusing our attention on thinking patterns led us to conclude that the basic difference between the drug user and the criminal who did not use drugs lay in the cutoff of fear. This mechanism allowed a criminal to eliminate temporarily the fears that were deterring action (see Chapter 6, Volume 1). To be sure, the drug user had committed many crimes without drugs. But there were other crimes that he thought of but could not bring himself to commit without drugs because he was blocked by fears of being apprehended and pangs of conscience. Having discovered this, we commented, "The drug user is the fellow who really shouldn't be in crime because he can't be comfortable with it." The nonuser was a more effective criminal in that he did not have the additional "hassle" with drugs and thus was not in as much jeopardy.

We still believed that the primary role of drugs was to offer escape from problems, environmental or intrapsychic. As we became more critical of the self-serving accounts of all criminals, we obtained a clearer understanding of the role of drugs. Drugs enhanced cutoff of deterrents, enabling the user to do what he otherwise was afraid to do. But we also noted another element. The drug user was not simply escaping from something—he was moving toward something that he wanted very much. Early in our study, one criminal had said, "On drugs, I could do anything." This aspect of drug use, overlooked at first, was coming more and more to our attention.

As we developed techniques for training the criminal to report his daily thinking, we were in a better position to see the world as the criminal viewed it. A significant finding was that although drugs *per se* did not make a man a criminal, they facilitated criminal thinking; they permitted the criminal to elaborate his fantasies, and they increased the amount and speed of his thinking about crime and exploitative sex. The drug user who was "on the nod" while using heroin appeared to be inert and in a dreamlike state, but his mind was racing with criminal ideas. Although we were focusing mostly on opiates, other drugs had a similar impact on thinking. We were able to study this thinking firsthand as it was reported on a day-to-day basis in long meetings with people who were using drugs both on the street and in confinement.

Drug users said that they were in search of the "high." They defined the high as "feeling great," and they wanted to continue to feel that way. Initially we accepted the idea that a high was a kind of euphoria or state of elation. Only as we dissected thinking patterns did we come to understand that this was not the case. When a user was high, he regarded himself as all-powerful: he could do anything and everything. Nothing would stand in his way. One drug user summed up the effect of drugs by saying that he felt great because "I feel ten feet tall."

We were beginning to understand more about why a person, fully cognizant of the dangers and risks, persisted in drug use. Drugs gave him "heart" or courage and facilitated exciting thought and talk, which led to actions that were criminal. "Nothing could be further from the truth than that people use drugs just to feel 'high' in the sense of comfortable, relaxed, and easy." What we had said of the criminal nonuser was true of the user. Both wanted to be "ten feet tall," but only the user needed drugs to achieve this.

When using drugs, each man believed that he would not get "hooked." Under drugs external deterrents were eliminated, and he was afraid of nothing. This was the criminal "superoptimism" (Chapter 6, Volume 1), in which he was certain that he was immune from apprehension. Conscience fears also were eliminated: "When I'm craving drugs, I don't want to be bothered by my conscience."

As we traced the drug user's thinking from his flow of ideas before a crime to his thinking after its commission, we found that drugs had served several purposes. First, fear was cut off so that he could commit the crime. After the crime these fears returned; the user again resorted to drugs to diminish them. Finally, by eliminating fears for a while, the user could celebrate his success and then prolong the state of excitement by repeating the offense or committing others.

As we came to view drugs as facilitators rather than simply as a means of relieving distress, we discovered the tremendous impetus they gave to sexual fantasy, talk, and exploitative action. Without drugs the drug user, no matter how competent in the eyes of others, considered himself "half a man." With an optimal dose of certain drugs, he could maintain an erection for hours. His staying power gave him greater power over women. We observed, "Especially under drugs, his penis was a sword with which he could make others do what he wanted." It was not so much an enhancement of the sensuality of sex that the drug user sought but, rather, the admiration and buildup by his partner. As one man viewed his eight-hour sexual performance (under drugs), "I felt like Hercules." The prolonged use of a high dosage of a drug wiped out sexual interest altogether. We learned increasingly about the user's choice of a drug for sexual conquest, his sexual practices under the drug, and his regulation of dosage for optimal effects.

The user wanted drugs primarily for crime and sexual exploitation. However, there were other purposes. One man reported using drugs to summon the courage to visit his family, whom he had not seen in a long time. Another used drugs to summon the courage to tell us the truth when his marriage was at stake and depended on his revealing facts unfavorable to himself. Some sought religious experiences on drugs. Unanticipated effects were also experienced in a few cases. Drugs intensified suicidal desires or brought out psychotic features in the few with such predispositions.

We were also learning how drugs affect the user's judgment and performance when he is not in active crime. We studied his reading habits, his evaluation of his own creative work, and his and others' estimates of his job performance.

More important than the particular drug is the makeup of the person who uses it. In the course of our studies, we investigated the effects of a spectrum of drugs. It was striking that many different drugs were used for a given purpose. A man's choice of drug was determined by what he had heard and read, by his own experience, and by the availability of the drug. Very different types of drugs had the same effects, all acting to facilitate whatever the user wanted.

The psychologic determinants of "addiction" (physical dependence) were more prominent than the physiologic. We found that the process of withdrawal was not nearly as torturous as users had stated or were themselves led to believe. Indeed, physically dependent users reported the ease with which they stopped using drugs when it was required. Our observations, history taking, and experiments were eye-opening in what they revealed about the drug user's suggestibility. Just the knowledge that he was going to obtain drugs eliminated withdrawal symptoms. If he was not thinking about drugs but passed through a neighborhood where they were available, the withdrawal symptoms reappeared. With the decision to buy drugs, they vanished. Where drugs are involved, users are very suggestible. Having unknowingly injected sterile water, they reported getting high. The same was true when they pumped their blood back and forth with a syringe. We learned that "craving" referred secondarily to physical consequences, but primarily to the user's missing what he was accustomed to—not the drug itself, so much as the excitement along criminal lines that the drug offered. We dropped the term *addiction* because we found that the concept was based largely on ideas that did not withstand close scrutiny. Popular beliefs about drug use were significantly different from what we were learning from the criminal drug users whom we studied.

Retrospectively, we were surprised to see that we had continued to accept psychologic excuses for crime from the drug-using criminal longer than we had from his counterpart who did not use drugs. We were receptive to the drug user's complaints about life's adversities. We believed that if he learned to deal constructively with those adversities, he would no longer require drugs. It took more than nine years for us to realize that the drug user was searching for more than a peaceful existence. Even when things were going well (at least from the standpoint of a responsible person), the drug user was seeking drugs. Indeed, for the habitual drug user, being without a drug of some kind in his body was as unnatural as going without food. As we studied the user's thinking, it was evident that on the street he was not concerned with life's adversities. His primary quest was finding the excitement  that he wanted. His desire for the excitement that drugs offered was unrelated to events in life preceding drug use. Only if he had to account to others for his use of drugs did he recite a litany of personal adversity.

It is true that drugs did relax the user and, in some, facilitated sociability. However, what really put him at ease was criminal excitement. Like the criminal nonuser, the user is consumed by boredom,  self-pity, anger, and tension when he is deprived of the excitement of irresponsibility and violation—the oxygen of his life. When he is searching for that excitement, he is not thinking of what he wants to escape. Rather, he wants to go *to* something. By pursuing what is important to him, he manages in the process to escape what is objectionable, but it is what he wants that is primary; the escape is secondary. We concluded that the escape theme that we had subscribed to for so long was only another version of the victim stance that we had long before abandoned when working with the criminal who was not a drug user. Relating all his difficulties to an examining authority or therapist was basically a deceptive tactic, designed to blame others and absolve himself of responsibility. Some drug users had employed such defenses so often with parents, teachers, employers, law enforcement authorities, and others that they half-believed their arguments themselves.

What emerged so clearly after we finally dropped our view of drugs as an escape and of the user as a victim is the fact that the drug user, even on high doses of drugs, is very much in control. Drugs do not cause him to be irresponsible. In fact, if it is worth his while, he can give the appearance of total responsibility and do an adequate job.

# Recommended Reading

Bidinotto, R. J., ed. (1996). *Criminal Justice? The Legal System Versus Individual Responsibility*. New York: Foundation for Economic Education.

Burchard, J. D., and Burchard, S. N. (1987). *Prevention of Delinquent Behavior*. Newbury Park, CA: Sage.

Clarke, A. M., and Clarke, A. D. B. (1976). *Early Experience: Myth and Evidence*. New York: Free Press.

Dobson, J. (1988). *The Strong-Willed Child*. Wheaton, IL: Tyndale.

Douglas, J., and Olshaker, M. (1997). *Journey Into Darkness*. New York: Scribner.

Ewing, C. P. (1987). *Battered Women Who Kill*. Lexington, MA: Heath.

Eysenck, H. J., and Gudjonsson, G. H. (1989). *The Causes and Cures of Criminality*. New York: Plenum.

Hallowell, E. M., and Ratey, J. J. (1996). *Answers to Distraction*. New York: Bantam.

Hayes, E. K. (1989). *Why Good Parents Have Bad Kids*. New York: Doubleday.

Meloy, J. R. (1988). *The Psychopathic Mind*. Northvale, NJ: Jason Aronson.

Pileggi, N. (1985). *Wise Guy: Life in a Mafia Family*. New York: Pocket Books.

President's Task Force on Victims of Crime (1982). *Final Report*. Washington, DC: U.S. Dept. of Justice.

Rogers, J. W. (1977). *Why Are You Not a Criminal?* Englewood Cliffs, NJ: Prentice-Hall.

Samenow, S. E. (1984). *Inside the Criminal Mind*. New York: New York Times Books.

———— (1989). *Before It's Too Late: Why Some Kids Get Into Trouble and What Parents Can Do About It*. New York: New York Times Books.

Yochelson, S., and Samenow, S. E. (1976). *The Criminal Personality. Vol 1: A Profile for Change*. New York: Jason Aronson.

———— (1977). *The Criminal Personality. Vol. 2: The Change Process*. New York: Jason Aronson.

———— (1986). *The Criminal Personality. Vol. 3: The Drug User*. Northvale, NJ: Jason Aronson.

## Further Reference

An interactive videotape series on the change process:

Samenow, S. E. (1994). *Commitment to Change*.
   Part 1: *What Are Errors in Thinking?*
   Part 2: *Two Crucial Errors*.
   Part 3: *Overcoming Errors in Thinking*.
Distributed by FMS Productions, Carpinteria, CA.

# Index